Twenty years ago, I read *SoulTsunami*, and my soul was saturated by Len Sweet's inspiring vision of a future church that could swim in the fluid culture of the twenty-first century. Now, *Rings of Fire* has set my brain ablaze as he describes the spiritual hot zones that await twenty-second-century Christ followers. If you're ready to learn how to fight fire with the Spirit's fire, read this powerful book by my favorite holy arsonist.

TIM LUCAS, founder and lead pastor of Liquid Church, author of *Liquid Church: 6 Powerful Currents to Saturate Your City for Christ*

Too often in contemporary times, "Christian thought" is a practical oxymoron. For some, the exercising of faith is the relinquishing of curiosity and query that is at the center of sound thought process. Thank God for Len Sweet and his eternally curious mind. It is impossible to read Len Sweet and not think about what it means to be a person of faith. In *Rings of Fire*, Sweet guides us through multiple places of present and potential eruption in the world in which we live and profess faith. Many of these places influence and confront us every day, but we have detached them from our sense of being faithful. It is inescapable: We and our faith are definitely "in the world" (John 17:11).

GARY SIMPSON, associate professor of homiletics at Drew Theological School, leading pastor at The Concord Baptist Church of Christ

Len Sweet has once again written a guide for the future by asking questions we all need to answer. *Rings of Fire: Walking in Faith through a Volcanic Future* looks at the past, present, and then into the future to challenge the church to choose faith over fear and become all God meant for her to be.

DAVE FERGUSON, visionary for NewThing, coauthor of *Hero Maker*

Leonard Sweet is a prophet of sorts: He speaks of things he sees. We often hold prophets at bay because they challenge us with words describing a future that has yet to arrive. But when you find a prophet who regularly nails it, you pay close attention to what they say since you know that you will likely intersect with that future. Leonard Sweet's voice is so critically important for us to hear and embrace, because what he has seen and spoken will have a great impact on our lives, and he has already begun to identify how we should respond to a future that is rapidly settling on us.

GLENN BURRIS, president of The Foursquare Church

Just as seismic pressure forces magma to rise through the crust of solid rocks, creating a massive volcanic eruption, in *Rings of Fire: Walking in Faith through a Volcanic Future*, Dr. Leonard Sweet reveals to us the compounding, cataclysmic, global pressure points that produce a future world on fire. I encourage every Christian leader to read this earthshaking book and learn what it will take to walk in faith through a future world that will soon be upon us. Put down your old ministry maps and pick up *Rings of Fire* today!

DR. JAMES O. DAVIS, cofounder of Global Church Network, founder of Cutting Edge International

The gift of Len Sweet is the compelling way he draws us into current and future spiritual realities with imagery, facts, and bold prophetic vision. This book is his best so far (and they are all good). *Rings of Fire* is the shaking we need as the world shifts beneath us, as we wonder about the future of the church. Sweet not only demonstrates how twelve major social domains will impact the next century but also suggests strategic ways to embrace the fire.

DR. MARYKATE MORSE, mentor and author

What used to be a nice song has turned into a fiery reality. The world of the twenty-second century is a global ring of fire. Len Sweet—semiotician, storyteller, and prophetic seer of the future—masterfully helps us make sense of this new world full of erupting volcanoes. He guides us through the hot zones and hot topics of our day and shows us how to embrace this volcanic culture as followers of Jesus. This brilliant and timely book serves as a first responder's manual to a blazing new landscape. It is the primer for all who desire an eruptive faith, one that keeps up with Jesus while inviting others to God's fire to get warm. This book will assist and enable the church of the future to walk on lava!

STEPHAN JOUBERT, Extraordinary Professor of Contemporary Ecclesiology at University of the Free State, editor of Ekerk

LEONARD SWEET

with contributions and afterword from

MARK CHIRONNA

RINGS OF FIRE

Walking in Faith through a Volcanic Future

A NavPress resource published in alliance
with Tyndale House Publishers, Inc.

NavPress

NavPress is the publishing ministry of The Navigators, an international Christian organization and leader in personal spiritual development. NavPress is committed to helping people grow spiritually and enjoy lives of meaning and hope through personal and group resources that are biblically rooted, culturally relevant, and highly practical.

For more information, visit www.NavPress.com.

The Team: Don Pape, Publisher; David Zimmerman, Acquisitions Editor; Eric Stanford, Copy Editor; Ron C. Kaufmann, Designer

Published in association with the literary agency of Mark Sweeney and Associates

For information about special discounts for bulk purchases, please contact Tyndale House Publishers at csresponse@tyndale.com, or call 1-800-323-9400.

Library of Congress Cataloging-in-Publication Data
Names: Sweet, Leonard I., author.
Title: Rings of fire : walking in faith through a volcanic future / Len Sweet, with contributions and afterword by Mark Chironna.
Description: Colorado Springs : NavPress, 2019. | Includes bibliographical references.
Identifiers: LCCN 2019028375 (print) | LCCN 2019028376 (ebook) |
    ISBN 9781631463945 (paperback) | ISBN 9781641581349 (ebook other) |
    ISBN 9781641581356 (epub) | ISBN 9781641581363 (kindle edition)
Subjects: LCSH: Christianity—21st century.
Classification: LCC BR481 .S88 2019 (print) | LCC BR481 (ebook) | DDC 270.8/3—dc23
LC record available at https://lccn.loc.gov/2019028375
LC ebook record available at https://lccn.loc.gov/2019028376

Printed in the United States of America

25	24	23	22	21	20	19
7	6	5	4	3	2	1

Contents

Preface

A talent for following the ways of yesterday is not
sufficient to improve the world of today.
KING WU-LING OF ZHAO
(NORTHEASTERN CHINA), 307 BC

I LIVE ON A SMALL, HORSESHOE-SHAPED ISLAND called Orcas, which floats precariously on a 25,000-mile horseshoe-shaped arc of volcanoes. That connection of trenches, belts, plates, and subduction zones that encircle the Pacific basin is called the Ring of Fire. It boasts 75 to 80 percent of the world's volcanoes (452 active and dormant). Of the twenty-five largest eruptions in the last 11,700 years, twenty-two are located here.

Moving fault lines on the Ring of Fire generate earthquakes and eruptions multiple times a day. Most are too small to be felt or observed.[1] But sometimes the earth rocks and blows. The volcano that erupted in Hawaii in 2018 created rivers of fire that, when they hit the ocean, provoked dangerous chemical reactions, including a steam cloud of "laze" filled with shards of glass and toxic chemicals. As if the lava, acid rain, volcanic smog, sulfur dioxide, lahar, caldera, explosions, eruption plumes, debris avalanches, and fissures weren't enough, now Hawaii residents had to deal with the laze.

The world is now one global Ring of Fire.

Twenty years ago, I wrote *SoulTsunami* for the church as it entered the twenty-first century. *Rings of Fire* is written for the twenty-second century. Actuarially speaking, a child born after 2000 has a greater than 50 percent chance of living well into the next century, which means that right now our families and churches are forming and norming a twenty-second-century faith.

How are we doing?

Everyone is asking questions like "What is going on out there?" "How in the world did that happen?" "Why are we so polarized?" These are global questions, symptoms of structural shifts in society that impact the whole world. We are living on the other side of a cultural tsunami.

_____

Truth is a matter of eternity, whether it is truth evaded or truth faced.

PETER KREEFT,
HEAVEN: THE HEART'S DEEPEST LONGING

_____

We live in a world that is constantly, simultaneously, solidifying and lique-fying. In spite of our best efforts, the church is unprepared for the future and unpleasant when asked to think about it.

We are like the Haitian family so traumatized by the January 2010 earthquake that they fled to Chile—only to go through an even greater earthquake a month later. Or the Mitsubishi engineer Tsutomu Yamaguchi, who fled the bombing of Hiroshima during World War II, taking refuge in Nagasaki. Society is unraveling, and when you try to escape, turn your back on the unraveling, or join the denial lobby, you go from bad to worse.

I believe God is already present and active in these erupting volcanoes. The Way through and around and over them is already in the midst of them. Jesus calls his disciples to be first responders, those who run toward, not away from, the future.

This book is designed as a kind of first responders manual to help you assess the situation and assist the Spirit as the situation requires. The vol-canic metaphor finds its inspiration in perhaps the most astute interpreter of the US in our history: the politician and writer Alexis de Tocqueville. In 1848, he addressed the French National Assembly with these words: "We are sitting on a volcano. Can't you see that the earth is trembling again?"[2] The church needs to be more fiery than its culture. Only fire beats fire.

In a volcanic world, hot pockets are ready to blow and erupt at any minute, with constant explosions and sudden power surges. This kind of world needs the tribe of Issachar to re-form and rediscover their role in reading signs and knowing what to do.[3]

Ready or not, the future shows up. A default future arrives willy-nilly. A desirable future is birthed in blood, sweat, and tears. A faith that finds God in the past boasts roots, but a faith that finds God in the future bears fruits.[4] It is our prayer that this book will help the church thank God, not just for what has been but also for what is coming as the church ventures forth into this volcanic culture with a red-hot, eruptive faith, bringing old and new together in innovative, probing, playful, and paradoxical ways.

The Dead by the Side of the Road

When it comes to the future, the church is in the dark—not only unable to see the forest for the trees but also lost in the bark. The church of the future will be impossible to locate on a spectrum of left or right, only forward or backward. It is apostasy not to be in one's own time, both for the disciple and for the church. The ecclesiastical equivalent of sinning against the Holy Ghost is not to be open to the future.

In this book we take a fresh look at the global megatrends affecting the church of the twenty-first and twenty-second centuries—the "hot zones" worth keeping a watchful eye on, the "hot topics" that we can't avoid discussing, and the front-burner issues making for a "hot church," along with some "hot takes" to stimulate further consideration down the road. We approach these megatrends from a faith-based rather than a fear-based posture. We have no interest in "keeping up with the times" but rather in keeping up with Jesus and opening up to God's presence in the times we're in. Jesus the Bread of Life is unchanging—the same yesterday, today, and forever—because the Bread is constantly changing, freshly baked for every time and clime.

Most Americans write hundreds if not thousands more words a day than they did ten or twenty years ago.

ANNE TRUBEK,
THE HISTORY AND UNCERTAIN FUTURE OF HANDWRITING

The church is in the state it's in partly because it has mistaken the *Zeitgeist* ("spirit of the times") for the *Heilige Geist* ("Holy Spirit"). Every time-and-technology "sign" opens up a biblical way forward and a "sign of the Spirit." A church that incarnates the timeless and the timely at the same time yields timefulness.

Mark Chironna made an addendum to an old adage: "When one door closes, another door opens. But the hallway is a hellway." Gregory Boyle, a Jesuit priest and the founder of Homeboy Industries, reflected that revised adage when he adopted the phrase "line the hallway" as an image statement for Homeboy Industries:

At Homeboy Industries, I tell our senior staff that part of our task is to "line the hallway," to make that distance stretching between the old and new versions of one's self a comforting one. We encourage and cajole with a constant tenderness as the tentative soul takes steps toward the fullness of becoming. The hallway can be long and the lure to return to an old, tired, but known and safe version can be compelling. And those who line the hallway haven't arrived fully either. Our mutual accompaniment with each other along the way pulls us all over the finish line. It's about the "rehab of the soul," as one of our senior staff puts it. We all line the hallway on this good journey with only gentleness in our rucksack and our own brokenness within reach.[5]

Rings of Fire shows how a Christian can walk that hallway and line that hallway, all the while looking for doors to open that will let the Kingdom future "in." As Jesus uses the term, the Kingdom is that desired future where God reigns in justice and in peace.

We call for the cultivation of semiotic awareness and a prophetic role for all disciples, what we might call (in the spirit of Issachar) the "prophethood of all believers."[6] If a prophet is one who speaks for the future, we must somehow all be prophets now.

This prophetic role of the laity was recognized by the Second Vatican Council (1962–5). There is a prophetic role, which is a matter of "ends" from a religious perspective; there is a pragmatic role, which is a matter of "means" from a political-economic-social perspective. We need both the prophetic and the pragmatic. Most often there is a tension between the two. Seldom do the prophetic and the pragmatic elide into one calling, or one book.

Reality helps by terrors which transcend the parrot-wisdom of trivial experience.

SØREN KIERKEGAARD,
THE SICKNESS UNTO DEATH

Hence the concluding call for a new order of Issachar. Even though Ossip Flechtheim coined the term *futurology*, Jesus is its original inventor. Jesus comes to his disciples from the future and pulls us forward more than pushes us from behind. When Jesus taught us to live abundantly, he taught us to live *out of* the past, to live *in* the present (not in the past), and to live *into* the future. You can't live in the past and go forward. To study Jesus is to study the future.

"I have a thousand and ten thousand things to say to you. My heart is full of futurity," wrote William Blake to Thomas Butts.[7] How many of our hearts are "full of futurity"? In this book we will forget about the thousand or ten thousand futurities and will consider a precise set of futurities from the twelve major domains of twenty-first- and twenty-second-century life:

> › politics and power
> › business and economics
> › science
> › technology
> › health and healing
> › environment
> › religion
> › culture (pop and high) and communications
> › arts
> › governance
> › education
> › family and relationships

Based on our research into all twelve domains, we have organized our findings along a fivefold grid: text, textures, tensions, triggers, and trajectories.

> › *Texts* are the primary resources and hard data that tell us in black-and-white what is going on—facts on the ground about the future. But all data has to be interpreted, and data often leads us astray. The words *figure* (number) and *fictitious* come from the same Latin roots: *figura*, meaning "to shape into," and *fingere*, meaning "to mold" or "to dissemble." You can't trust the data, but you still need data. Go figure.

> › *Textures* are how the hard data is experienced in emotions and motions. Facts alone are never the whole story—it's the space between the facts where the story appears.

> › *Tensions* are the fault lines on the front lines. We pluck revelatory threads out from an all-too-uneven cultural fabric.

> › *Triggers* are those wild cards that could explode at any minute.

> › *Trajectories* are the winds blowing in a certain direction and the identification of artifacts from the future.

Rings of Fire continues the approach I've taken in three of my earlier books. They were lonely at the time of their releases, but their observations proved out and set the table for the work of this book.

FaithQuakes (1994) was originally drafted as a manifesto to be released by a multiracial, multidenominational group of twelve US evangelicals after a 1991 Moscow meeting with Mikhail Gorbachev. It argued that the church must prepare for a succession of cultural earthquakes impacting the home, the workplace, our relationships, and our mission.

SoulTsunami (1999) served up ten appetizers of future food the church needed to get used to, including glocalisms and the dechurched movement.

Carpe Mañana (2001) roughed up the church a bit with a series of switches:

> from manual to digital
> from linear to loop
> from word to image
> from vast to fast
> from "make sense" to "make sense"
> from "Who am I?" to "What is to be done?"
> from sharp to fuzzy
> from outer space to inner space
> from clockwork orange to web green

As the world—not just the West—wobbles on its axis and smoking volcanoes flare up all around us, *Rings of Fire* comes as the main course of this now-twenty-year meal: How do we distinguish our state from our fate? The state, as observed by Bill Emmott in his *The Fate of the West*, is "demoralised, decadent, deflating, demographically challenged, divided, disintegrating, dysfunctional, declining."[8] In such a world of decivilizing forces, when civilization itself seems to be blowing up, the path to the future must be one that recivilizes life and culture.

We are aware of the colonial baggage that the phrase "civilizing gospel" carries, but our emphasis now is not on the subjectivity of civilizing but on the bedrock strength of gospel, which teaches us all how to be human again, which was at the heart of Jesus' mission. The colonial mission was one of spreading a Jesus gospel stamped "Western." We are calling the church to spread a Jesus gospel stamped "Human."

Every historical era is . . . multitemporal, simultaneously drawing
from the obsolete, the contemporary, and the futuristic.

MICHEL SERRES,
CONVERSATIONS ON SCIENCE, CULTURE, AND TIME

God's church will always have a future. It is God's mission, not the church's mission, and God's mission will be carried out, with or without our tribes and traditions. This is made uncomfortably explicit in the story of Hosea, who has three children by Gomer: Jezreel ("God will sow"), Lo-Ruchamah ("No Mercy"), and Lo-Ammi ("Not My People").[9] Hosea's second and third children were living reminders that God is not captive to our capitulations, not an accomplice to our idolatry.

Sometimes God works not by addition, nor even by multiplication, but by subtraction. The children of God were still the children of God, even after the ten northern tribes were lost. The divine seems to enjoy working through a faithful remnant, the critical mass of "two or three," not a mishmash gabagool of majority-rules compromise or middle-of-the-road mediocrity.

The mountains quake before him and the hills melt away. The earth
trembles at his presence, the world and all who live in it.

NAHUM 1:5

God's mission now takes place on a landscape where volcanoes are erupting all around us, eruptions that bring in their wake lava flows, magma rock, and vents and fissures that open with unpredictable flurry and fury. You can live on a territory carved out by volcanoes. Just visit Iceland. In Iceland you can even walk on lava.[10] But it's a very different life and walk.

You can survive mega seismic quakes and tsunamis too. Just ask Tokyo, which felt a major seism registering 9.0 on the Richter scale, the biggest in Japan's history and the fourth largest recorded in the history of the planet, that occurred off the Pacific coast of Japan's Tohoku region on March 11, 2011, and rocked central Tokyo for six minutes. Tokyo survived relatively unscathed, but only because they were prepared by decades of strict building codes, shake-proof innovations in construction, broadcast alerts, and evacuation drills.

In this book we don't give models or blueprints or fill-in-the-blanks formulas for moving into the future. What we do give are strategies, schemas, scenarios, story lines, and metaphors. Much of what we say will be sweeping. But some "sweeping" arguments are as necessary as brooms. In a book that is by definition sweeping, we did not feel bound to solve a problem. It's enough to call attention to the breakage and warn people not to step there.

When accosted with new information, the women in Toni Morrison's novel *Beloved* "fell into three groups: those that believed the worst; those that believed none of it; and those, like Ella, who thought it through."[11] When confronted with new technologies or information, the church has fallen mostly into the first two groups. It reflexively believes the worst of it or believes none of it would ever happen. Each ring of fire in the pages that follow is a summons for the Ellas to emerge.

We have enough scientific knowledge and enough technical means
to ward off the threats that are said to hang over the world;
now all we need is to actually want to ward them off.

RENÉ GIRARD,
WHEN THESE THINGS BEGIN

The last prayer of the Bible is "Even so, come, Lord Jesus!"[12] This prayer is how the first Christians greeted one another—a departure from the conventional Jewish greeting "Shalom" ("Peace"). They knew their times were troubled and tormented and that the only shalom they might find in this life was the peace of the coming Christ.

Oh, my loving brother,
When the world's on fire,
Don't you want God's bosom
To be your pillow?

"FIRE SONG" (APPALACHIAN CHORUS)

Wake up! The world's on fire! "Wake up, sleeper, rise from the dead, and Christ will shine on you."[13]

Introduction

*The secret for harvesting from existence the greatest fruitfulness
and the greatest enjoyment is to live dangerously! Build your cities on the slope
of Vesuvius! Send your ships into unexplored seas! Live in war
with your equals and with yourselves!*

FRIEDRICH NIETZSCHE,
THE GAY SCIENCE

THE DRAMA OF HUMAN EXPERIENCE is always played out on the stage of culture. Is culture your bosom buddy? Is culture your enemy? Or is culture your inevitable companion on the journey? You can't escape culture, nor would it be good if you could.[1]

Having culture as a bosom buddy can lead to collusion (or syncretism). Having culture as an enemy can lead to condemnation.[2] Having culture as a companion on your journey can lead to its own problems.

We do not get to pick our ambient culture. God has determined our appointed times.[3] You and I are part of an arranged marriage, made and chosen "for such a time as this."[4] The *Zeitgeist* ("spirit of the times") is not the enemy but the context in which the *Heilige Geist* ("Holy Spirit") wants to be released and unleashed. The church spends more time slandering its moment than in savoring and saving its moment. If we loved the world as God so loved the world, we would love it well and love it to life.

On the Side of the Angles

But we live "our times" not as the world lives its time. In a holy triangulation, we are to be "in" the culture but not "of" the culture. The Christian faith interacts with the culture always at an angle to it.[5] To live incarnationally is not to live out of time or out of place but to live in time and in place in a way that is not in-time or in-place. In this respect Jesus promised to make his disciples "anglers of people."[6]

There has never been a present that has accurately comprehended itself historically, let alone interpreted the present adequately for the future. We

1

rush in where angels fear to tread. How do we keep the charge (and keep charged) for a lifetime of ministry and mission?

If Darth Vader can be converted, anything is possible. In *Star Wars: Episode III—Revenge of the Sith*, a climactic battle takes place where Anakin (whom we later know as Darth Vader) makes a pact with the devil. The background of this final crossing over to the dark side is a sea of fire, or lava, on a planet filled with nothing but volcanoes. The lava at the end opens into hell.[7]

Look around you in any direction—socially, politically, economically, religiously. Can you see the slow flow of lava? How can you miss the fire fountains swarming the sky? The music industry did not see it in 1999 when it celebrated the most profitable year in its history. When it was pointed out to top executives at a London consultation that something else was going on that could change this in a nanosecond—something digital and streaming—the executives laughed and cut short the consultation as a waste of their time. CDs would rule forever, they said. Consumers would never prefer access to ownership. Within the year, "mp3" overtook "sex" as the Internet's most popular search term.[8]

Are we living in "the best of times" or "the worst of times"? Is the world hotfooting it to hell in a handbasket? Or is the world ambling to paradise, with the better angels of our nature at the wheel? Is the future a promised land of milk and honey or a hellscape? War, disease, poverty, and despair have always been part of human history. Are they getting worse or better? Will they always be with us?

We must meet the challenge rather than wish it were not before us.

JUSTICE WILLIAM J. BRENNAN JR.,
SPEECH GIVEN AT GEORGETOWN UNIVERSITY

Some say we are living among the endings, the postludes, the codas of a great tradition. Some say "our times" are an "age of enrichment." Some say we are living in an "enlightenment age" as the Internet births a whole new civilization and new technologies make possible a whole new human. Others say we are teetering on the edge of Armageddon, an age of lurking catastrophes, with our new vernacular of technology a veritable alphabet of apocalypse, a syllabus of horrors. Will scientific shouts of "Eureka!" be greeted by shouts of praise or shrieks of horror?[9]

Should our response to the future be bounded enthusiasm or stiff-upper-lip despair? Or maybe our palates should get used to a sweet and sour fricassee of honeyed hopes and braced-to-face realities?

A Die Progress Unit (DPU) is the amount of time it takes human beings to achieve enough progress that the shock of bringing a time traveler to your era would kill them. In hunter-gatherer times, a DPU stretched over hundreds of thousands of years. Post–Agricultural Revolution rates were reduced to about twelve thousand years. The post–Industrial Revolution world has moved so quickly that a person living in 1750 would only need to go forward a few hundred years for the disparity between the world she knows and the world in which she suddenly finds herself to stop her heart.[10]

We believe 2050 will be a coming DPU for anyone reading this book. We live in a science-fictional world. Our children may well experience multiple DPUs in their lifetimes, a shock to the psyche never before experienced, much less imagined in human history. The world we used to call home is going up in smoke. Our descendants will have multiple worlds go up in smoke in their lifetimes.

Oh, it needn't come to that!

ALICE TO HUMPTY DUMPTY

Scholars who take the most data-driven, hardheaded, chapter-and-verse demographic probes of where we are today end up in a very optimistic place. Wealth is more evenly distributed than it was two hundred years ago, one of many trends that need to be rescued from their reputations. In the twentieth century, which medieval historian Ian Mortimer believes was the "most-change century" of the last thousand years,[11] USAmericans were 92 percent less likely to perish in a fire, 96 percent less likely to die in a car crash, and 95 percent less likely to die on the job.[12] Humanity is also becoming less violent.[13]

People in the world are getting smarter, living longer, getting better educated. Thanks to the trifecta of free markets, free trade, and free enterprise, people of modest means throughout the world can now live better than the rich of the not-so-distant past. The "poor" enjoy luxuries that robber barons such as the Rothschilds and Rockefellers couldn't imagine.

When you brought your produce to market in the agricultural age and you looked at how the royalty lived in that moated castle, little could you imagine that in the industrial age people would live the same way. In the industrial age, when you worked on those railroads and looked at how the millionaire robber barons lived in remote mansions, little could you imagine that in the digital age this is how people would live. When you freelance in the digital age and look at how the billionaires live, where things they don't want to do are done for them, little can you imagine that in the future this is how you will live, liberating you for what you find impressive, persuasive, immersive.

Even today, residents of the poorest places on the planet, the favelas in Rio de Janeiro and the squatter camps of Africa, enjoy TVs, air-conditioning, and stereos, with many of the homeless even owning supercomputer phones with apps geared specifically to them. Advances in medicine, including genetic therapy and breaching the blood-brain barrier, open up whole new possibilities for healing some of the most intractable diseases, such as Alzheimer's, Parkinson's, and cancer. In the words of the archbishop of Canterbury, Justin Welby, "The greatest expansion of riches, and reduction in poverty, famine and general want, has been under the market economies."[14]

There is so much hype about future technology that if it does anything less than make the earth move, it will be deemed a failure. The more responsible and critical antipessimists include Julian Simon (*Hoodwinking the Nation*), Bjørn Lomborg (*Global Crises, Global Solutions:*), Matt Ridley (*The Rational Optimist: How Prosperity Evolves*), Peter Diamandis and Steven Kotler (*Abundance: The Future Is Better than You Think*), and Kevin Kelly (*The Inevitable: Understanding the 12 Technological Forces That Will Shape Our Future*). The outlines of their arguments are as follows:

› Food is more abundant and available.
› Clean water and good sanitation are increasingly available.
› Life expectancy is longer.
› Poverty has fallen dramatically.
› Global living standards are skyrocketing
› War and violence blight fewer lives.
› Increasing wealth has benefited the environment.
› Literacy is widening and deepening.
› People are increasingly free of despotic authority.
› Equality is increasingly experienced and demanded.
› Advanced agricultural technology such as farmbots will raise crop yields by as much as 70 percent by 2050.[15]

> More than a billion people have been lifted out of poverty in the last fifty years.[16]
> Ethical consumerism is becoming the norm, with some grocery chains carrying only fruits that have a fair trade label.[17]
> Ethical audits of organizations and corporations are now the norm, not the exception, and any nation without an ethical dimension to its foreign policy is scorned and marginalized.
> Globally, there was a 37 percent decrease in executions from 2015 (1,634) to 2016 (1,032), according to Amnesty International.[18]

So far, so optimistic—but not for two authors in particular. Swedish intellectual Johan Norberg and Harvard cognitive scientist Steven Pinker showcase the variety of ways the world has "progressed" over the last three centuries to blunt the scourges facing our ancestors. Pinker's books are less a paean to progress than a panegyric for reason and the Enlightenment. In his hatred of religion as a regressive force, Pinker fails to realize that his vaunted "Enlightenment values" are mostly a gift to the world from Christianity.[19] He also fails to admit that rationalism in the wrong hands and without the constraints of religion have given us some troubling gifts: Leninism, Maoism, Stalinism, and Nazism.[20]

People may say what they like about the decay of Christianity;
the religious system that produced green Chartreuse can never really die.

H. H. MUNRO,
"REGINALD ON CHRISTMAS PRESENTS"

Because of the nature of media, where good news is no news, no news is bad news, and bad news is good news, daily headlines countermand this glowing picture. Addicted to adrenaline and fueled by TV-cabled anger, we are captive to the "availability heuristic"[21] and the Zeigarnik effect.

The "availability heuristic" is cognitive science's way of talking about how the human brain privileges the probability of what is most memorable. What do we remember most? The most horrific and shocking. The longer an incident stays in our thoughts, the more "available" the memory, the more we believe similar incidents happen frequently, and the more blind we are to actual reality. In short, mind mirrors media: It privileges bad news over good news.

The Zeigarnik effect is named after Lithuanian psychologist Bluma

Wulfovna Zeigarnik. She noticed in 1927 how people better remember unresolved, incomplete events than resolved, completed ones. In relational terms, if you want to get over a relationship and move on, you must give it an ending. If it's open and unresolved, like major disasters and uncertain developments, you have trouble putting it to rest.

The world is as healthy, wealthy, and wise as it's ever been. Things have been getting better for Europeans and USAmericans since 1800 and for the rest of the world over the past seventy years. To be sure, hunger, pollution, terrorism, poverty, and sickness are facts of life for many throughout the world. Still, in historical perspective as well as in absolute terms, these ills are on the decline. To be sure, there is huge inequality in the world, but the floor of that inequality is not nearly as low as it has been, even if the upper regions of that inequality are getting bigger. In short, the rich are getting richer, and the poor are getting less poor, but the rich are getting so much richer that in comparison it seems as if the poor were getting poorer.

So if life keeps on getting better, and we make better magic every day, why do we live in a time of tumbling hopes, despairing fears, and depressive spirits? Why do we keep folding our magic carpets or use them as tapestries? Depression is the mind's waterboarding of the spirit. Depression rates are climbing almost everywhere, as are drug abuse and addictions. An array of addictive and compulsive habits is always on display.

People may be doing better in every way, but they don't feel they are and are depressed about it and looking for ways to escape all the success. Technology has brought us to the edge of utopia and to the edge of psychological and environmental dystopia.[22]

It's almost as if Jesus had diagnosed our condition: "What good is it for someone to gain the whole world, yet forfeit their soul?"[23] It's almost as if Jesus' warning were coming true: "Watch out . . . life does not consist in an abundance of possessions."[24] It's almost as if higher wages won't bring happiness and higher life expectancy won't bring happiness, for only the Bread of Life will satisfy.

The hungry sheep look up, and are not fed.

JOHN MILTON,
"LYCIDAS"

If you do not listen to the world in stereo, the louder channel is the bad news. And when bad news is all you hear, the handwriting is on the wall:[25]

› A world where anti-Semitism is on the rise.
› A world that has lost half the planet's topsoil in the last fifty years.
› A world that has heated the atmosphere to dangerous thresholds, even (some say) beyond the point of no return.
› A world with such acidified oceans that the future of saltwater fish is in question.
› A world where soon seas will have as much weight in plastic as in fish.
› A world where humans have ushered in the greatest mass extinction since the wiping out of the dinosaurs.
› A world that has militarized the public schooling of its children— already in some neighborhoods police officers outnumber guidance counselors or nurses.
› A world that has criminalized addiction and throws those addicted into jail with set sentences, jails that are hotbeds of high drug activity and addiction.[26]

An apocalyptic spirit is pervasive: moral panics of ecological collapse, technological dystopia. So many zombies in popular culture you can't keep up with them. More than 60 percent of New Yorkers believe the end of the world is imminent.[27]

Maybe every age is equidistant from eternity. At the end of every technological advancement, the ones who invented the technology are still human and prone to waywardness.[28] Maybe the best is yet to come because the worst is already here. Maybe Umberto Eco was right in his claim that "technology moves like a crayfish, in other words, backwards."[29]

Never underestimate nostalgia and its power to idealize the past and demonize the present.[30] Headlines capture and catalog the doomsayer's handbasket, filling it with a cornucopia of fears about the worsening of the human condition that make the appetite for nostalgia all the more sweet.

But where nostalgia is a slow buzz, vertigo causes disorienting spells of dizziness and the "spins" that turn apocalyptic anxieties into flare-ups. Vertigo is as much a psychological reaction as a physical one. Why don't you get queasy, light-headed, and dizzy from looking down from a plane window? From a high window or the top of a building, you have to stop looking down before your head "spins" from the dizzying sense of space below. We measure space by what we can calibrate. If we can't calibrate it, the space is less threatening. Who's to say the same isn't true with time?

Is Your Body of Christ Pregnant?

Reversing the tide of one million youth leaving the church per year is the most significant domestic evangelism challenge in American history.

PINETOPS FOUNDATION,
THE GREAT OPPORTUNITY: THE AMERICAN CHURCH IN 2050

The twenty-first-century church in the West has the two worst illnesses any species can have. The first is a reproduction crisis. We cannot reproduce the faith in our children, our communities, our churches, and our world. When any species can no longer reproduce itself, we classify it as *endangered*.

The only thing worse than having a problem is the failure to be aware of the problem you have. That's the church's second illness—anosognosia, or the ignorance of illness.

This is the time for the church to find itself, to learn to be itself, and for new panoramas and pathways to address the world's most urgent challenges. We can get ahead of social change. We can be a player in the formation of the future. But only those who are the most nimble and fleet-footed in the face of change are positioned to make the greatest contributions for the future.

"Reform!" the Duke of Wellington is said to have complained. "Aren't things bad enough already?"[31] Rumbling, erupting, and exploding volcanoes signal the time for volcanic drive and cyclonic energy among us, to carve anew some breath-giving vistas of the future. Bob Dylan's "The Times They Are A-Changin'" may have worked for the twentieth century, but the soundtrack for the twenty-first century may be Wagner's "Ride of the Valkyries." Or if classical music is not your thing, try Johnny Cash's "Ring of Fire."

PART ONE

Hot Zones

1

HOSTILE CULTURE

I created every one of you with a burden of sin—guilty from the moment of birth. Then I loved you so much that I made a woman pregnant so she would give birth to me and I would become my own son so that I can have myself killed as a sacrifice to myself in order to save you evil sinners from the burden of sin that I created you with in the first place.

SALAFIST TRACT HANDED OUT BY SUNNI ISLAM EVANGELISTS
IN 2018 ON THE STREETS OF BIRMINGHAM, ENGLAND,
SUMMARIZING CHRISTIAN THEOLOGY

THE EDITORS OF *GQ* MAGAZINE selected some of their favorite writers to challenge "received wisdom" about classic pieces of literature. The panel was instructed to select twenty-one books they believed were overrated and could be struck "from the canon." Number twelve on the list of "21 Books You Don't Have to Read" is the Bible.[1]

The *GQ* editors chose to ban the Bible from any required reading lists because "it is repetitive, self-contradictory, sententious, foolish, and even at times ill-intentioned." In the Bible's place the recommended reading is Ágota Kristóf's novel about a world without empathy, *The Notebook* (1986).

Welcome to our (new) world, church. It's a world we helped create. We asked for it.

The volcanic twenty-first century will call for the most creative evangelism and shrewd apologetics the church has seen since the first century. If ever the time is ripe for tilling, planting, and watering the soil, it is now. But best not to underestimate the challenge. We may be the least "formed" and worst prepared generation of Jesus disciples in history facing the greatest challenges the church has ever faced.

The life of Christian faith is now lived in an unfriendly environment. But "unfriendly" means different things in different times. For example, parochial schools and private Christian schools are under attack in Great Britain for promoting inequality by their existence. It is not uncommon now for weddings to be officiated by someone with no more than a notary public authority. But this is low-level "unfriendly." Christians in the West have no idea what it means to suffer for one's beliefs.

We will. Soon.

"Whom You . . . Denied before the Face of Pilate"

It is not easy to face or outface the "face of Pilate."[2] Never has been. How many times have we shrunk back in fear, even repudiated our faith under the pressure of power and the peril of authority. "The face of Pilate" can be religious authority, political authority, or pop culture. But Jesus as Lord often takes a pass, a back seat, or even a sycophant sit-down when faced with the powers of the state.

Not until the fourth century did the early church talk about the "cross" so much. Prior to then, this symbol of torture and death was a daily reality for them. The first Christians loved the symbol of the fish (*ichthus* in Greek, its letters standing for "Jesus Christ Son of God Savior") and clung close to cheerful, culinary images of Jesus partly because persecution had made life so difficult. Followers of Jesus today don't seek out crosses to carry, but when you cross the grain of culture and church, you get splinters and splintered, which become our "thorns in the flesh," and even sometimes, if they become cross-spangled banners, our "crosses to bear."

Paper cannot wrap up a fire.
CHINESE PROVERB ON HOW TRUTH WILL ALWAYS WIN OUT

Most recent estimates are that one in ten Christians worldwide (200 million+ brothers and sisters) are being persecuted or discriminated against.[3] Between February 12 and 15, 2015, the Islamic State of Iraq and the Levant (ISIL) beheaded twenty-one "people of the cross," Egyptian Coptic Christians kidnapped in the city of Sirte, Libya. They were slaughtered on the beach opposite Al Mahary Hotel in Sirte. Their last words, spoken by each as their heads were cut off, was "Lord Jesus Christ."

Do we know any of the names, even one, of the Coptic Christian martyrs? The early church passed on the names of the martyrs and spoke them out loud as part of the Cloud.[4] The world needs to hear these names, famous or not. They deserve it. We deserve it. The air deserves it—not just to clear the air but to clean the air.

Words like Asia Bibi are air cleaners for every household. Asia Bibi is the name of a Catholic woman sentenced to death under Pakistan's blasphemy laws. At the same time, we also need to remember those of other faith traditions who have been or are being persecuted for their beliefs, such as the Syrian archaeologist and director of antiquities who was beheaded trying to protect the Palmyra museum from its destroyers. ISIL hung the body of Khaled al-Asaad from a pillar with a placard on it reading, "Director of Idolatry."[5] Why are we not weekly in worship lifting up prayers for "all persecuted Christians" and referencing some by name?

Some scholars have noticed the sharp contrast between the relative indifference of Christians to the fate of fellow Christians around the world and the care and concern of Muslims to the plight and predicament of fellow Muslims, as Muslims, or Jews, as Jews.[6]

It is time for the church to toughen up in dealing with the world today. Jesus sent his earliest disciples out into a world that killed them. He sends us out to a mocking and maligning world, but most of us are still alive. In the language of Nassim Nicholas Taleb, we must learn to be an Antifragile Church that can embrace vulnerability and weakness and celebrate the positivity of stress.[7] To be "antifragile" is to trust the order behind the chaos, to flourish from random environments rather than established settings, and not to be afraid of antifragile preaching that can take place outside the normal patterns (systems) of church. YouTube, Facebook, podcasts, and other digital formats (screens) are a few antifragile ways to preach in a hostile culture.

That feeling of wanting to jump up and down is one of the ways that scientists measure joy.

DESIGNER INGRID FETELL LEE,
"WHERE JOY HIDES AND HOW TO FIND IT"

"Blessed are you when people hate you," said Jesus, "when they exclude you and insult you and reject your name as evil, because of the Son of Man. Rejoice in that day and leap for joy, because great is your reward in heaven. For that is how their ancestors treated the prophets."[8] How many Christians are jumping up and down in the good times, much less in times of persecution and suffering? Maybe we do not leap and jump for joy because we've forgotten the reward now and the future reward? As we see in the Beatitudes, joy is one of the ways God measures faithfulness.

Different tribes engage in the practice of dog-whistling—sending out signals that only those who know the lingo and liturgy of the subculture will recognize. The twenty-first-century church has its own equivalent to this: the God-whistle.[9] As the future unfolds, we will need to practice the God-whistle so our distinctives are clear and conformed to what God is whistling over us and for us.

Tears melt God's heart and bind his hand.
PURITAN THOMAS WATSON,
THE BEATITUDES

A medieval fable tells about a young woman who died early in life but was a troublemaker in heaven—so much that she was expelled but told that if she would return with the gift most valued by God, she would be welcomed back.

So she searched the ends of the earth for what God might value most. She brought back drops of blood from a dying patriot. She brought back some coins that a destitute widow had given the poor. She brought back a leaf from the Bible that one of the greatest preachers had used over a lifetime. She brought back some dust from the shoes of a missionary laboring on a remote island. She brought back many things such as these but was always turned away.

One day she saw a small boy playing by a fountain. A man rode up on horseback and dismounted to take a drink. The man saw the child and suddenly remembered his boyhood innocence. Then, looking in the fountain and seeing the reflection of his hardened face, he realized what he had done with his life. And tears of repentance welled up in his eyes and began to trickle down his cheeks. The young woman scooped up one of these tears in a lachrymatory and took it back to heaven . . . and was received with joy and celebration.

Repentance is a word seldom heard or used anymore. But *apologize* (from the weak French word *apologie* and the strong Greek/Latin word *apologia*) may begin to approach the depth of *metanoia*, or "repentance," which David Bentley Hart consistently translates into English as "change of heart."[10]

By *apologize*, we mean what John the Baptist meant when he began his ministry with the words "Repent, for the kingdom of heaven is at hand."[11] True apology is not escapology but eschatology. This may include the traditional "apology," as Pope Francis has demonstrated in his willingness to apologize to abuse victims.[12]

Unfortunately, when the church doesn't want to engage in substantive thought about something, it issues an apology. For example, in 1917, at the four hundredth anniversary celebration of the Protestant Reformation, the primary emphasis of Anglicanism was to claim that the purest heir of the Reformation (although it started in Germany) was the Church of England. In the course of my lifetime, the Church of England has lost 75 percent of its membership.[13] The five hundredth anniversary in 2017 featured a quasi-apology from Justin Welby (archbishop of Canterbury) and John Sentamu (archbishop of York) for the hubris of the previous celebration.[14] This kind of groveling is almost enough to give *apology* a bad name.

Telling the truth is the only proper way of restoring dignity.
LITHUANIAN POET TOMAS VENCLOVA,
MAGNETIC NORTH

The first work of grace is the first word of grace: *Repent.* Like John the Baptist, Jesus began his ministry with this word: "Repent, and believe in the gospel."[15] Peter based his most famous sermon around it: "Repent and be baptized."[16] Paul could not stop reminding the churches that God "commands all people everywhere to repent."[17] Martin Luther's first of 95 Theses was the affirmation that when Jesus called on people to repent, it was a call that reached to every corner of life. Beginning in 1775, the Second Continental Congress calendarized specific "National Days of Prayer and Fasting," which featured calls to "repentance," a tradition that was periodically observed throughout US history and most memorably reinstituted by President Abraham Lincoln during the Civil War.

To apologize, in our sense of the word, involves a 3-m response: a metanoia (change of heart), a metamorphosis (change of behavior), and a metastasis (change of being). It is more than a time like Lent, when we confront our shortcomings and celebrate our passions; it is a daily lifestyle of conversion.

> Everyone does wrong. The ultimate in doing wrong is failing to recognize you've done wrong and apologize for doing it.
>
> We've done wrong in placidly occupying our privileged perches in Christendom.
>
> We've done wrong in going down the rabbit's hole of leadership rather than keeping our eyes on the prize of our high calling as followers of Christ Jesus.[18]
>
> We've done wrong in not trusting the Holy Spirit to speak the vernacular.
>
> We've done wrong in a lack of humility for the blessings of our birth.
>
> We've done wrong as trustees of God's creation. Planet Earth is headed toward environmental meltdown. God isn't doing this. We are.

The biblical call to repent is the call to come home, to return to where you came from, to turn from waywardness, and to hoist the heart toward paths of homecoming and hope. Augustine said he found out too late in life that God promises forgiveness to those who repent but not repentance to those who sin.[19] Or in the words of Paul, who never abandoned apologetic preaching for kerygmatic preaching, as some suppose, "Do you despise the riches of His goodness, forbearance, and longsuffering, not knowing that the goodness of God leads you to repentance?"[20] To believe in repentance is to believe there will be repentant murderers who will meet their victims in paradise, to believe there will be repentant slanderers who will meet those they slandered in heaven, to believe there will be repentant thieves who will meet those they've plundered in heaven.

Even as the heart is mourning its loss, the soul is rejoicing in its find.
SUFI APHORISM

William Temple, archbishop of Canterbury from 1942 to 1944, said that "to repent is to adopt God's viewpoint in place of your own. . . . In itself, far from being sorrowful, it is the most joyful thing in the world, because when you have done it you have adopted the viewpoint of truth itself, and you are in fellowship with God."[21]

Has there ever been a better definition of repentance than this from C. S. Lewis?

Fallen man is not simply an imperfect creature who needs improvement: he is a rebel who must lay down his arms. Laying down your arms, surrendering, saying you are sorry, realising that you have been on the wrong track and getting ready to start life over again from the ground floor—that is the only way out of our "hole." This process of surrender—this movement full speed astern—is what Christians call repentance. Now repentance is no fun at all. It is something much harder than merely eating humble pie. It means unlearning all the self-conceit and self-will that we have been training ourselves into for thousands of years.[22]

When Jesus called for people to repent, he was calling them to take on the courage of a child: who is open to life, not armored in defenses and weaponized with victimology; who is receptive to risk—the risk of becoming all of who they are, which is the essence of the abundant life promised to all who grow into childhood. Unless, therefore, we become as a child and are willing to repent, we cannot be his disciples or "see" the kingdom of heaven forming all around us.

"There is hope in your future, says the Lord"[23] is the bottom line of repentance.

"These Days, These Days"

A missional people and a missional church don't get to pick their day and place. Like the prearranged marriages of times past, someone else (God) chooses your love, and you love God's choice. Anything less is a church out of place, and a displaced church cannot be a doxological church, since nearness to God is at the heart of the value of a place. There is a field of study called *psychogeography*: the effect of place on human emotion and behavior. We need a new branch of study called *theogeography*: the effect of place on faith, community, and mission.

Volcanic eruptions prompt evacuations. Few things are harder in life than moving from settled positions where we feel safe and comfortable to unknown territory where we must find our places and set up new positions. The church now finds itself being evacuated from its established perch in society and must find new homes, all of which are in precarious danger zones. These evacuations taking place are not just cultural but also intellectual.

Question: The number of people on Twitter who follow a
religious leader, house of worship, or pastor?
Answer: Two percent.

SEE PINETOPS FOUNDATION,
THE GREAT OPPORTUNITY: THE AMERICAN CHURCH IN 2050

Christianity is the future's go-to honeypot for ridicule and abuse. In the aftermath of volcanic eruptions, the belief that the Bible is a sacred text with salvific solutions for a world gone wrong appears in the same category as the belief in fairies, leprechauns, and unicorns. Already more Brits are convinced of the existence of ghosts than they are of a divine Creator or even of heaven.[24]

In our lifetimes we've gone from "Please pray for. . ." to "If you're the praying type, you might consider praying for. . ." to "No more thoughts and prayers" or "Your thoughts and prayers are as effective as tots and pears."

The gospel has always gone against the grain, but the grain has been friendly grain until now. From here on out, it's hostile grain.

When North American Christians do anything in the future in public or even semipublic arenas, they can expect fire fountains to erupt from the pent-up anger seething at the bowels of the earth. Any Christian practice will be problematic, from praying in public to making the sign of the cross.

This hostility is extending beyond Christianity to religion in general. One of the most popular answers to the question "What is the one single thing anyone could do to make this world a better place?" has become "End all religion." Indeed, in a recent and disturbing development, advocates for human rights may or may not include "religious freedom" in those "human rights."[25]

Increasingly, numbers of people are being raised in households where Christians in particular, and religious people in general, are viewed as inferior in every way: morally, intellectually, socially, and culturally.[26] This flippant dismissal of people of faith is not unheard of in history. Scottish biographer James Boswell (1740–95) hurried to the deathbed of philosopher David Hume (1711–76) and found him "lean, ghastly and quite of an earthy appearance." Boswell unabashedly asked Hume about his views on the afterlife, and Hume admitted that philosophers John Locke and Samuel Clarke had turned him off to faith. Besides, Hume added, "the Morality of every Religion was bad." When Hume heard someone was religious, he immediately assumed "that he was a rascal." Boswell then pushed further and asked if Hume wouldn't like to see some of his friends who had recently died again. Hume owned that he would but added that none of them "entertained such a foolish, or such an absurd, notion."[27]

Catholic schools are under attack in Great Britain for being "socially divisive" and for running "monofaith" establishments. They are now under quota constraints to accept no more Catholic students than would consti-tute 50 percent of its student body. This "faith cap" is to preserve "social cohesion and respect," even though this means Catholic schools are being asked to discriminate against Catholics. The Catholic church has agreed to compose its student body of up to 30 percent non-Catholics, but that is not enough for the government.[28]

We can expect religiously motivated violence to increase and the free exercise of religion to be constrained at every turn. Religious freedom itself will be an increasingly contentious notion. In the 195 countries of the world today, diversity and pluralism are losing out to the imposition of a religious monoculture[29] or a ban on religion, which is itself a religious position.

For example, France has banned all "conspicuous religious signs" as a new dress code for members of its parliament. No crosses, no menorahs, no crescents, no symbols showing personal religious beliefs are allowed, and a neutral dress code is enforced.[30] Ironically, early Marxists argued against such restrictions of religion, advocating for the freedom of reli-gion because ultimately they believed freedom of religion would free people from religion.[31]

Government is not the major offender in twelve of the twenty-three worst countries for the waning of religious freedom. The primary culprits are "non-state militants," another name for terror groups and the new Puritanism across all religious traditions. For some, the free exercise of reli-gion is "blasphemy."[32] There are also many nations (Indonesia, for example) who profess tolerance and acceptance of religious diversity, but never a word is spoken publicly against attacks on Christians and other religious minorities.[33] Some Indonesian Christian churches include in their weekly liturgy a "Martyr's Moment" to remember those in their communities who died or had their houses burned because of their faith.

Being a Christian will "appreciate" in cost, and there are no "trivial" costs. A "cost" can be as high as losing your head, but a cost of loss of friends, rejection by family members, and mockery by society are still real hurts, real costs causing real pain, and you really feel all these losses. This new hostile environment will lead to "bivocational ministry" (a dangerous term, since there's only one calling) as the new norm for the church, largely surpassing that of the "professional" paid pastor, although the pastoral role and the culture of church will need to change to accommodate the new realities.

If we were to go ahead with a purge of religious ideas from our account of human worth, human dignity, and basic equality, it is an open question how much that purge would take with it.

NYU PHILOSOPHER JEREMY WALDRON,
ONE ANOTHER'S EQUALS

Pastors as Development Officers

Given this climate of hostility, no longer can the church count on special favors from the state in any arena, especially and including finances. The end of tax-exempt status for religion is within view. This means that pastors and churches must rethink the whole arena of "stewardship" and fund-raising.

Elsewhere we have framed this transition as the shift from "stewardship" and its theology of giving to "trusteeship" and its theology of receiving. In stewardship one gives to God a portion of what one has. In trusteeship one receives for oneself a portion of what is God's. "Freely you have received; freely give," Jesus said.[34]

The Greek word *oikonomos*, from which we derive our word *economy*, is comprised of two Greek words: *oikos*=house; *nomos*=rules or laws. An *oikonomos* is someone who manages the house or *oikos* (property) of the owner according to the *nomos* of the owner. Christians frequently act as if we're the owners. But it's not *our* property. It's not *our* estate. It's not *our* wealth. It's theologically incorrect to say "ours" about anything we have, because followers of Jesus own nothing. We are trustees for the true owner. The money may be in our bank accounts; the title may be in our names; but we are only the trustees of what is in the bank or on the deed.

Everything that is not given is lost.

INDIAN PROVERB

No one "gives" to God. We only "give back" to God. "All things come from

You, and of Your own have we given You."[35] The implications for the future of traditional churches are revolutionary:

› Every pastor is now a fund-raiser and is never not involved in a capital campaign.
› Every church needs a cash cow and every pastor a second occupation.
› Every church needs to digitize their giving as much as possible and use offering plates only symbolically.
› Every church needs to get used to paying taxes.
› Every house of worship needs to be prepared to be a "housing project"—providing space for marginalized people such as immigrants, the homeless, the sick and dying, and the elderly.

The very ability of the editors of *GQ* magazine to take on an established canon and replace it with their own divinations is a gift of Christianity to the world. Toleration and liberality come of a Protestant concern for the individual's unmediated access to the divine. The rejection of public power to enforce religious orthodoxy has its historical origins in European Protestant traditions. Even atheists who claim to live a "moral life" are living a morality shaped and "haunted"[36] by centuries of Jewish-Christian teaching. As Matthew Parris wrote, "Whether or not we ourselves believe in God, we've all soaked up the ethical teachings."[37]

One of the most hapless figures in church history is Michael Servetus, the Spanish theologian, physician, and Renaissance humanist. In fleeing the Catholic Inquisition in 1553, he made the mistake of hiding out in John Calvin's sanctuary—Geneva, Switzerland. Servetus's views on the Trinity made him as despised by the Protestants as by the Catholics. When Calvin found out he was hiding in Geneva, he had him hunted down and imprisoned and then personally masterminded his prosecution as a heretic. Servetus was burned at the stake ten weeks later.

Other wings of the Reformation movement were aghast at what Calvin had wrought. One of the outraged was French Protestant preacher Sebastian Castellio (1515–63), a onetime apprentice of Calvin who fell out with his mentor when he was the only clergyman who remained in Geneva to care for the sick and the dying after an outbreak of the plague in 1643. Castellio responded to Calvin's denial of freedom of religion with a statement that strikes at the heart of all human freedoms: "To kill a man is not to defend a doctrine. It is to kill a man."[38]

Escape or Engage?

The temptation of the church of the future will be to escape, not engage, such an unsafe culture. Or if it engages, to let the world set the terms for weapons. But as Castellio himself wrote, "When Servetus fought with reasons and writings, he should have been repulsed by reasons and writings."[39] We must learn to use some new weapons in the future (weapons we actually should have been using in the past) if we are to engage the culture.

Besides, we are not given a choice of only going into those nations and cultures where the soil is open and receptive to the gospel. The great ommission is a command to "go into all the world,"[40] not just places where the soil is already tilled and the climate is conducive. All soils have one thing in common: They need to be seeded by the Good News. But every soil differs in color, topography, living organisms, and mineral content. The point of Jesus' story about the four soils[41] is not that we shouldn't plant in problem soils but that we need to know what we're up against. The church of the future will need more R & D than ever before if it is to keep its divine appointments.

There are times when fear is good. It must keep its
watchful place at the heart's controls.

AESCHYLUS,
THE ORESTEIA

Volcanic soil is some of the richest soil on the planet. Lava burns the ground at first but then enriches the soil with fertilizing elements such as iron, phosphorus, potassium, magnesium, and the blood of the martyrs. A slow process called *chemical weathering* turns a destructive eruption into an enlivening enrichment, a luxuriant lava soil in which things like coffee, tea, and chocolate thrive. Hawaii's Kona coffee is prized worldwide because soils that began as pumice from volcanic eruptions produce better coffee than soils that began as sediments deposited by rivers.

There are privileges that come when the church has a limited and liminal role or is lambasted and flamed—the privileges of suffering, sacrifice, constant misunderstanding, and forgiveness.[42]

One of our heroes is Eivind Berggrav (1884–1959), the Norwegian Lutheran bishop who resisted the Nazi occupation of Norway and refused to cooperate when he was instructed to change the liturgy to reflect the politics of National Socialism. When threatened by his Gestapo interrogators—"We will have you shot"—the bishop calmly replied, "Go ahead. Shoot me. And what will you do then?" That kind of confidence only comes from Christ.[43]

> WALKING IN FAITH

1. Western Christianity is beginning to face some "Pilates," whether in the form of religious authority, pop culture, the court of public opinion, or the power of the state. As we navigate these pressures, in what ways are we denying Christ and pushing his lordship to the back seat of our lives and faith communities?

2. A volcanic culture is best approached not with the force of a fist, but with the force of a fable. In her work entitled *Wired for Story*, Lisa Cron says, "We think in story, which allows us to envision the future."[44] The story that breathes life through the church is *his* story. Which stories within his story empower you to envision the future?

3. The essence of the abundant life is being receptive to the risk of becoming who you are. Part of the risk is in repentance, which is Jesus' call for us to take on the courage and openness of a child. In what specific ways or instances has repentance allowed you to "see" the Kingdom of heaven forming all around you?

PEDAGOGICAL AND ANDROPOLOGICAL REVOLUTIONS

[Children] should be taught not the little virtues but the great ones.
Not thrift but generosity and an indifference to money; not caution but
courage and a contempt for danger; nor shrewdness but frankness and a love
of truth; not tact but love for one's neighbour and self-denial; not
a desire for success but a desire to be and to know.

NATALIA GINZBURG,

THE LITTLE VIRTUES

HIGHER EDUCATION TODAY is poised right where the Roman Catholic church was on the eve of the Reformation, where the British Empire was on the eve of the American Revolution, and where Humpty Dumpty was on the wall just before his great fall: elitist and removed from the hoi polloi and the future in a culture that values equality above elitism.

Two-thirds of US students start some sort of tertiary education after high school, choosing from some four thousand institutions of higher education. Both numbers will only drop precipitously, partly because the digital revolution and financial realities no longer require the leave-home rite of passage to become a "wandering scholar."

Factory-model, industrial-style, fill-in-the-blanks learning has never been replaced by models of learning that fuel and fill up the mind and enchant the human spirit. VR (virtual reality) has not lived up to its promise of transforming education. But it will.

The proof is in the pudding. The words *rich* and *well educated* no longer go together, as Vietnam, one of the poorest countries in the world, does better than the US in math, science, and reading. The 10 percent of Vietnamese kids who are most disadvantaged do better than the average USAmerican child on tests in these three subjects.[1]

Open a school, close a prison.
ATTRIBUTED TO VICTOR HUGO

Our methods of education are part of our culture and its practices. As cultures shift, methods of education need to adapt or risk becoming irrelevant, uninteresting, and/or ineffective, at least when it comes to engaging and impacting the community at large. If science, music, and other art forms evolve across time and cultures, why not education? When you can spend $180 a year at masterclass.com to get twenty-four sessions on writing with Malcolm Gladwell, or on filmmaking with Martin Scorsese, or jazz with Herbie Hancock, or architecture with Frank Gehry, or the art of performance with Usher, or singing with Christina Aguilera, or cooking with Gordon Ramsay, or writing for television with Shonda Rhimes, how much longer do you think someone will pay $80,000 a year to study at one of our colleges or universities?

Here are some commanding themes that will be key components of any responsible educational models for the remainder of the twenty-first century. In place of "education," we are calling it "enchantment learning."

10 Commandments of Enchantment Learning

1. Thou shalt have no other subject higher than the student. Corollary: Kill the learning box misnamed "the classroom."[2] The real classroom for learning is the world.

2. Thou shalt not make for yourself graven images of any technology, nor bow down to any tablet, whether print or digital, nor worship any culture, whether Gutenberg or Google. Thou shalt learn to speak and communicate in the vernacular of the culture you are in.[3]

3. Thou shalt not take the name of your profession in vain. Corollary: Don't "teach." Design and organize learning instead.[4]

4. Thou shalt remember the sandbox, where learning is fun. Keep the playground holy.[5]

5. Honor the Cloud, the gifts of your ancestors, so that you may live long into the future by not confusing relevancy with recency.

6. Thou shalt not forget Moore's law, which is breathing new life, thanks to AI chip making. Half-lives of knowledge are getting shorter and shorter.[6]

7. Thou shalt defy Illich's law at every opportunity, which predicts that it's only a matter of time until any bureaucracy will create the very condition it was organized to prevent.

8. Thou shalt not commit an MOOC (Massive Open Online Course).[7] In the future, students will be allowed to specialize earlier and earlier (like athletes do today). There will be fewer generalized diplomas, only certificates of competencies or credentialing in skills that are required by the marketplace. The name of the education game is individualized, customized, tailored learning experiences. Learning systems must be based on new academic paradigms that shift from passive learning modes to active learning modes, especially ones where students learn habits of mind and habits of the soul at their own rates and in their own areas of special interest.

9. Thou shalt not play it safe but instead take risks and dance the failure shuffle. ("Shake the dust off your feet," said Jesus.[8]) All learning requires unlearning, which requires tremendous courage.

10. Thou shalt not commit a factory-model, cookie-cutter pedagogy. Thou shalt not covet your neighbor's YouTube, nor his Facebook, nor his Instagram, nor his zip code. Thou shalt be an original, a one-off, and cultivate one-off originals.

Only well-educated and technically competent persons can destroy civilization. . . . Education is not enough. Educated men staffed the atomic plants and designed the Buchenwald furnaces.

JUSTICE ROBERT HOUGHWOUT JACKSON,
CHIEF US PROSECUTOR AT THE NUREMBERG TRIALS

> WALKING IN FAITH

1. If preoccupations with microaggressions, cultural appropriation, and no-platforming are making true education impossible, what adjustments can restore education—and our expectations of education—to effectiveness and relevancy?

2. How might embracing a theology of failure (see chapter 17) free educators and students to embrace risk within the learning process?

2

DEVOLUTION REVOLUTIONS
AND THE COLLAPSE OF
NATION-STATES

IN BOTH WORLDS OF UNLIMITED CYBERSPACE and contentious physical borders—worlds both virtual and literal—the question, What is a nation? is of pressing urgency.

St. Brendan, a sixth-century Irish monk, voyaged across the North Atlantic in search of the legendary Isle of the Blessed. He came face-to-face with an erupting volcano, "shooting up flames into the sky . . . so that the mountain seemed a burning pyre."[1] The dangers of lava bombs falling on sailing vessels and setting them ablaze was an ever-present one.

It still is. Especially to ships of state.

In 1589, the English Privy Council used the word *state* to describe a place with fixed borders and a fixed government. The word had been in currency for only a couple of decades. It was political philosopher Thomas Hobbes (1588–1679) who developed the concept of the state as the locus of political sovereignty.[2] The "nation-state" is a subsequent invention, emerging in its current form in the same decade that gave us the "denomination."[3] The latter came out of the Westminster Assembly of Divines in 1643; the former came out of the Treaty of Westphalia in 1648, which ended the Thirty Years' War. It is no accident that these two "mediating structures" are both coming apart at the seams and at the center.

A globalized, digitized world is moving away from nation-states and denominations, away from independent, monolithic models of governments and corporations and toward interdependent, polylithic models. Boundaries are, as a consequence, becoming more problematic, which means their defensibility is both more intensely contested and more high maintenance. The question is whether the national sovereign state remains a worthy instrument of social life or is becoming increasingly clumsy for a world of mass migration, terrorism, globalism, and climate change.

A global economy is not unprecedented. Between 1880 and 1914 there were high levels of world economic integration. That system was demolished by thirty years of war and depression, generating a backlash that fostered national self-sufficiency and localization.

Let goods be homespun whenever it is reasonably and conveniently possible;
and above all, let finance be primarily national.

JOHN MAYNARD KEYNES,
"NATIONAL SELF-SUFFICIENCY"

The one thing we all share is . . . uniqueness. The hallmark of our universality is our particularity. Nationalism becomes a negative force when it is narrow, prejudiced—when you can't see beyond the rim of your own plate. Positive patriotism is different: You are able to love your country while seeing the delights and excitements of what is on others' plates.

It wasn't too long ago that scholars cheered "the end of history": Liberal democracy, with its attendant open markets, globalization, and rule of law, was bringing an end to all this nationalistic nonsense. But something is up. Have you noticed? The more "global" we get (or as Thomas Friedman would describe it, the more the world "flattens"),[4] the more frizzy, fluxy, boingy, slippery the world becomes. Equally prominent to the fading influence of the West is the worldwide populist backlash against globalism and corresponding emerging tribalisms.

Many still see globalization as inevitable. Guinness sells more beer in Nigeria than it does in Ireland.[5] And in the long run, the inevitability of globalization may be true. But also in the long run, as John Maynard Keynes once said,[6] we're all dead. Meanwhile, in the short run, globalization can go into reverse, and as of this writing the nationalist chickens have come home to roost.

As Albert Einstein expressed it in a letter to G. S. Viereck in 1921, "Nationalism is an infantile disease. It is the measles of mankind."[7] The more global we become in our consciousness and citizenship, the more every country is undergoing a surge of nationalist fever and even tribal fervor. Add to that the fact that laws written for nation-states no longer work when some of our greatest threats are coming from non-nation-states, and preemptive intervention, up to and including warfare, is now a national strategy.

The dismal failure of all centralized statist and collectivist approaches does not mean that free-market capitalism has won. Chinese capitalism is very different from the capitalism practiced in the US. In China, there is no inclusion of democracy in private enterprise but an authoritarian political order with a redistributive ethic.

The linkage between religious belief and economic behavior, first proposed by sociologist Max Weber in his 1904 book *The Protestant Ethic and the Spirit of Capitalism*, has not been fashionable in recent years, as economists have given moral arguments the dismal dismissal. The good news is that current studies are showing that God and mammon have more to do with each other on a wallet level than previously anticipated.[8] Some, like Nobel laureate Jean Tirole in his book *Economics for the Common Good*, have argued for the moral limits of the market.[9] Ethics must become fundamental to economics, and morality affects economic behavior in essential ways.

In a world that is tearing itself apart into tribes, we need to look for new modes and models that bind everyone together.

Much of modern research and study went to foreign affairs and military campaigns. But the real story of the twentieth century was in internal affairs and conflicts.[10] Foreign conflicts in the twentieth century resulted in 33 million casualties. But domestic conflicts resulted in 170 million deaths.[11] And of course, internal conflicts then lead to regional collapse and international conflicts. You might even say there is a global civil war going on, as the planet has become one big Afghanistan, one spread-out Syria.[12] We have in our lifetime seen whole countries—East Germany, the Soviet Union, Iraq, Somalia, Yemen—crumbling in front of our eyes. Yet every country is undergoing a surge of nationalist fervor as the devolution revolution takes entities back down to their most tribal tiers. You're not surprised to see it in places like Poland, Austria, Hungary, and Ireland, but even those nations most known for their cosmopolitan flair and flavor, such as England, France, Italy, Australia, Scotland, and Sweden, are undergoing surging tribalisms.

The greater the integration of the world community, the greater the hunger to hold on to identity markers: languages, cultures, traditions, histories.

Japanese Americans don't want to "blend into whiteness," hence the birth of young people's participation in tea ceremonies and learning about kimono etiquette and the art of taiko drumming, not to mention pilgrimages back to Japan. And countries such as Israel, Taiwan, and Mexico encourage (and sometimes subsidize) hegiras back to homelands and mother countries.

Tribalism doesn't end at the national border. Secessionist movements are proliferating around the world: separatist Moro in the Philippines, Uighur separatists in China, ISIL in the Middle East. Scotland and Wales constantly debate cutting off from Mother England. Russia is encouraging eastern Ukraine to secede. Secessionist movements are stirring even in the US. In November 2006, the First North American Secessionist Convention was held in Burlington, Vermont. Hosted by the Middlebury Institute, the convention had delegates from eighteen states. Both the Alaskans and the Hawaiians want their countries back, and talk is increasing of a Second Vermont Republic. Similarly, there is talk of a "Cascadia," composed of parts of Washington, Oregon, Idaho, and British Columbia (axis of Seattle-Vancouver, Portland, Boise).[13] "Calexit" and "Texit" make ritual appearances every election. The Lone Star State of Texas is constitutionally able to secede, and some people are already signing their location as "Texas Republic." Every souvenir shop in California is filled with California Republic clothing and artifacts. "California values" are proudly touted as of more consequence and correctness than US values. A first failed attempt at devolving California into three or four states will be followed by many others, as well as an attempt to give Native Americans the eastern half of the state as their own independent nation.

People need boundaries to establish who they are. The question of the future is, How local do these boundaries need to be? Are they nation-state boundaries? Are they smaller than that, say city-state boundaries? Are they market-state boundaries? Do people today need multiple boundaries for their multiple identities?

City-States and Urbanburb Culture
As the nation-state diminishes in importance, city-states become the control centers of the global economy.[14] Already mayors of some cities have more power than presidents of some nations. Population density and economic energy will be increasingly yoked and concentrated. The boundaries between urban and suburban are becoming so blurred that the hub of missional activity in the future will be in urbanburbs.

More than half the world's population are now urban dwellers, a number that will climb to two-thirds of the planet's population in the next twenty years and 80 percent within the lifetime of most reading these words.[15] Cities constitute at most one percent of the planet's landmass, but they pack into that space more than half the world's population and the majority of its physical structures and infrastructures.[16]

We've come a long way from Ur, the city of Abraham, from which emerged Judaism, Christianity, and Islam. The early church didn't have denominations, but they did have factions based around cities (Antioch, Rome, Jerusalem, Alexandria, later Constantinople). The Bible begins in a garden, but it ends in a garden city. Every great city has a countryside, but we are bound for the city of God, not the countryside of God.

A megacity is defined as a city of more than 10 million people. In 2000, there were fewer than twenty megacities, only four of which were in industrialized countries. By 2030, there will be forty. Tokyo is currently the largest megacity—home to 38 million people, more than the entire population of Canada. Shanghai is China's largest city, with more than 25 million people.

The cities most capable today of sustaining themselves as nation-states include Singapore, Los Angeles, London, New York City, Shanghai, Sydney, and Hong Kong.[17] If you want a feel for the future, go to Singapore. The nation gained independence from Malaysia in 1965. Singapore has 5.6 million inhabitants, almost all of them living in high towers. Each with a population of at least five million, these city-states need not answer to anyone.

From 2010 to 2016, large cities accounted for 73 percent of their nation's employment gains and two-thirds of output growth.[18] From 2010 to 2014, just twenty counties accounted for half the new business formation in the US. The suburbs now house more poor people than do the nation's urban centers.[19]

The big divides in the US are not between red and blue, or interior and coastal, or cosmopolitan and parochial nationalist, but apartheid divides between rich and poor in cities themselves. More than a billion city dwellers, or one-sixth of the world's population, are living in squatter settlements. The number of slum dwellers is expected to double in the next couple of decades.

Instead of cities of light soaring toward heaven, much of the twenty-first century urban world squats in squalor, surrounded by pollution, excrement, and decay.

MIKE DAVIS,
PLANET OF SLUMS

Every great city has distinct small-town neighborhoods with the soul of a village. Every great church is a community with the soul of its neighborhood and the mind of Christ. If there is "no there there," as Gertrude Stein famously said of Oakland, California, then it is not a city.[20]

Corporate States or Market States

The Big Five—Amazon, Apple, Alphabet Inc. (parent company of Google), Facebook, and Microsoft—are essentially new forms of nationhood. They are corporate states, not nation-states, with corporate diplomacy now as important as political diplomacy. In Ernest Cline's dystopian vision of the future (*Ready Player One,* 2011; now a Spielberg film, 2018), the world is governed by corporations, not nation-states.

The church was once the bedrock on which communities were built. Facebook will be that for the future if Mark Zuckerberg has anything to do with it. When Facebook crashed in some cities during the summer of 2014, many people called 911.[21]

Google aims to be, according to cofounder Sergey Brin, "the perfect search engine . . . like the mind of God."[22] The Apple Store on Fifth Avenue is the most photographed image in New York City.

The global economy is in the grip of big corporations. In the future, machines may devour us. So may corporations. The US agriculture industry, like the US airline industry, has consolidated down into three megaconglomerates.

Micronations

Off the coast of Dubai is the Nakheel islands, billed as "The World." A private archipelago of three hundred islands is being built to form a map of the globe, with waterways patrolled by private security. Individual islands sell from $10 to $40 million apiece. Or you can look into the twelve-deck cruise ship condominium complex known as "The World" that allows people to create homes on board the ship while they travel the world.

You can purchase a small island as an autonomous country where there is "open citizenship" and people who don't live there can still be citizens in a form of virtual citizenry.[23] Or you can declare the plot of ground you own, no matter how small, as a micronation and secede from the country you are now a part of.

Partnerships, Alliances, Liaisons, Strategic Alignments

Germany's leading sociologist, Ulrich Beck, was a champion of the European Union and a confessed Europhile. He saw the nation-state as an outmoded structure and guarantor of security.[24]

The European Union is as highly centralized and bureaucratized as any of the European nation-states that are collapsing in its embrace. The European Union is an "abstract social space where the sole principle of legitimacy now resides in human rights"[25]—open to anyone and anything that upholds universal humanity and a relational universe. No mediating institutions (like nations or denominations) are necessary, but they are tolerated if their reactionary features are checked.

The church cannot expect any nation-state not to pursue and act in its national interest, but it can help redefine and refine what its national interest is. In an increasingly interconnected world, a universal church with exclusive claims, conspicuously local mission, and a high tolerance for paradox can help the whole world find its footing.

> WALKING IN FAITH

1. It is no accident that the "mediating structures" known as nation-states and denominations are coming apart at the seams and at the center, and it was probably no accident that they both appeared in the same decade in the seventeenth century. In what ways does an unbounded commitment to the preservation of these entities ignore or deny this undoing?

2. In your view, is the "inevitability" of globalism negated by the current riptide of hypernationalism? Are they opposing forces or two sides of the same coin? How does greater integration of the world community produce a greater hunger to hold on to identity markers?

3. How is corporate nationhood manifesting in the current culture? What new levers of corporate power are being revealed from a market-state perspective?

GLOBAL REFUGEES AND MIGRANTS

All Christians are called to be hospitable. But it is more than
serving a meal or filling a bed, opening our door—it is to open ourselves,
our hearts to the needs of others. Hospitality is not just shelter
but the quality of welcome behind it.

CATHOLIC ACTIVIST DOROTHY DAY

IN A CULTURE THAT ENCOURAGES US to be the lord of our lives and lord it over others, we hear another voice: *You are your brother's and sister's keeper.* The question is, How do you define "brother" and "sister"? And "keeper"?

In 1941, 769 Jewish refugees from Romania were stuffed onto a 75-year-old, 240-ton yacht bound for Palestine. After ten weeks, it had only reached Istanbul. The engine had broken down, and the British and Turkish governments wrangled over protocols for the coming and going of the refugees. With no British guarantees to enter Palestine, the Turks towed the disabled boat out to sea and abandoned it to the waves. On the night of February 24, 1942, the crippled ship, dead in the water, was dealt a death blow by a torpedo fired in error by a Soviet submarine. The ship sank with only two survivors.[1]

As it was then, the global refugee crisis is one of the great moral challenges of our time.[2] There are now about 250 million migrants worldwide, a population about the size of Indonesia, the fourth largest nation in the world.[3] A world of incessant volcanic activity can't stop making migrants and refugees any more than a new mother can stop making milk. In a world of global warming, the crumbling of the postwar order, and decivilizing meltdowns, the refugee crisis will only get worse. Environmentally induced migration alone will displace tens of millions of people. That means the world will be getting more xenophobic and xenophilic at the same time.

For a tradition whose founder started out life as a child refugee in a foreign land, who was born in a "barn" because there was "no room at the inn," and grew up as a displaced person in a village a long way from the family homestead, Christianity should treat refugees like royalty. We often treat them like refuse.

In fact, Christians are "more likely to be anti-immigrant" than "nones" in almost all of the fifteen European countries surveyed by the Pew Research Center.[4] The refugee and migrant crisis, which can only get worse, not only will define Europe's and North America's character and future but will also define the character and future of Christianity itself because it strikes the heartbreak note of a lived faith. It hits both chambers of the heart of faith —first, a love of kith, kin, and neighbor as part of the common good, and second, a hospitality to the strangers and aliens in our midst—and it can break the heart if not cared for.

Slovenian cultural critic Slavoj Žižek champions the refugee crisis as "one of the major global challenges of our time." The church's failure to protect the vulnerable, honoring their needs and rights while at the same time honoring the needs and rights of citizens and residents, "will have far-reaching implications." But Žižek also argues that the answer to the refugee crisis is neither "throw open the borders nor pull up the drawbridge."[5] Refugees need to respect and learn the culture of their hosts, and hosts need to learn and respect the culture of their guests.

The gifts that guests bring to the host culture is symbolized every time we eat a bagel. Bagels were brought to the US by Jewish refugees from Russia, and so even though they are Eastern European in origin, they came to be known as "Jewish." Poland is the most likely country of origin for the bagels brought from Russian Jewish refugees. But don't attempt to tell a New Yorker that. They get really defensive about their bagels.

The voyage of discovery is not in seeking new landscapes but in having new eyes.

MARCEL PROUST,
LA PRISONNIÈRE

Toward the end of the fourth century, Ambrose, bishop of Milan, scoffed at the useless wealth and art galleries of the pagan temples and cults Julian the Apostate had tried to restore since he took over as Roman emperor in 361: "Let them count up how many captives the temples have ransomed, what food they have contributed for the poor, to what exiles they have supplied the means of living."[6]

In a poem about Chiune Sugihara, the Japanese vice consul to Lithuania who issued thousands of exit visas for Jews fleeing the Nazis, Irish poet and archaeologist Caitríona O'Reilly puts into monosyllabic simplicity a tribute that tugs at the heart:

> *Some just know*
> *that love must be put into action or it is not love.*[7]

Unfortunately, our disaster and refugee relief is still medieval, tossing food and coins to those lined up outside the doors of churches. Turf wars among international humanitarian agencies are utter embarrassments. We need a "Humanitarians Anonymous"[8] where relief professionals can confess their sins, overcome their doctrinal disputes among themselves, and focus on the need.

A starving child knows no politics.
RONALD REAGAN

Paul was a Jewish nationalist, bent on the extermination of resident aliens and outliers like Christians, and he was venerated for his violence and zeal. Yet Paul became the one who stood up to Peter and insisted that one's identity as a Jesus follower transcends all distinctions of race, ethnicity, nationhood, and class.[9] The theologies of both Judaism and Christianity fought against distinctions of nation and race and class: There is only one God, Creator of all humanity, not nation-gods who conquer other nation-gods, and there are no racial or economic differences before God.

Jesus rebukes every us versus them, erases every in versus out, banishes every elite versus outcast, and calls us to a strange Kingdom of living and loving where Calvary levels all. To disrespect any person is to slap the face of Jesus and to slander that person's Creator, God.

Remember only that I was innocent and, just like you, mortal on that day,
I, too, had had a face marked by rage, by pity and joy,
quite simply, a human face!
WALL INSCRIPTION AT YAD VASHEM HOLOCAUST MEMORIAL,
JERUSALEM

> WALKING IN FAITH

1. How do (even wealthy) nations approach mounting refugee needs in light of the perception of finite resources? Is the perception the problem, and if so, what truths can be brought to bear?

2. Does the church mimic the views of nations in this regard? How does the church help to resolve the plight of refugees?

3. Is the church fully assuming its role, or is the church receding in some ways? Explain.

3

CHINAFICATION

THE NEW SUPERPOWERS are China, India, and the united Arab region.

The collapse of the US and of the West generally as the world hegemon is clear. What is unclear is what or who will take its place. The most globally connected and sophisticated cities in the world are Bangkok, Singapore, and Kuala Lumpur. The Association of Southeast Asian Nations will be the fourth largest economy by 2050. What makes a developed country is not the poor having cars but the rich using public transit.

Time has made the East more West. But China is now as Western as it will get. China in the future will make the West, and the world, more Chinese, more Eastern. It is said the world can get a cold from USAmerica's sneezes. It will get the flu from Chinese rhinitis.

From the standpoint of sheer numbers, China will be the world's most populous Christian nation by 2040. Some scholars are even arguing for 2030 as the date when there will be more Christians in China than in Mexico, Brazil, or the United States.[1] Buddhism is currently the most popular religion in China, with 250 million adherents. The Communist Party remains officially, aggressively atheist and views all religious activity as destabilizing of the social order. But since 1979 it has officially recognized five faith traditions: Buddhism, Daoism (practiced among Han Chinese), Islam, Protestantism, and Catholicism.

Although China's Christian roots date back to the seventh century, the last forty years saw a record turnaround for the Christian faith in China. During the 1970s, all public expressions of faith were banned, something Mao started twenty years earlier. If China does overtake the US to become the world's largest Christian nation,[2] it will be the greatest single revival Christianity has ever known. Like the early church, it will have taken place in a culture of persecution where those not willing to have state control over religion (e.g., house churches, Pentecostals, underground Catholics, Falun Gong, Tibetan Buddhists, and Uighur Muslims) face daily harassment, from closed job doors to locked prison doors, and the criminalization of religious behavior, from wearing long beards to giving children religious names (common Muslim practices prosecuted in Xinjiang).

Catholicism in Chinese is *tian zhu jiao*, literally "the teachings of the heavenly Lord." Protestantism is *jidu jiao*, literally "Christ Teachings." Then there are numerous Christian cults and movements. In Chengdu, the capital of China's Sichuan Province, there is Eastern Lightning, a Christian cult whose millions of followers believe that Jesus lives on earth as a Chinese woman.

A conservative estimate for the number of Chinese Protestants is 60 million (some say it's more like 100 million). Perhaps as much as half of these belong to the underground Protestant church free of state control.[3] A conservative estimate for the number of Chinese Catholics is 17 million.[4]

Jiang Zemin, just before he retired as general secretary of the Communist Party of China in 2002, is reported to have said he would propose to make Christianity the official religion of China.[5] Whether this was spoken in jest or not, it reveals the loosening grip of ideology on the Chinese people and the appeal of Christian faith.

An increasingly affluent, sophisticated, and cynical society, China needs the narrative of revived national greatness to buttress claims to legitimacy, claims that will be more and more insistently contested in the years ahead. To what extent a surging Chinese nationalism will fuse with a surging rise of Christianity to form a new civil religion is one of the great unfolding stories of the future. Before leaving China, one high-ranking Chinese executive invited us to pray with him (and the many others he said were like him) that China would soon become "the first truly Christian nation ever." Then he said with a smile, "You Americans claim that status, but you know you never really were." The church can expect the future of church-China relations to be a roller coaster ride, like the one we are on now, with the papacy in the midst of a rapprochement with the party while at the same time, the *Economist* reports, "The Chinese government has recently stepped up efforts to block the sale of Bibles online and to stop children from attending churches."[6]

The "three taboos" in China—Tibet, Taiwan, Tiananmen—will drive the plotline of the China story in ways yet to be decided. What is clear is that what President Xi calls the "sinicisation" of religions in China will bring the dragon back in the story of Christianity, if Xi follows through on his promise to make sure all religions in China "serve the highest interest of the state and the overall interest of the Chinese nation: supporting the leadership of the CPC [Community Party of China], supporting the socialist system, and adhering to the socialist way with Chinese characteristics."[7]

It is highly symbolic that Jesuit paleontologist and philosopher Pierre Teilhard de Chardin wrote his most famous manuscript, *The Phenomenon of Man* (1955), while in China. What China has been able to accomplish in a relatively short time is a monumental tribute to the "phenomenon" that "man" can be.

This tribute to "the phenomenon of man" is a historic one as well as a contemporary one. China's tradition of innovation and invention is legendary to the history of civilizations. Nine thousand years ago, the Chinese were drinking wine (made from rice, honey, and fruit) and using alcohol to sterilize and purify. Three centuries before Christ, the Chinese invented the magnetic compass and the crossbow. It took almost fifteen hundred years for Europeans to learn how to make paper after it was invented by the Chinese in 105 BC,[8] a skill that made possible Johannes Gutenberg's printing press—and the Chinese themselves began printing six hundred years before Gutenberg. China invented gunpowder in the second century. They created the first chain drive seven hundred years before the Europeans. Before the second century AD, the Chinese were using built-in rudders in their water vessels. Don't tell the Italians, but the Chinese were the first to eat noodles, at least four thousand years ago. China built a big, beautiful Great Wall two centuries before Christ, a wall now being dismantled in large sections and bulldozed to make way for roads and even one Starbucks.[9]

And China *is* building roads. In 1989, China had only 168 miles of freeway. By 2015, China had 22,500 miles of freeway, the same as the US interstate highway system. By 2025, they will have added more than

30,000 miles of highway. Communist China is successfully using capitalism economics to maintain its power and expand its infrastructure—without protecting workers' rights or human rights. Yet in China, only 3.1 percent of the rural population is below the poverty line. The US figures are 12.7 percent.[10]

No one predicted that China, with its strong and controlling Communist Party, would turn out to be one of the orgies of capitalism. China seems to be rewriting the rules of economics in more ways than one. For reasons no one can yet fully understand, China has managed to transform itself in record time from the world's factory to an industrial park of innovation and technology and local brands with their own intellectual properties. As of 2018, China's share of global science and engineering publications has overtaken those from the United States.[11] It has gone from factory floor to top-drawer R & D by refashioning capitalism with targeted state involvement, bureaucratically allocating capital and credit, tightly controlling money flowing in and out of the country, manipulating currency, protecting sectors from competition, and bungling state-owned enterprises.[12] Maybe China's success in pioneering a new form of capitalism has something to do with the mind-set of an old Chinese proverb: "Better a diamond with a flaw than a pebble without."

There are 41,000 Chinese restaurants in the US—more than McDonald's (14,000), KFC (4,500), and Burger King (13,000) combined. Our new saying ought to be "As American as Chinese takeout."

What does this geopolitical shift that is China's surge back to global prominence mean for Christianity and the church?

› Any Christian apologetic that does not take China into account is irrelevant to the world in which we live.
› The church needs to re-Orient toward the East, not always pivot West.
› Every religious book published needs to be translated into Mandarin.
› Every Christian child needs to learn another language than their native one, with Mandarin and Spanish the two top picks.

When is the last time your church has displayed Chinese art like chinoiserie, or offered a course on Chinese culture and religion, or served an authentic Chinese meal? China will be our primary conversation partner in the future. It is time we learned to listen and speak to each other.

> WALKING IN FAITH

1. Statistically speaking, China will be the world's most populous Christian nation by 2040. Christianity is flourishing in a repressed society and waning in the American democratic republic. Why?

2. What implications might result if China makes the future West more Chinese, more Eastern?

3. What role might the Chinese tradition of innovation and invention play in the Chinafication of the West? What future conditions in the West might already be developing in support of Chinafication?

4. How is the meteoric rise of Christianity reflective of China's innovative history?

WORLD RELIGIONS, ESPECIALLY ISLAM

Tradition makes the incredible credible.

POLITICAL PHILOSOPHER LEO STRAUSS,
PLATO'S REPUBLIC

WHEN POPE JOHN XXIII MET WITH a Jewish delegation to the Vatican, he introduced himself to them as "Joseph, your brother." He honored their closeness to God and acknowledged their rich historical patrimony with Christianity.

God's prior activity in individuals and cultures is widely recognized in Christian theology by various names: *prevenient grace* (Wesleyan), *common grace* (Reformed), *general revelation* (Catholic). When the Good News is named and proclaimed, it comes as a two-edged sword: One edge critiques some features of that culture, and the other edge fulfills that culture's deepest needs and dreams and is "a confirmation of its prophecies, and an interpretation of its greatest religious symbols and stories."[1]

When Paul saw an altar "TO AN UNKNOWN GOD" in Athens, he referenced the altar and worked that into his sermon: "The One whom you worship without knowing, Him I proclaim to you." He then quoted a Greek pagan poet as witness to the Jesus as revealed in Scripture.[2]

It is not an option but an obligation for religious leaders of all faiths to speak and meet together and explore common issues related to the greater good of humanity. Global religious conflict is on the rise, when the future needs it to be on the wane.

And yet we live in a culture than can agree to agree but not agree to disagree. If we disagree, someone dies, war is declared, an offense is registered, and the opposing voice must be silenced. In other words, we have no idea what pluralism means.

Pluralism means agreeing to disagree. It is not our differences that divide us. It is our refusal to recognize, respect, and learn from our differences that divides us. Pluralism doesn't mean we accept Hindu or Buddhist or atheist teachings, but it does mean that our Christian faith is enriched by the encounter with other traditions.[3] One can nod admiringly at Gandhi's famous claim that "different religions are beautiful flowers from the same garden" while shaking one's head over his follow-up clause: "or they are branches of the same majestic tree."[4]

Interreligious dialogue presupposes deep formation in the Christian faith, which is a momentous assumption. But when that formation is present, conversion can occur. When Jesus found genuine and even superior faith in people from outside his own Judaism,[5] he celebrated it and taught from it. And yet he still affirmed that salvation is from the Jews.[6] Encounters with other religions were not a threat to Jesus but a common thread throughout his life, starting from the very beginning.

Interreligious dialogue is not dialogue between religions.
It's dialogue between believers.

FRENCH CARDINAL JEAN-LOUIS TAURAN

Christianity is enriched by encounters with other religions. When Christians see how Muslims value prayer, we are prodded to "pray continually." When Christians see how Buddhists value *moksa*, or "harmony and equilibrium," we are inspired to be "anxious for nothing." When Christians see how various religions value nature, we learn to "consider the lilies."[7]

In the context of local cultures, the emerging indigenous Christology expands our understanding of Christian salvation. For some cultures and religions, Jesus the Redeemer and Savior resonates most. For others, Jesus as guru, or as liberator, moves people to their knees. Ultimately, everyone comes to "Messiah, Son of God." But everyone has to start somewhere in particular.

The church should be excited to sit down at the table with passionate people of all faiths, engaging them in conversation and learning from them. Can we be "hosts of heaven" like we are hosts in our homes? Can we hear "heaven," not just as a location above and beyond us, but as a living presence and lifestyle among us? Can we be "heavenly hosts" to conversations that speak for all of humanity?

This imperative is most immediate in relations between Christianity and Islam.

Self is a thorn in the flesh.
Zen is another thorn to dig it out with.
When self is out, throw both thorns away.
ANCIENT ZEN SAYING

A fifth of the people now living—1.8 billion people—are Muslim, in all their diversity and wonder. There are many forms of Islam—in places from Paris to Tehran, from Istanbul to Dearborn, Michigan.[8] Up until now, Sunni scholarship has dominated Islamic studies, but Shia scholars are now starting to be taken seriously, and the monopoly of the Sunni view is being challenged.[9]

Meanwhile, there are more Christians in Indonesia, the largest Muslim nation in the world (26 million Christians), than in Canada (24 million Christians).

Religion is like a swimming pool—all the noise is at the shallow end.
ANGLICAN THEOLOGIAN WILLIAM H. VANSTONE

Christianity's twentieth-century sparring partner was communism. Christianity's twenty-first-century ideological rival is twofold: consumerism[10] and Islam. Islamism, a reform movement within Islam that has declared holy war against the West, is an option on the table for the world's disaffected and ostracized.[11] This branch of Islam coexists alongside a mainstream Islam that is becoming both more respected and more respectable. Many of our kids will live to see the inauguration of the president of the US featuring a swearing-in ceremony with one hand on the Koran.

Nevertheless, Islam is not the fastest-growing religion in the world. Christianity is. Since the fall of communism, the 100-million-strong Russian Orthodox Church has been building or reopening churches across Russia at the rate of three a day.[12] But Islam *is* the fastest-growing religion in Europe and North America and the dominant faith in more than forty countries. Already there are more mosques than churches in much of France, and this will proceed apace through Germany and the rest of Europe. Demographically, Islam has already won much of the West.

This is why Libya's Colonel Muammar Qaddafi (1942–2011) mellowed as he aged, even sometimes purring like a cat (that just swallowed a mouse): "Allah will grant Islam victory in Europe—without swords, without guns, without conquests. The fifty million Muslims of Europe will turn it into a Muslim continent within a few decades."[13] In the eternal wonder of who wins and who loses, Qaddafi concluded that Allah had already stepped down demographically to declare Islam the winner of the twenty-first century.

What makes Muslim culture so incomprehensible to Christians is that to be born Muslim is to live and die Muslim. To choose or change a religious commitment is a very Protestant notion in countries where faith is based largely on submission to authority.

Christians must learn to stop comparing the worst in Islam to the best in Christianity.[14] It seems as if we willfully misunderstand such concepts as *jihad* or *umma* or *takfir* or shamelessly stereotype Muslims.[15] Something can be recognizably Christian without being legitimately Christian. Something can be recognizably Islamic without being legitimately Islam.

Nothing regresses like progress.

E. E. CUMMINGS

Just as Christianity has been co-opted as a civil expression of Western or USAmerican culture, so Islam is now being co-opted as a civil expression of Arab culture and Arab power rather than a faith religion. But *Arab* and *Muslim* do not necessarily go together. Four out of five Muslims are *not* in the Middle East. Arabs constitute only a minority percentage of all Muslims—80 percent of all Muslims are non-Arabs.

The most populous Muslim country in the world: Indonesia
A big chunk of India: Muslim
The southern part of the Philippines: Muslim
The seven "-stans" in Central Asia (Afghanistan included): Muslim
Most of northern Africa: Muslim

There are recognizably Arab, African, and Southeast Asian forms of Islam. West African Islam has grown through pacific, not coercive, methods.[16] Expect the emergence of a European Islam. Will there be an American Islam?[17]

Of course, the geographic heart of Islam is the Middle East: The holy sites of Mecca and Medina are both on the Arabian Peninsula—Mecca, the birthplace of Muhammad, and Medina, the tomb of Muhammad.

Islam is not an "Eastern" or "Oriental" religion as distinct from Judaism or Christianity. All three traditions emerged in the Fertile Crescent, and for two thousand years the primary context for their development remained the Mediterranean. The three great monotheistic religions—Judaism, Christianity, Islam—share more than a lot in common.

Christianity began as an offspring of Judaism. Islam was an offspring of Christianity. Islam kept much of what Christianity carried over from Judaism—divine transcendence, providence, creation, divine justice and punishment, the devotion of the people to God—and built on it. One book of the Koran is dedicated to Mary.[18] Mary herself is mentioned more times in the Koran than in the entire New Testament.[19]

There are Jewish circles that revere Jesus as the greatest defender of the Halakhah since Hillel the Great. There are Muslim circles that revere Jesus ('Isa) as the Great Prophet and messenger of end times. We have met Muslims and Jews who have a higher view of Jesus than many Christians we know, especially students we teach.

But there are some very real differences. Both Jews and Muslims reject the Incarnation and the notion of God as triune. Even the concept of translating sacred writings is anathema to Muslims, for whom the Koran is inimitable (*i'jaz* in Arabic) and untranslatable.[20] Conversion is a strange concept in Islam, since in Muslim theology everyone is a Muslim. Muslims see both Judaism and Christianity being restored to their original true forms by means of the Koran.[21]

Islam is a comprehensive culture, a totalizing system of life: religious, social, political, economic, educational, judicial, and military systems expressed in religious terminology. Surah 3:19 of the Koran states categorically that Allah's religion is Islam.

Jews and Christians take for granted the separate identity of religion and politics, faith and power. In Islam, there is no distinction. In Arabic, there is no word for "citizen" or "citizenship."[22] So the leaving of temporal affairs to the state and letting religious authorities handle sacred matters is a foreign concept.[23] Sharia law (in one of four forms) is the law of the land in Afghanistan, Iran, Mauritania, Saudi Arabia, Somalia, Sudan, Yemen, and some Islamic states in Nigeria.[24]

True progress consists not in being progressive but in progressing.

BERTOLT BRECHT,
BRECHT ON THEATRE

During the period from the eighth to the eighteenth century, a portion of which we in the West mistakenly call the Dark Ages, and half of which we equally mistakenly call the Christian era, Islam was the leading civilization on the planet. Muslims stood at the forefront of history.[25] Some have argued that it was "the Muslims who lived during the eighth to twelfth centuries who taught the West how to think."[26] One of the earliest dedicated psychiatric hospitals was built in Baghdad in AD 805.[27] One Christian apologist in southern Spain complained that "all talented young Christians read and study with enthusiasm the Arab books; they gather immense libraries at great expense; they despise the Christian literature as unworthy of attention."[28]

In the ninth century, when science barely existed in Europe, the greatest center of scientific research in the world was the House of Wisdom in Baghdad. Historians laud polymath Ibn Khaldun (1332–1406), with his cyclical view of history, as the precursor to Machiavelli, Vico, Montesquieu, Hegel, Marx, Durkheim, and Toynbee. Sociologists claim Khaldun as the founder of their discipline. Marxists claim him as a prophet of dialectical materialism. Capitalists claim him for his advocacy of supply-side economics and the Laffer Curve.

One can be ahead of one's time in one area and behind in another. The rate of adult literacy in the Arab world today is lower than almost anywhere else. Literacy rates in such cities as Cairo and Damascus may well have been higher in the late Middle Ages than in cultured cities like Marrakesh, Morocco, in the early twentieth century.

As disciples of Jesus, we can learn a lot from Muslims, just as we can learn from Jews, Buddhists, Hindus, and atheists. The Spirit cannot be separated from Jesus and the Scriptures, but he can be at work in the hearts of all people of any, all, or no religions. In 1986, at the World Day of Prayer for Peace at Assisi, Pope John Paul II prayed with Hindus, Buddhists, Muslims, and Jews, reminding everyone that "the Spirit, who is at work throughout the world, is particularly active in the hearts of those who pray."[29]

But Christians also have something unique to offer to these conversations:

We offer Jesus. Bob Roberts, a Southern Baptist pastor in Keller, Texas, is showing the rest of the church how to do both from his pastor perch at Northwood Baptist Church.[30]

In AD 917, two envoys from the Byzantine court in Constantinople traveled to the fabled city of Baghdad, the largest city in the world outside of China and the heart of the Abbasid Empire. Upon reaching the caliph's compound, they were taken on a tour of twenty-three palaces, including the palace of the tree, with its astonishing automata; the palace of the one hundred lions, where wild beasts began "sniffing them and eating from their hands"; and the palace of paradise, where eunuchs slaked the ambassadors' thirst with iced water and sherbet. Thirty-eight thousand wall hangings, elegant carpets, and exquisite jewels were displayed to showcase Islamic culture and impress the visitors with this cosmopolitan city whose residents spoke Aramaic, Persian, and Arabic and where the Muslim majority coexisted peacefully with thriving communities of Jews, Christians, and Zoroastrians.[31]

The envoys had been sent to negotiate a cease-fire between the two empires and to organize a prisoner exchange. But if the rulers of Byzantium and the Muslim rulers of Baghdad were enemies, they still treated each other with decorum and dignity.

It is easy to forget that fourteen centuries of relationships among Christianity, Judaism, and Islam have often been dynamic and fruitful. Historically, there is no ingrained and inevitable antagonism between Islam and the West. In the long and complex history of these three great communities of faith that trace their roots back to the same revelation to Abraham (see Genesis 12:1-2), barbarism and inhumanity have been plentiful, to be sure. But there have also been many instances when the Menorah of Judaism, the Cross of Christianity, and the Crescent and Star of Islam (really the Ottoman Empire, but that's another story) encountered one another with mutual enlightenment and respect.

In today's geography, the first people of substance to honor the Christ child came at great expense from Iran, Iraq, and Saudi Arabia. There were Arabs at the manger, pagan outsiders paying homage before Jewish insiders. And yet despite this, some of the greatest volcanoes humanity has ever faced are looming on the horizon. One of these volcanoes is an uncomfortable truth: Either all cultures and all religions are morally equivalent or they are not.

If they are morally equivalent, if we really are all climbing the same mountain, just on different paths, then all human individuals are *not* endowed with the same human rights, because some religions, some cultures, differentiate rights for men and rights for women, the disabled, the young, the elderly.

If we *are* all endowed with the same human rights, then all cultures are not morally equivalent, and all religions are not equal. Those who believe in solidarity with the world's oppressed must be willing to take the risk they are right. There are morally superior ways of being in the world.

A fanatic is someone who can't change his mind and won't change the subject. Any time anyone attempts to build genuine solidarity between those divided by religion and culture, you can expect to hear the silencing shouts of the fanatics.

Fanaticism is an equal opportunity silencer. Its enforcement extends to every religious tradition and to every movement within that tradition, whether the waters are being stirred up in the pools on the right and left or the puddles and muddles in the middle. But to criticize Islam is not inherently Islamophobic, any more than to criticize Christianity is inherently Christianophobic or to criticize Judaism is inherently anti-Semitic. Islamic intellectuals need to be able to criticize features of the Islamic heritage without the threat of fatwa or the stigma of submitting to colonialism.

And yet whenever someone says that Islam needs to undergo a reformation like the one Christianity underwent in the sixteenth century, a historian can only cringe and mutter under their breath, "Have you read the story of the Protestant Reformation and the violence and fanaticism it released in the bloodstream of Europe?" Instead of an "Islamic Reformation," we need to encourage an Islamic public theology that recovers its rich heritage of intellectual inquiry and hospitality.

The intellectual stagnation and sclerosis of the Arab and Muslim world needs to be challenged from within. Greece, with a population of 11 million, translates more foreign books into Greek every year than do 300 million Arabs into Arabic. More books are translated into Spanish each year than have been translated into Arabic over the past thousand years. The Prophet Muhammad claimed that every century or so a *mujaddid* ("renewer") would be sent by God to restore Islam to its true form. The faith always required constant renewal and rebooting—as it does today.

The vitriolic relationship of violence to faith needs a fresh appraisal in all religious traditions, especially Christianity, Hinduism, and Islam.[32] But whether this ring of fire becomes an abyss or a horizon depends on how we answer Jesus' question, "What are you looking for?"[33]

> WALKING IN FAITH

1. In a culture that cannot agree to disagree, how does fanaticism drive society's biggest issues away from resolution? How is the church caught up in the fray: Are we defusing angst or throwing fuel on the fire? How so?

2. On the macro level, how does relativism feed the "absolutism" of fanaticism?

3. On the micro level, how do cognitive distortions feed the "absolutism" of fanaticism?

5

THE PUBLIC SQUARE

To blossom, human beings need public spaces that enable play,
freedom and social contact without any ties to consumption.

LAIA JUFRESA,
"SPEAKING OUT OF THE SILENCE"

IF WE ARE TO ADDRESS OUR COMMON PROBLEMS and not blow all asunder on a shrinking and shriveling planet, we must come together and listen to one another. And what's one of the highest gifts you can give anyone? Listening to them. For most people, being listened to and being loved are virtually indistinguishable.

The problem is, there is no longer a public arena, a commons green for listening—only a commons for talking points and distinct, competing publics. A public square has been replaced with public squares. We don't so much have a lack of solidarity as a clash of solidarities based on religious, national, sexual, and ethnic lines. We must bring back the village green, the public square, the commons.

Can the church be the body of Christ amid the realities of violence, politics, and power without becoming corrupted by violence, politics, and power? We can if we exercise the prophethood of all believers: "Oh, that all the LORD's people were prophets and that the LORD would put His Spirit upon them!"[1]

There is an inherent public nature to the Christian life. The public life of Christianity embraces both personal and social interests, both of which may include politics. Preaching has enormous public significance, which is different from political significance.

What is the best way for the future church to interact in the public arena? Nick Spencer, research director at Theos, a Christian think tank in Great Britain, argues that neither of the current methods of "privatization nor privilege" are the ways of the future. In privatization, the church stays out of the public arena. Privilege decrees that it's our culture to begin with and Christians have a special dispensation to mix religion and politics and get their way.[2] Spencer recommends instead that the church only enter the public arena for the public good.[3]

Good poetry is usually written from a background of conflict.

WILLIAM EMPSON,
SEVEN TYPES OF AMBIGUITY

It must be said: Any entrance into the public arena is enough to give you high blood pressure and low self-esteem. Hyperbole and bathos are the occupational hazards of speaking in and writing for the public square. No community deserves the name "community" if it is only comprised of people who think alike, talk alike, walk alike. So the church must get used to not always getting its way and to supporting and sustaining people who think very differently than we do. Even though Voltaire never said what people attribute to him—"I may disagree with what you have to say, but I shall defend to the death your right to say it" (a biographer put those words in his mouth in 1906)—it still doesn't negate the truth that people of all faiths and no faith must find ways to become allies, partners, sisters and brothers in the mutual mission of a better world.

But beyond the cheese and chocolate, the strangeness and the disaffections, which the church must get used to, the public square needs healing before it can truly be a public commons. Right now there is little calming "green" or shared "commons" in the village commons or the village green. Where is the worst place for a serious discussion of any issue anymore? Where is the last place one expects a resolving of tensions, conflicts, and clashes of values in society? The public arena. The psychogeography of the public square is toxic, which in part explains (but doesn't explain away) our bulimic emotionality that swings from emotional starvation to emotional extravagance. But just as Christians must sometimes sit in the smoking section, so Christians must enter the public square.

The Christian never has an excuse to be mean or self-righteous. When every issue is hoisted on the banner of ultimate right and wrong, when everyone is self-righteous in their signaling virtues, when everyone is competing in the Oppression Olympics, when every opposing view is approached as a takedown of an opponent or enemy, when the terms are set in stone and unequivocal . . . then conversation, much less compromise, is made almost impossible.

There are many ironies in this, three of which are worth mentioning. To open the ironic curtain is to find . . .

› *The intellectual irony:* People who oppose "dualism" and "dualistic thinking" the most are often the very ones who demonize those who think differently and try to silence their viewpoints.
› *The cultural irony:* If truth is nothing but a social construction, how can a culture denounce injustice with such vehemence on the basis of oppression and righteousness?[4]
› *The religious irony:* At least for Christians, the wicked and wrong are there not for us to feel better about ourselves but to pray for and humbly call to repentance and conversion.

Social media parrots the public square, but it sets the table for prophetic engagement with a particular menu: First, an obligatory indignation cocktail. Next, an appetizer of wounded outrage and wallowing in victimhood. Then a bottomless buffet of public shaming: Say one stupid thing, and there will be rolling outbursts of online ridicule, including abuse and death threats by instantly marshaled mobs of the righteous—an echo chamber that quickly becomes a gas chamber. It's a final meal offered to a digital culture on death row.[5]

The British politician Sir Oliver Letwin has registered a severe warning for the public square if it is not to be blown apart by what he calls "conviction politics" and "conviction politicians." Entrenched parties are tightening their grips over the public arena. Swelling numbers despise politics and see parties as part of the problem, serving the interest of the oligarchy rather than the people. Then there are people (on both the left and the right) who want their values legalized in society. Letwin argues that "society holds many basic, irreconcilable values—beauty, truth, prosperity, freedom, equality, virtue and justice—none of which can claim overriding significance." If politics cannot become what he defines as "civilization in the service of itself," then the decivilizing forces of the twenty-first century will win.[6]

The worst places are where God does God's best work. And the worst times are when God does the most amazing things. When the church was most corrupt and least "good" (late fifteenth, early sixteenth centuries) was precisely when it conducted and sponsored one of the most revolutionary bursts of creativity in all of art history. The after-parties are often better than the parties.

Back to the prophets, who hang crucified between the past and the future, the actual and the ideal. Every one of us was slapped into being; we all need slaps now and then to bring us back into being. But nobody loves being slapped. Likewise, nobody loves to tell people what they most hate to hear. In spite of the abuse and the attack, the misconstruals and the hate sites, followers of Jesus must exercise the prophethood of their calling as well as protect the backs of those who provoke. Rather than punish the "provokers," we need more people whose ministry is provocation, even if we don't agree with their provocativeness.

The word *prophet* appears more than three hundred times in the First Testament and more than one hundred times in the Second Testament. The Hebrew word for *prophet* is *naviy'* (nahvi), which literally means "mouth-piece" for God, a speaker whose voice speaks for the divine.[7] When Paul instructs us to "quench not the Spirit" and "despise not prophesyings,"[8] it is another way of saying, "Quicken, not quench, your prophetic fire."

How does God convey the prophetic word and quicken the prophetic fire among prophet-disciples? Prophetic discourse in the public arena comes in the following forms:

> *Nataf* is a prophetic word that drips and drops like rain. It is heard in the slow, gentle droppings of the truth, the soft raindrops of the presence of God and the healing resin or anointing oil that consecrates for mission and ministry. In a noisy, discursive world, where conflict of opinion is weaponized for personal destruction, the prophetic exercise of *nataf* helps prophets serve as architects of restraint.
>
> A primary means of prophetic discourse in the *nataf* mode is ritual. Ritual is subjunctive, not subjective. In ritual you are prophesying your way forward, symbolically acting as if something were true, and in so doing making it so. The future church needs more ritual, because ritual restores trust, and trust is the flywheel of faith.

> *Massa* is "the burden of the Lord" placed on us by the hand of the Lord. The mark of a prophet is the ability to recognize a problem before it becomes an emergency. That's a burden that has been placed

on our hearts that other people may not even understand or recognize. Prophets must all be willing to be educated in public.

Part of our prophetic calling is to faithfully carry a burden for a particular issue or situation. We may carry that burden for a little while or for a lifetime. But carry it we must, and with critical detachment combined with lived commitment. We often bear burdens we don't understand or comprehend. But the Scriptures tell us that "God spoke to our ancestors through the prophets at many times and in various ways."[9]

There are hundreds of ways of carrying our burdens—often forgotten, however, is with the handles of music and the arts. This is stated explicitly in Scripture: David set apart those "who were to prophesy with lyres, harps, and cymbals."[10] It is promised that the Spirit of the Lord speaks through us.[11] The prophetic function of the arts has yet to be integrated into the life of the church.

All prophets have a Tarsus period, when they come to their senses and present themselves to Jesus and say, "Whatever you want, Lord, I will do."

> *Naviy'* is prophetic discourse that flows forth or gushes out like a fountain. There are times to keep silent; there are times to speak.[12] There are times when silence itself is speech. Sometimes the loudest and strongest prophetic witness to empire is silence. When Jesus stood before empire, he said nothing. Pilate asked a question, and Jesus invoked silence. When Jesus was encouraged to get political, he rejected the violence of "this world" and invoked the power of God. When he did get physical, he lashed out in the courtyard of the Temple, not in the court of Pilate or Herod.

When the church is always nagging the state, protesting this or that, its prophetic voice is muffled. But when the church disciplines its witness to gush forth the seriousness of its distress at the momentous moment, the impact is magnified.

I need thy thunder, O my God;
thy music will not serve me.

JOHN DONNE,
DEVOTIONS UPON EMERGENT OCCASIONS

When we burst out with prophetic witness, what we lift up is not politics or policies but Christ and his mission.[13] Nothing neuters a prophet faster than seeking popularity and applause.[14] Politics is "the art of the possible." Faith is the art of the impossible. The creative possibilities of the art of the impossible are what move humanity forward. As the story of David and Goliath makes clear, the power of faith wins over the power of the state.

Perhaps one of the best words for the future is the nonpolitical word *synod*. *Synod* comes from *synhodos*, which brings together the Greek *syn*, which means "together," and *hodos*, which means "path," "road," or "journey." The path forward to a positive future for the church and a healthy public square for everyone is a way of life found in following the Way, who transcends all isms, all ideologies, and all politics. Will the church take a "synod" and together (*syn*) walk the way (*hodos*) into the Way of Christ?

> *For this is love's prerogatives—*
> *to give, and give, and give.*
>
> JOHN OXENHAM

Our mission is to make people's lives narratable—to show how their lives make sense and make meaning in the larger story: not the Hollywood story or the Silicon Valley story or the Wall Street story or the White House story or the United States story, but the Jesus story. A future is found in the church's solidarity with his story.

> WALKING IN FAITH

1. How can the church put into effect Nick Spencer's recommendation to only enter the public arena for the public good? How does the church avoid the sense of privilege (which Spencer discourages) when advocating for the public good?

2. In a world where conflict of opinion is weaponized for personal destruction, prophets are needed to serve as architects of restraint delivering *nataf:* slow, gentle droppings of the truth, the soft raindrops of the presence of God and the healing resin or anointing oil that consecrates for mission and ministry. What specific examples of *nataf* have you witnessed in recent times? How many "prophetic exercises" have contradicted this idea?

ACID BATHS OF IRONY

*If virtue becomes vice through some hidden defect in the virtue;
if strength becomes weakness because of the vanity to which strength
may prompt the mighty man or nation; if security is transmuted into
insecurity because too much reliance is placed upon it; if wisdom
becomes folly because it does not know its own limits—in all
such causes the situation is ironic.*

H. RICHARD NIEBUHR,
THE IRONY OF AMERICAN HISTORY

WHAT IS AT THE TOP of the list of things you dislike? We'd put people who feel the need to make lists of things they don't like.

That's irony. Did you groan? Say "Make it go away"? Better get used to it. Faith is now forged in a furnace of contradictions and complexities. The ability to ironize one another, along with iron-sharpening-iron discipleship, are two of the most important ways we can arm and armor ourselves for the future.

Let's try a couple more from the past, present, and future:

› If you want to learn about alien invasions and alien ancestors, you go to the History Channel.
› We live in a country that opposes all torture, beginning with water-boarding. But we take you out in a nanosecond with drones.[1]

———

*I thought how ironic it was that I'd dismissed dog meat as a cultural idiosyncrasy
in Vietnam; that "who am I to judge?" extended to Islamic laws in Uzbekistan
and Buddhist temple restrictions in Cambodia, but not to Republicans, hunters or
gun owners. I'd shaken my head at the prejudices some nations had for their closest
neighbors, only to discover that, among my cultural neighbors, I was just as prejudiced.*

LIZ DODD,
"WELCOME TO THE NEW WORLD"

———

Christians in particular, and USAmericans in general, tend to be tone-deaf to irony, satire, and even sarcasm. Critic and satirist H. L. Mencken (1880–1956) thought the disability was so severe that he developed a special backward-sloping script (he called it "ironics") to clearly indicate irony whenever it stared you in the face. There is a punctuation mark, called an "ironieteken" (⸮), meant to identify irony and sarcasm for those who simply don't "get it"[2]:

You don't have to love irony, but you do have to come to appreciate it. The more often opposite things happen at the same time, the more we'll have to learn to live with it. In a culture that scoffs at supernatural healing but can't get enough of supernatural horror, that applauds the "Big-Bang" immaculate conception of two hydrogen atoms but mocks the coming together of the Holy Spirit and Mary in the Virgin birth, the ability to keep going in the midst of the encircling irony is a survival skill of the first order.

Henry David Thoreau made his living working as a surveyor, and the irony of his measuring the forests and fields for those who developed the land and cut down the trees didn't escape him. A biographer wrote that his profession "made him complicit in destroying the forest" he loved.[3] But he still didn't stop mapping the land.

Uprightness and uptightness do not go together. God lives in laughter, lightness, loyalty, love, spontaneity. Life is not a joke, and yet life is jovial, joyful, playful—full of beauty, wonder, oddness, and sadness. The life of faith that can sustain us into the future is in view in Luke 10:21-24: After his disciples came back from their mission trip, "Jesus rejoiced in the Spirit."[4] That little phrase, *ēgalliasato tō pneumati tō hagio* in Greek, means Jesus celebrated, danced, prayed, and let the Spirit loose. We are invited to do the same.

In the history of the church, you see the playful, witty, whimsical side of liturgical life in festivals of the church and the microarchitecture of cathedrals: dragons and gargoyles leering out of the darkness and skulking in their niches; crowds of mythical creatures lurking in the lofts; all sorts of naturalistic foliage unfolding on every open surface.

All literary style . . . is made up of such coincidences, which are a spiritual sort of puns. That is why style is untranslatable; because it is possible to render the meaning, but not the double meaning.

G. K. CHESTERTON,
IRISH IMPRESSIONS

There are lots of ways to take the Lord's name in vain. To call yourself a Christian and to have undergone a humordectomy is one of them. So is living a fuddy-duddy faith. Christians are experts at creating and fostering coincidences, the things G. K. Chesterton called "spiritual puns." You might even call it a stylistic thing.

Others might not get our puns. Christians may also be known for "inappropriate" laughter at odd times and over random items. The sublime in every tragedy, and the tragic in everything sublime, prompts in us the kind of incongruous laughter ancient Greek playwrights expected during their tragedies.[5] To laugh in the face of suffering is not to show disrespect but to honor suffering with the ultimate in respect: laughter as well as tears. The apostle Paul was never more snarky and sarky than when talking about his own afflictions and suffering.[6]

We began this section with a quote from the historian H. Richard Niebuhr. Let's exit this ring of fire with a quote from his older brother, one of the four greatest theologians in US history, Reinhold Niebuhr:

> Humour is, in fact, a prelude to faith; and laughter is the
> beginning of prayer. . . . The intimate relation between humour
> and faith is derived from the fact that both deal with the
> incongruities of our existence. Humour is concerned with the
> immediate incongruities of life and faith with the ultimate ones.
> . . . Laughter is our reaction to immediate incongruities and
> those which do not affect us essentially. Faith is the only possible
> response to the ultimate incongruities of existence which threatens
> the very meaning of our life.[7]

> WALKING IN FAITH

1. Not recognizing and "appreciating" sarcasm and life's ironies leaves one open to being overwhelmed by impossibility. How can the church better balance seeming contradictions with our guiding truths?

6

THE DISUNITING STATES OF AMERICA

The last thing to collapse is the surface.
ALBERT EINSTEIN

EVERY COUNTRY IS BORN TO DIE. There are no exceptions. Greece was once the greatest civilization in the world. Now it is the poorest country in Europe. Mighty Athenian democracy, the highest expression of the ancient world, fell and failed. USAmerican democracy can fall and fail too. Are we doing ministry in the twilight years of Pax Americana?[1]

The United States of America is broken—not just its systems, its structures, its politics, or its processes, but most of all the spirit of its people. Trust in the American Dream has withered and weakened, and with it a respect for the nation's heritage, hopes, and future.

The US once stood as a proud beacon of hope and a promised land of freedom for the underdog, the dreamer, the outcast, the risk taker. US citizens today feel like they are living some Nietzschean nightmare, not the American Dream.

The US once was proud of its "melting pot" and "salad bowl" status as a land of opportunity for all. Today there is no unified "American" identity but only a concatenation of interest groups and identity politics. (When an identity crisis is permanent, it's no longer a crisis but a condition.)

The US once held all its diverse components together on a declaration of "self-evident" truths about a government of/by/for the people. Today truth is not self-evident but self-constructed, fabricated from the moist finger in the winds of opinion research and social media.

The US once was celebrated as the greatest nation on earth, first in math, science, innovation, infrastructure. The US has since fallen to the rear of almost every category, and no one is in agreement as to how best to measure greatness.

The US was once a beloved nation, respected and revered abroad. Today it is one of the three most hated countries in the world for its arrogance, attitudes, and actions. The loss of faith in the vision of America that fueled the dreams of the world for the last two hundred years is as stunning as a shooting star. The shared narrative that inspired loyalty and love is not only not being shared; the primary sense is also that something is wrong with America's primal story to begin with.

Therefore, be it perceived: Ministry will now take place as the American Empire comes to an end in what can only be called the Disuniting States of America. "Our time" is one of dusk and dawn, vespers and lauds, valediction and vision.

You're not going to like what comes after America.

LEONARD COHEN,
BOOK OF LONGING

The eagle has fallen. It is writhing on the ground, critically injured. Can it be healed? Should the church have a role in healing it?

The US is a divided country, with many splits and more splinters occurring almost every day. There is the divide between the under and working classes versus the middle class and upper class. There is the college educated versus the "uneducated." One of the least understood divisions is between urban and rural, which in many ways surpasses the divide between North and South, coastal and flyover. USAmerica is now back to being a brawling, fractious society coming apart at the seams but without sufficient distance from the unraveling fabric, which is flailing the faces of its sleeping citizens.

We may not be fighting a physical war with two visible sides, but might we be at an even worse crossroads, fighting a "virtual" war split into hundreds of shards, perhaps thousands of factions who refuse any and all satisfactions? It is now trendy for an American to be anti-American, and that's the norm on many college campuses and in many cities. Patriotism among the young, who have never been told they can love their country without being xenophobic, or introduced to the difference between positive patriotism and negative nationalism, is so low in some places it is virtually non-existent.[2] It was not their fault that many of them were able to get through the US public education system without reading the US Constitution and the Declaration of Independence.

Patriotism is the love of the dishes of our childhood.
PHILOSOPHER LIN YUTANG

Humans are built on story. Our common values as a nation, as Rousseau put it many years ago, are expressed in ritual forms that take the shape of a "civil religion." If humans run on stories, and stories are the bloodstream of the body of humanity, the right story at the right time can change everything and help people and nations move forward through anything. Is it time for a new "civil religion" based on a new story of our nation and our world?

Just as religion functions in its purest form as a balm, a bandage, a binding up, a healer for a broken people, so too can civil religion be a binder for a broken nation—but only when its people adhere to common stories, songs, icons, celebrations, and values. For more than two hundred years, the US has had a powerful, unifying story that issued in a strong civil religion gluing the nation together with a great stability, unity, and even a mythological veneration.

USAmerica has now become a nation of all pluribus, no unum, and filled with civil religious agnostics. In order to create new unity, we need a new civil religion, one that celebrates not a certain politics or faith but the core of what it means to be human, to love, to honor, to be in mutual yet reciprocal relationships, and to respect human differences.

This new civil religion does not marry (make one) but marinates (keeps two by the presence of a third) human difference. It does not attempt to fit in but to fit together the diverse stories of the past. It refuses to mandate common beliefs but celebrates all beliefs in common. It is out of living in the commons of the creative tension of juxtaposed differences that our best creativity, our best innovations, our best selves emerge. We must not demonize our polarities but build a bridge over them and then "get over it."

All human beings are born free and equal in dignity and rights.
ARTICLE I—UNIVERSAL DECLARATION
OF HUMAN RIGHTS, UNITED NATIONS

In fact, the whole world needs a new civil religion. Perhaps its greatest expression will be in the sports arena. A sporting occasion is seen by Catholic theologian Daniel O'Leary as "a festival of both God and of humanity—because, in light of the Incarnation, these two mysteries can only ever and always be celebrated together."[3] Nelson Mandela once looked around the world and noted how sport brings hope and peace to places of despair.[4] This is apparent today in Pakistan, where there are an equal number of television channels devoted to cricket as are devoted to Islam. In global civil religion, real battles are replaced by ritual warfare on fields of play.

At the 1936 Olympic Games in Berlin, the world record holder for the long jump, Jesse Owens, was watching his dream slipping away. He had fouled his first two jumps in the preliminary round. His blond German rival, Ludwig "Luz" Long, took him aside and coached him in how not to get that final foul. Owens took his advice and went on to win the gold medal. Long took the silver. Hitler stormed out of the stadium.

Owens later paid tribute to his rival: "It took a lot of courage for him to befriend me in front of Hitler. . . . You can melt down all the medals and cups I have and they wouldn't be a plating on the 24-carat friendship I felt for Luz Long at that moment."[5]

In the words of Daniel O'Leary, "There is more to sport than the gold of the medals; there is the gold of the spirit."[6]

Italian historian Enzo Traverso argues that a collective memory of the Holocaust is the grounding for a new global civil religion. Its early shape is already apparent in its temples (Holocaust museums), its festivals (Holocaust Remembrance Day), its priests (Elie Wiesel, Primo Levi, Victor Frankl, Anne Frank), and its saints (memorialized victims). Of course, Traverso is quick to point out that Holocaust memory has done little to forestall or lessen subsequent atrocities (Bosnia, Rwanda, Syria).[7]

Out of shared narratives of our humanity and virtual connections, a new global civil religion will emerge to support justice, peace, and the integrity of creation. This global civil religion would transcend all nationalism and revitalize both our tribal and global villages—a pesto of manyness. In place of a country eating its own seed corn, a global civil religion would provide a new space for dream seeding, a new global commons for innovative imagining, and a new kind of iconography that can sustain a new kind of world for a new kind of human.

There is only one God, Creator of all humanity, not nation-gods who conquer other nation-gods, and there are no racial or national differences before God. Most importantly, our people need to be sensitized to a God who works across national boundaries and loves a child from Chihuahua as much as a child from Chicago.

> **WALKING IN FAITH**

1. It is now trendy for Americans to be anti-American. On many college campuses and in many cities, anti-American sentiments are the norm. How is the presence and/or absence of story involved in the development of this condition?

2. What might a new civil religion—one that celebrates the core of what it means to be human, to love, to honor, to be in mutual yet reciprocal relationships, and to respect human differences—look like? How would this civil religion accomplish its aims, and how is the model distinct from any current model?

PART TWO

Hot Topics

7

TOLERANCE OF DIVERSITY,
TOUTING OF UNITY

Iucundum nihil est nisi quod reficit varietas.
[There's nothing pleasant save what variety freshens.]
PUBLILIUS SYRUS

LAVA SOLIDIFIES INTO ROCK—different kinds of volcanic rocks. All rocks of volcanic origin are igneous rocks, but all are diverse in almost every way. All are also beautiful, and most are useful for building a foundation for the future: andesite, dacite, basalt, rhyolite.

The gift of Pentecost is Spirit—and Spirit turns persons into personalities, each one of which finds their uniqueness in Christ.

Master of Multiplicities

"There is a river whose streams make glad the city of God," the psalmist sang, "the holy place where the Most High dwells."[1] The one river has many streams. And it is those streams that make glad the city of God. God loves diversity. God loves manyness. Like Jesus, we are masters of multiplicities who dance around a core of Oneness—"One God and Father of all, who is above all, and through all, and in you all."[2]

Just look around. No two faces are alike. No two fingerprints are alike. No two minds are alike. No two mosses or coral reefs are alike. All of New England has 1,200 plant species, while the Amazon has more than 80,000 plant species. A square mile of Amazonian forest may be home to as many as 23,000 distinct forms of life.

To put on the mind of Christ doesn't mean we'll all end up thinking alike or that we'll merge and submerge all our differences; but it's a true coming together where the manyness of the body of Christ can truly emerge in our oneness in the mind of Christ. When the Church Universal turns away from business models of organizational leadership and instead begins to trust and obey the Spirit, the global church will not march in step but dance in sync.[3]

Diversity means division and diversion only when it is not seen in its true light—as divine divulgence and dividend. The One-and-Only Jesus makes a world of difference. When you've met one Jesus follower, you've met one Jesus follower. The more Jesus lives in us, the more unique, original, and one-of-a-kind we become. The way to be yourself is to be with Christ.

Christ does not say to me, "Be yourself." He says, "Be with me."
BROTHER ROGER OF TAIZÉ

The word *Christian* is itself cosmopolitan, suggesting discipleship as at ease with diversity and at home in diverse cultures. *Khristos* is the Greek literal translation of Hebrew and Aramaic "the Anointed One"; the ending is from the Latin "*-iani.*" Thus a Greek and Latin word jumbled together from Hebrew and Aramaic names the religion. Those who were the first to use the word *Khristianoi* around AD 50 were from Antioch, a Greek-speaking city on the edge of Syria. The very word *Christian* is Pentecost made plain.

The church of the future needs a heightened awareness of its own cosmopolitan origins and diversity of cultures. The words *Christianity* and *West* seem to go together, but the truth is quite different. It began as an export from the Middle East. It today boasts Orthodox traditions in both Byzantine and Oriental forms, and it embraces the oft-forgotten and beleaguered Assyrian Church, which spread from what is today Iraq to India and to the Pacific during the first millennium. Even today the truest ring of the gospel is struck when sounded in its natural Semitic idiom.

Irish poet William Butler Yeats is famous for his foreshadowing of a future where the center cannot hold and the centrifugal forces win. But the "center cannot hold" is not a building metaphor but a motion metaphor about a falconer and his falcon.

Turning and turning in the widening gyre
The falcon cannot hear the falconer;
Things fall apart; the centre cannot hold;
Mere anarchy is loosed upon the world.[4]

Yeats's center is the falconer. When the falcon loses hold of the falconer, everything goes into free fall and free-for-all. Jesus is the Falconer, who is always the same but always on the move. When Jesus is lost sight of by the church, "anarchy is loosed."

The future of humanity depends on this intricate interplay of unity and diversity, the dance of falconer and falcon, with no less diversity but much more unity. People can have double or even multiple identities, but not without a core identity. We still have not plumbed the depths of what it means that the unity of the Spirit issues in a diversity of gifts.

To work toward a common dream, you need cognitive diversity, even the embrace of those who disagree with the common goal to begin with. You need people who think differently as well as look, labor, and love differently in order for true diversity to take place. But diversity must be in the service of unity. Otherwise the wheels fall off and the world whirls apart.

It is only recently that humans have come to tolerate diversity. Sebastian Castellio was one of the first Reformed Christian proponents of religious toleration, freedom of conscience and thought. But the concept of tolerance did not catch on until the seventeenth century following the Wars of Religion. Toleration did not mean you agreed with those hateful Protestants (or Catholics, depending on which side you were on). Toleration did not mean you had to platform or showcase the theology or ideology you found false. But toleration did mean you would not ban it, or burn it, or try to shut it up or shout it down. Toleration was first intended for the hearer. Today toleration has become just the opposite—it is not the hearer who must tolerate but the speaker who is to shut up about what's controversial out of deference to the hearer.[5]

The vitality of USAmerican religion is, historically speaking, precisely its disjointedness, its pluralism, its diversity. It was unplanned liberty and self-governing improvisation that made the Anglo-American colonies so much more formidable than those of other Europeans. But the vision of God's providence in this new promised land of future beckonings held the diversity and disorder together.

Only when difference has its home, when the need for belonging
in all its murderous intensity has been assuaged, can our
common identity begin to find its voice.

MICHAEL IGNATIEFF,
THE NEEDS OF STRANGERS

The notion seems to be that the more diverse we become, the more silencing we need for diverse views, even and especially ones with which we disagree. Hence the expansion of hate-speech laws, first in Europe and then in the US, which will increasingly entangle the church because already in Europe any Roman Catholic opposition to abortion is prima facie "hate speech." But more diversity of culture, religion, and ethnicity ought to lead to more *expressions* of cultural, religious, and ethnic diversity in all aspects of life. In other words, more diversity of opinion, not less diversity of speech.

Color is broken light. We love to gather around the rainbow, but the seven colors of the rainbow are nothing but refracted light. We live in a rainbow refraction of truth, not the blazing white light of truth. God did not make us color-blind but color-blessed and color-bright. Even Jesus, the One Light, appears in rainbow form as the bridge to the divine: Wherever Jesus appeared in some pieces of art in Christian history, and especially in Italian Renaissance art, there was likely to be a rainbow nearby, lurking in rubble or rain. The rainbow was more than a symbol of God's covenant with the earth; it was an earthly earnest of the celestial body of Christ. On the cross, the Broken Light enables us to see in color. We need the solitary rainbow colors, but we also need the solidarity of Light.

And yet we operate within a culture that makes orthodoxies poisonous and heterodoxies cleansing. We celebrate diversity and difference, but at a superficial level, never quite achieving the solidarity and unity intended as their outcome. We should never forget that it was diversity and difference in the service of solidarity and unity that brought down Nazism, one of the great evils of the twentieth-century world. We live as one, or no one lives. We live as one world, or there will be no world.

The stamp of difference only makes a difference when it is set on what is joined, not what is disjointed or fragmented. "We, being many, are one body in Christ, and individually members of one another."[6] Civilization cannot build a future solely upon people's differences. Only evil would prefer fragmentation above concord. The future will never be secured by choosing sides but by embracing the whole. United we live, divided we perish.

In spite of all the unity-in-diversity rhetoric, this is a culture that increasingly prefers to live in tribal enclosures and economic cocoons. Victimology is a virus that has infected everything and everyone, including the church. Victimhood is never a victory. Every healed "victim" who goes on to heal others and not just therapize themselves can attest to one thing: No one gets better by being excused from carrying responsibility for the consequences of their choices and actions.

The common vision of much contemporary social protest is simply emotional release. But "protest isn't the same as self-expression."[7] Geysers of anger and emotion, rhetoric and rants, do not a strategy make. Any spirit that weakens community or undermines communion with Jesus does not come from the Holy Spirit.

This is a world that can blow up in the fist of a single fighter. Violence is counterproductive. Nonviolence works and has more power to change the world than violence.[8] When Kurt Vonnegut's son Mark claimed conscientious objection during the Vietnam War, Vonnegut wrote a letter to the draft board. It ends, "He will not hate. He will not kill. There's hope in that. There's no hope in war."[9] The church is a wielder of soft power. The world majors in wielding hard power.

Let everything that has breath praise the Lord.
Learn to praise God
in metrical psalms,
in Hebrew yadahs,
in English magnificats,
in Ukrainian kyries,
in Gaelic lullabies,
in Peruvian glorias,
in Appalachian shape notes,
in Gregorian chants,
in Latin rap,
in hipster hop,
in nu metal,
in earworm claymation melodies for children,
in Southern gospel,
in hill-country blues,
in suburban pop,

in Ethiopian tizita,
in all the crazy cacophony that love for God has inspired in humans.

And then learn to hear and celebrate God's holy name in the sounds
  of other religious traditions:
in Buddhist throat singing,
in Hindu raga,
in Muslim nasheed,
in Taoist yin and yang tones,
in Shinto kagura,
in Sufi qawwali.

In a remarkable presidential address before the 1996 meeting of the American Studies Association, Patricia Nelson Limerick, the premier historian of the American West, warned about the state of a discipline when its scholarship focuses exclusively on the pieces and parts and not the whole. "Imagine a [*sic*] ecologist looking at an ecosystem, and deciding that she or he really found the study of soil tiresome and pointless, and thus would only look at the role of air and water."[10]

Sociologists, anthropologists, historians, psychologists have wonderfully explored the experiences of cultures formerly excluded from the story. But in all the excitement, said Limerick,

We have backed away from any vision of common ground; we
have, instead, divided American life into a set of experiences—
Catholic, Protestant, Muslim, Jewish; male and female,
heterosexual and homosexual; Indian, Anglo American, African
American, Mexican American, Asian American.
    For what were very good reasons, did we over-accent cultural
differences?[11]

Might all this accent on diversity, she continued, have "unintentionally cut some of the ground out from under empathy, compassion, fellow feeling, and understanding?"[12] And while we will (and should) continue to hear about "separate destinies, separate cultures, separate and fragmented units of identity,"[13] might it not be time for scholars out in the public arena to start reweaving the foundational fabric "of interrelatedness, of our intertwined destinies?"[14] Fragmented lenses of race, gender, class, ethnicity have made it difficult to envision a unified culture of consensus, not just a culture of dissent and dissonance. "Even if we wanted the people of the United States to have separate and pure identities and histories, we are about five hundred years too late for that purity."[15]

Unfortunately, this prophetic address fell like a stone into the vast academic abyss. The problem Limerick highlighted twenty years ago has only gotten worse. You cannot build a future on diversity without commonality.

Those of us who have kids have all been taken for the same ride. We shudder to think about it, with its candy chorus that gives instant diabetes: "It's a small, small world."

> WALKING IN FAITH

1. There is at the very least a *perceived* tension between diversity and unity. As a biblical model, however, we know that unity-in-diversity is both achievable and desirable. How does it encourage others-centeredness and devotion to the body of Christ?

2. Practically speaking, how might this others-centeredness release us from a misdirected trust in sameness and into the flourishing wholeness in which expressions of diversity knit us together?

IDENTITY CRISES GALORE AND GALLOPING

AT THE TIME OF THIS WRITING, the number one TV show is *This Is Us* and the number one song is "This Is Me." That is no accident. Identity issues drive all we do. They show up in our politics. They show up in our religions. They show up in our obsession with zombies—individuals without agency.[1]

God's question to Hagar in the wilderness in Genesis 16:8 haunts each one of us. The hunger and hunt for identity is a driving force of the modern world. But the nature of the self in an age of simulacra, pseudonyms, avatars, gender/racial fluidity, "the wisdom of crowds," and online friends makes having an identity a massive maze of conquest and confusion.

Western Christianity is in permanent identity crisis. For the first time in a millennium of history for much of the West (and soon in the US), Christianity is no longer the default identity for the majority of its population. The percentage of US citizens who claim to be Christian is plummeting (from 85 percent to 75 percent in the last twenty-five years). For the first time in a thousand years, Christianity is now in the minority in England and Wales. What is more significant, Christianity is not the default identity even for many who poll as "Christian." Their go-to identity is found in other arenas, like class, gender, race, sexuality, politics, and ideology, with ethnicity and sexuality now eclipsing class and religion in forming identity movements, and social divisions ("Eurasianism," "white power," etc.) all responding to their sense of impending threat. No wonder the church no longer knows what it means to "pastor" anymore, and pastors themselves are in a state of professional disquiet.

Identity politics can work as well on the left as on the right, and it is no wonder that identitarian movements on both spectrums are on the rise from Austria to America. What is fueling the bloodshed in Arab countries is not Shia/Sunni sectarianism but manipulation of identity politics.

Fourteenth-century Arab historian and Maliki jurist Ibn Khaldun identified the key health of a culture by taking the temperature of its *asabiyya*, an Arabic word meaning "social solidarity" or "frame of reference." The Israeli American sociologist Aaron Antonovsky (1923–94) echoed Khaldun in his insistence that a sense of social coherence is the heart of positive well-being. Without a strong frame of reference or "sinewy strength" in group identity to make sense of what is happening around them, the health of the person or group frays and falls apart from the inside out.[2] Once lost, it is not easy to get one's *asabiyya* back.

No matter how much wealth or success a civilization might have, no culture is any stronger than its *asabiyya*. The loss of *asabiyya* means the death of a culture.[3] The only justification for public education is for a society to pass on to its children and youth the *asabiyya*, the coherent values it prizes and seeks to preserve. Not the politics. Not the information. Not merely the tools and techniques of learning. The public school system used to be the crucible of *asabiyya*. It is now a battleground of incoherence.

Issues of identity and authority are related. What ties them together is narrative. The importance of a narrative compass for identity formation cannot be emphasized enough. The words *author* and *authority* are more than similar. Whoever you allow to author your story is your authority. Identity requires the union of opposites: fixity and fluidity, permanence and permeability.

Put another way, identity requires the stability of one author and the pliability of multiple story lines. A new humanity that does not need to define itself in any storied particularities of family, faith, or community—only in abstract principles—is something never before encountered in history. A universal without a particular is something truly new. A generic, unknown, anonymous Supreme Being, untethered from any particularities of tribe or tradition, religion or community, is a divine-human relationship of unprecedented appearance.

Parents have tried to base and build an identity for kids on values ("Christian values"), views ("Christian worldview"), virtues ("classic Christian virtues"), and verses (versitis). You can pretty much classify all Christian colleges according to one of these four "missions." But identity requires a narrative foundation. The church doesn't lose its kids when they go to college. We start losing them in middle school. We lose children in the church when we send them out of worship to children's church or Sunday school. This is one reason why Jesus kept insisting, "Let the little children come to me."[4]

Why are meals over a table so important—to family, faith, nation, planet? First grub, then gospel. Identity is forged from shared stories, symbols, images, and ideas that resonate across a constituency. The best place to learn those stories is around a table. If there are no shared narratives and metaphors, there is identity confusion and collapse. The Jesus story is the tapestry that signifies and validates Christian identity. Jesus is the secret formula that brings new life and renewal to everything it is applied to, and that is the "secret law" of church. Two of the six Resurrection stories involve sharing food with Jesus. It is time to bring back the table and banish the children's table.[5]

After the resurrection, Jesus didn't show up at the temple, but around the dinner table, [thus] reframing where He is to be found.

HEATH HOLLENSBE

What we as a church need to inculcate in our children, and evangelize to our culture, is that what really matters is not how others look at you but how you look at them. Do not draw your identity and worth from the gaze of others. You are not worth more when someone looks at you than when they don't. We draw our identities in Christ: When he is allowed to author our stories and thus be the authority of our lives, we become part of God's Kingdom.

Every life story is worth telling, but God designed yours to be a masterpiece if Jesus is its author and the Spirit your editor. To surrender your life to God and pivot your life story around your Creator is not the negation of the human being but the summation of the human being; not the annihilation of the self but the realization of the self.

> WALKING IN FAITH

1. Christianity is no longer much of the West's default identity, even for many who poll as "Christians." Instead, identity is found in class, gender, race, sexuality, ethnicity, politics, and ideology—and social divisions are organized along those lines. By what practical means is the spiritual reality of identity in Christ restored?

2. How will the exploitation of concretized social divisions become less effective in the future, and what role will the church play?

8

SEXULARISM

The trouble . . . with a sick and purely physical sexuality is that in it the
whole person is not involved. The bodily libido is temporarily satisfied, but
the heart and mind do not participate and therefore they are not quieted by
the encounter. Sexuality without love never achieves fulfillment, for when
sexuality breaks free from love, it can never be total. This is probably the
reason why there have seldom been so many sexual problems as under
the sign of our modern emancipation.

HELMUT THIELICKE,

BEING HUMAN . . . BECOMING HUMAN

IF AN ALIEN WERE TO WATCH SITCOMS FOR THE FIRST TIME, it would think
that the biggest trivial pursuit among earthlings was sex. "Sexularism"[1] is
an approach to life that views and values everything and everyone through
a lens of sexuality.

At best, the church's default position has been that sexuality is something that can be left to take care of itself, and the less said the better. At
worst, many homegrown Christians grew up in sex-negative strands of
Christianity,[2] which may help explain why Christians are so fascinated by
other people's bodies and what those bodies may have been up to. During
the filming of *Cleopatra* in 1963, the Vatican accused Elizabeth Taylor of
"erotic vagrancy."[3]

Why is the sinless life often synonymous with the sexless life? Why
is the Hindu religion known for fifteen hundred sex positions and the
Christian religion for one? And why has the culture detached sensuality
from sentiment?

Only God could have created the pleasures of sex. As a matter of evolution, reproduction would be merely mechanical and functional, a simple

exchange of bodily fluids. Instead, for humans (and maybe for dolphins), sex is not just urge and duty but also play and pleasure. Humans are the only "animal" that has sex face-to-face, making sexuality relational—humanistic, not animalistic.[4] The twentieth century's most erotic song, George Gershwin's "Do It Again" (best sung by Judy Garland or Diana Krall), showcases the relationality that is inherent to human eroticism:

When your two lips were pressed to mine.
When you held me, I wasn't snuggling.
You should know I really was struggling.

Sex is an intimate holiness, a daily mysterium, an embodied sacramentum that images the *yada* ("knowing" in Hebrew) presence of the Creator in our every instance of our every day. We connect with God in the flesh.[5] The physical is the channel for the divine. Sex is one of God's most creative dreams and delicate designs. Yet the church has had a hard time seeing the flesh in general and sexuality in particular as part of discipleship.

Meanwhile, this is a culture that sexualizes everything it touches. Language itself has become so corrupt and so sexualized that there are fewer and fewer innocent words left in the English language. Yet at the same time, communications between the sexes are in deplorable shape and going downward, while mistrust of each other is at an all-time high and going higher. The very ways we talk about sex are indecipherable. Here is a question from a final exam in a religious studies course given at NYU:

Mindful of Michael Warner's caution that "you can reduce
religion to sex only if you don't especially believe in either one"
(*Tongues Untied*), consider the relationship—even the "analogies"
(to use a loaded term)—between religion and sex, and/or between
religious and sexual identities. How might such analogies disrupt
conventional oppositions between religion and sex (and in
particular between conservative religion and gay gay [*sic*] sex)
and/or admit the possibility of both rupture and continuity in
narratives of personal identity?[6]

And the question is . . . ?

Rituals of mating and dating have changed radically in our lifetimes and will change even more. How far we have come in our grasp of sexual dynamics is reflected in three incidents, all of which were intended as compliments in their day but today cause the listener to blanch:

› Missionary physician/organist Albert Schweitzer didn't like lipstick, not because he was against cosmetics, but because he said it added unnecessary hazards to a stolen kiss.[7]

› Actor/director Orson Welles once congratulated Jamaican-American supermodel/singer Grace Jones's performance style by saying, "Certain people seduce an audience, flatter an audience, beseech an audience. Grace, you rape an audience—your show is a sexual assault."[8]

› The 1957 song "Thank Heaven for Little Girls" is a casualty of a culture that has lost its innocence and/or discovered its guiltiness: "Thank heaven for little girls / For little girls get bigger every day."

The church may gussy up its pretensions and moralisms in a gospel goulash of piety and smugness, but we really have no idea what it is to help people have healthy and whole sex lives in a digital culture. Maybe the church could take its cue from fairy tales like "Sleeping Beauty": When it was foretold that Beauty would die if she pricked her finger on a spinning wheel before her sixteenth birthday, her parents chose to rid the kingdom of all spinning wheels instead of teaching her how to use a spinning wheel properly. They sent her away and sheltered her from the spinning wheel world. Sure enough, right before her sixteenth birthday she found a spinning wheel and was curious. What was it? How did it work? What did it do and make? And what do you know—she "pricked" her finger, drew blood, and died.

No one need be alone with her aberrant desires, and no desires were aberrant.

EMILY WITT,
FUTURE SEX

When the church has dared to look at sex theologically, it has spent its moral and ethical capital on the negative side of the ledger. All the negative condemnation has shortchanged the giftedness of sex—its genius as a binding force, its inspiration to the human imagination in the creation of great music, poetry, and art; its role as a motivator and ensurer of family stability.

Here are at random a number of questions pastors and disciples will be asked to address during the lifetime of everyone reading these words:

> How do you insulate kids without isolating them?

> How will you train kids in the moral muscles of "Don't click"—important survivor words for "Don't quit" in a world that tests and tempts and teases and taunts and traps them with clickbait?

> How do you compel kids with the vision that "true love waits,"[9] when, given early onset of puberty and long-delayed marriage, they'll be waiting longer than any generation in history?[10]

> How do you counsel couples regarding lifetime commitments, when "lifetime" means a hundred years or more?

> When you are asked to marry a man to two women, or a woman to two men, what will you say and on what basis?

> When you are asked to marry a human to a transhuman (see chapter 15) that looks and acts like a human in every way, what will you say and on what basis?

> How can the body of Christ support the making of babies and support of children during the decline of marriage and the nuclear family?

> How is your church repositioning its pastoral care to accommodate new forms of conception, childbirth, and child care?

> How will you make the increasing numbers of children who are being raised in homosexual families feel at home as part of the church family?[11] (We have come a long way since 1944, when the major textbook in pastoral counseling dismissed homosexuality as "just not the pastor's problem."[12] The failure to treat the LGBTQ community with dignity and grace is a primary factor in why Christianity is seen as outdated at best.)

> What ethical guides will you provide church members regarding robot slaves, including whether it is moral to use them as sex toys?

> What is sexy, anyway? In the medieval past, wealthy women were the most desirable to men. Therefore the more fabric a woman wrapped around her body, the more sexy she appeared. Muslims operate by a different standard of "sexiness" than the prevailing culture. Why not

Christians? What would be a Jesus definition of a "sexy Christian" in terms of fashion and design? What might a "sexy church" look like?[13]

The schizophrenic nature of this culture is nowhere more apparent than in its attitudes toward sex. On the one hand, sex is becoming increasingly criminalized, stigmatized, and placed under surveillance. Child pornography laws are being applied to teenagers who share pictures of themselves with their peers. Sentences for certain sexual offenses now far exceed those for murder.[14]

On the other hand, the sexualization of culture is more and more pervasive, symbolized in the iconic brass plaque once put over the door to the Playboy mansion in Chicago by former Methodist Hugh Hefner: *"Si Non Oscillas, Noli Tintinnare,"* or "If you don't swing, don't ring." The pervasiveness of sex is evident everywhere in the soundtracks of the culture, from hip-hop to heavy metal, and in the story lines of TV and movie scripts. For a long time, one of us thought Meghan Trainor's 2014 hit "All About That Bass" was paying tribute to the most important musical instrument in any band, only to learn after watching the video that it was a body anthem celebrating fuller figures.

Farmer/poet Wendell Berry wrote, "Sex . . . is less safe now than it has ever been. What we are actually teaching the young is an illusion of thoughtless freedom and purchasable safety, which encourages them to tamper prematurely, disrespectfully, and dangerously with a great power."[15]

According to Sam Williams of Bay Marin Community Church, "smart sex" requires four things:

Intimacy. Intimacy means more than sharing your body; it's sharing your burdens and blessings and dreams. "I've observed something," Williams shares. "It's hard to kiss and talk at the same time! And when kissing starts, talking stops."

Commitment. In relationships, premature sexual involvement short-circuits three really important things: objectivity, growth into maturity, and trust. In Williams's words, "Spend a life—not a night—together."

Maturity. Maturity is deferred gratification, the ability to say an immediate no for a longer yes. Of all the requirements for "smart sex," this is the one that carries the most cultural weight. Indeed, one of the loudest cases now being made for teenage sexual responsibility is not based on tenets of religion or covenants of relationship but on future prospects for career opportunities. The older the age of sexual activity, the greater the level of maturity and the higher the rate of academic success.[16]

Love. Williams did not quote poet and monastic Gil Bailie, just as he did not quote Wendell Berry. But Williams's "smart sex" requirement of love is best conveyed in Bailie's response to a question from an interviewer:

Nietzsche said that if you destroy the Christian ethic, you can destroy Christianity without ever having to challenge its creed, and this is exactly what's happening in our world. The Christian moral ethic around sexuality is essentially a way of encouraging the sexual experience to fulfill itself in this moment of communion that is not just physical but also spiritual. If you turn sexuality into a kind of athleticism, or into a recreational activity, or into the equivalent of shaking hands, you destroy the arena in which most people experience the Christian mystery.[17]

> WALKING IN FAITH

1. How has the piety-and-smugness approach to sex affected you and those around you? Do those who need and even desire guidance feel free to seek it within the church? If not, how is a lingering self-consciousness and shame in the mere mention of sex barricading redemptive avenues?

2. Which tendencies in your church bode well in countering the sexularization of the culture? Which ones are raising red flags about the body's ability to incarnate Christ?

3. How has the mantra of "safe sex" on the one hand and the criminalization of sex on the other multiplied sexual perils for our youth?

9

GENDERS AND GENDERING

He and she *are not sufficient to encompass this new heaven, new earth.*
LAST WORDS OF THE NOVEL *THE NIGHT BROTHER,*
BY ROSIE GARLAND (2018)

THE WORLD OF GENDER IS BLOWING UP, spinning out of control. If you think the temperature is heated now, it's time to put on some bunker gear, or maybe even a hazmat suit. The issue of homosexuality, which has buzz-sawed its way through every one of Christianity's rooms and antechambers, pales in significance to the gender-bending of the future.[1] One scholar diagnoses our current malady as "gender obsession disorder."[2]

Some of the biggest Vesuvius moments of the future will be gender. Is gender a "social construct" or a scientific reality? Even if it is a biological reality, does that make it a metaphysical reality? Or is gender an individual mind-set subjectivity? Furthermore, even if gender is biologically set, how many "genders" are there? Is the connection between biological and grammatical gender fixed or tenuous? What does it mean for us that a Hebrew name for God—Elohim—is grammatically plural but not gendered? There is nothing that will set the church's teeth on edge and make its belly growl more than questions like these.

On any scale of relative hotness, issues of gender are poised to release the most vigorous pent-up energies of the planet. What stirs people up today is not politics but gender politics and sexual politics. When lava mixes with mud, it moves from slow to thunderbolt. When lava-hot gender mixes with the mud of politics, it's time to start dodging debris avalanches.

To grow up in an online world is to be weaned by an imaginary universe where there are no traditional identity markers. This world offers to everyone a rich feast of fantasy and illusion that is gripping and captivating. The premodern world legislated for the norm and allowed for no exceptions (which were always present but kept hidden). The modern world legislated for the norm and allowed for the exceptions. Today's world legislates for the exception and allows for the norm.

Can you build a solid identity on a fluid gender? What does it mean for the church to accompany people with compassion on these precarious journeys through the super volcano of sexuality[3] while at the same time being ever ready to give witness to the "faith which was once for all delivered to the saints"?[4]

Given the diversity that exists within every religious tradition on issues of sex, gender, dress, etc., we are realizing that it is difficult if not dangerous to draw lines between culture and religion. But gender identity may be where the fault lines of culture and religion grind and grate the most in the years ahead. For example, Western culture worships self-determination and the freedom of the individual to define themselves any way they see fit. This ideology of the individual clashes against a Christian theology of God-determination, where "you are not your own,"[5] where we find our identity (and die to self) for the good of others and the glory of God.

Gender has entered a posttruth era. The world is increasingly confronted with the thorny issues of alternative facts, virtual realities, and artificial intelligence. Trans rights is the number one civil rights issue of the first half of the twenty-first century. A Rubicon was crossed in 1993 when the Barbie Liberation Organization swapped the voice boxes of Barbie and GI Joe dolls. Barbie now barked "Eat lead, Cobra!" while GI Joe cooed, "Let's go shopping."[6] The gendering of childhood is one of the key battlefronts of the future.

Which way the culture is headed can be glimpsed already in the decision in June 2015 by the *Oxford English Dictionary* to include the word *cisgender*, or *cis*. It means "designating a person whose sense of personal identity corresponds to the sex and gender assigned to him or her at birth."[7] In the eyes of the culture, "cisgender" people are the simple people who safely settled in their default setting; "transgender" people are the adventurous ones with more complicated sexual identities.

My God, deliver me from my god.

MEISTER ECKHART

Issues over gender are already smoking volcanoes, but they will only spew more fire in the future. The Fula people of sub-Saharan Africa boast twenty genders in their language.[8] In Australia, adults are allowed to register their sex as "unspecified" on legal documents like passports.[9] And in New York City, there are now at least thirty-one genders officially recognized, with fines in place for those who persist in not recognizing a person's preferred gender.[10] *Gender verification* will have the same associations in the future to what the word *segregation* does today.

The way forward through this thicket is always not around but through the Scriptures. In speaking of eunuchs, Jesus said that some were made that way, and some were born that way.[11] The eunuch "born that way" may be likened to the classification "intersexual," of which dozens of subclassifications are identified today.[12] Estimates vary widely and are necessarily speculative—with medical estimates ranging from 0.02 percent to 1.7 percent of infants being born with one of several possible intersexual conditions.[13] The issue of intersexuality and transgenderism is quite prevalent and in fashion in today's Western culture. Some Native American tribes celebrate "two-spirit" people who seem by their intersexuality to combine male and female attributes. In South Asia, "hijras" are considered neither male nor female.[14]

Is the tapestry that signifies and validates our Christian identity one of sex, or love? Pope Francis holds a position that gender theory is a form of "ideological colonization."[15] Gender, gender identity, and sexual orientation, he says, are not separate, distinct parts of our overall identity. But while he opposes the notion that gender can be chosen, he opens his arms to all LGBQT communities. To consider questions like these only by consulting ourselves and not being in relationship with those marginalized "poor" within our midst and without our walls, the church will further igloo itself in "frozen chosenness," its sacramental system will become more broken than it already is, and its hallowed rites of passage, such as bonds of matrimony, will seem ever more like bonds of acrimony.

In Acts 8, the Ethiopian eunuch returning from the Temple in Jerusalem is notably a direct violation of the Deuteronomic prohibition against anyone with sexual abnormalities being admitted to the Temple.[16] But the prohibition from Deuteronomy seems to be countered by a messianic prophecy from Isaiah:

> Nor let the eunuch say,
>   "Here I am, a dry tree."
> For thus says the LORD:
> "To the eunuchs who keep My Sabbaths,
>   and choose what pleases Me
>   and hold fast My covenant,
> Even to them I will give in My house,
>   And within My walls a place and a name
>   better than that of sons and daughters."[17]

The way of Christ is not a matter of male or female.[18] It is a third way. It's the way of the Holy Spirit in which we identify first and last as followers of Jesus.

> WALKING IN FAITH

1. How does the use of the term *cisgender* impact those who embrace their original gender assignments? How does it affect the "adventurous" ones who identify as *transgender*?

2. In which ways is the church's approach to the gender issue most accurate? In which ways can the message be conveyed with greater compassion?

3. How can followers of the Way resist the "ideological colonization" of gender theory without cutting ourselves off from redemptive conversation with people whose gender and sexuality are outside of historic norms?

10

SUICIDE CULTURE

MORE AND MORE PEOPLE ARE KILLING THEMSELVES, especially kids. At least so it seems, although some dispute the statistics. What is indisputable is that more and more people are obsessed with suicide, from the popularity of *13 Reasons Why* (2017) to the new release *First Reformed* (2018) to the new academic discipline called *suicidology*.[1] Suicide is an epidemic. All the signs are for it to become a plague in the future unless preventive actions are taken. Part of those preventive actions need to be theological and come from the church, which needs to see suicide not as a moral failing but as a conclusive cry of human pain and isolation and loss of identity.

Suicide has moved from the eleventh to the tenth leading cause of death in the US. It is still moving upward, and suicide rates have increased in almost every state since 1999 (some by more than 30 percent).[2] Suicide occurs among all demographics, including all religious groups. Every follower of Jesus has a different EQ as well as IQ. Some go down in the valley as much or more than they go up on the mountain. Others live in the valley and look up at the mountain. A few reside on the mountaintops. Each EQ state has its own susceptibility to suicide.

An urban legend reports that twenty-two veterans take their life every day, a number usually associated with vets of Iraq and Afghanistan but a number that can only come close if all combat vets are included, especially

Vietnam vets.[3] More generally, someone in the US takes their life *at least* every twenty-two minutes.[4] As a reminder that each of us is a custodian of the humanity of all of us, we are naming suicide the number "22."[5]

Behind all 22 statistics are stories of friends, family members, and neighbors, each one a tragic story. And at the base of every 22 story is a 273 story, a plummeting of the spirit to absolute zero, 273 degrees Celsius, a number hidden in the middle of the suicide prevention hotline: 800.273.8255 (TALK). Absolute zero is the lowest possible temperature where nothing could be colder and no heat energy remains in a substance.

Suicide happens when people in life reach 273. These people include musicians like Kurt Cobain and Avicii, writers like Virginia Woolf, Sylvia Plath, Ernest Hemingway, and David Foster Wallace; designers like Alexander McQueen and Kate Spade; actors like Marilyn Monroe and Robin Williams; gourmands like Anthony Bourdain. As least six people in the Bible took their own lives: Samson; Saul and his armor bearer; Ahithophel, who sided with Absalom in his rebellion against David; King Zimri of the northern kingdom of Israel; and Judas Iscariot.[6] But add to this number the many biblical outbursts of despair and depression that you find in the Psalms and among the prophets, such as this one from Elijah after being threatened by Jezebel: "I have had enough, LORD. Take my life; I am no better than my ancestors."[7]

Today, 22s can be caused by many factors:

About half of all 22s are due to mental illness. The World Health Organization (WHO) claims that one in four people around the world suffer from mental illness at some point in their lives. One of the growing professional fields of the future will be the mental health of infants. Does the rise in mental illness also tell us anything about the world we live in?

Depression is another big contributor to 22. The "pressures of life," once episodic routines, now seem to be incessant assaults. No wonder in any given week 15 million Americans will attend one of about half a million support group meetings. No wonder there are massive increases for all age groups in the rates of depression.[8] One researcher estimates that since the beginning of the twentieth century, "each successive generation has doubled its susceptibility to depression."[9] For those born around the First World War, the lifetime prevalence of depression was around one percent. For those born around World War II, the rate rose to 5 percent. For those born in the 1960s, it jumped to 10 and 15 percent. It's still climbing—44 percent of college students experience symptoms of depression, and one of the leading causes of death among college students is 22.[10] Antidepressants are now the most widely prescribed drug in the US, and their prescriptions are increasing. Depression is the number one cause of disability for people in developed nations.[11] Depression stalks the ranks of the clergy and clergy families.[12] In 1997, the Southern Baptist Convention founded a Wounded Heroes initiative to cope with the "toll of depression in their ranks."[13]

Despair is always described as dull, when the truth is that despair has a light all its own, a lunar glow, the color of mottled silver.

DAPHNE MERKIN,
THIS CLOSE TO HAPPY

We are all self-destructive. In some way, our lack of self-care means there is no living without killing oneself. Some work too hard, play too tough, eat and drink too much . . . any and all "too's" can leave the soul looking like a lunar landscape—dry, flat, and barren. Part of our self-destruction is not just the actions we take (sins of commission) but also our inactions (sins of omissions). If you purposely make choices that you know will lead to your destruction, even though they are not in and of themselves destructive acts, is this a form of suicide? We all make such choices every day with the desserts we eat ("To die for!") or the chances we take ("Get rich or die trying!"). It is especially important for Christians to keep this distinction in mind since the line between suicide and martyrdom can be hair thin.[14]

The mind can play tricks on you. In a culture with loss of impulse control and little training in deferred gratification, it is difficult to pass through times of mental trickery without taking precipitous and impulsive action such as a suicide attempt. Survivors of suicide attempts don't end up taking their own lives through future attempts an astonishing 90 percent of the time.[15] In this sense, suicide is largely preventable, as they found out in Britain when they reduced the number of aspirins in one package to a nonlethal dose.[16] With isolation and loneliness the primary breeding grounds for 22, you don't need ten or fifteen people. Just one friend's intervention can help prevent a 22.

The World Health Organization defines 22 as "a suicidal act with a fatal outcome," where a suicidal act is defined as "self injury with varying degrees of lethal intent."[17] The definition in a recent novel by Patricia Cornwell is more picturesque if less inclusive, but it showcases the element of impulsivity involved in 22s: "It's getting in the last pissed-off word. It's a big *so there*."[18]

Anthony Bourdain claimed in a 2016 interview that his purpose in life was to take care of his then nine-year-old daughter.[19] Apart from the question of whether taking care of your children is a high enough mission for a human (even animals do that), where does his 22 leave her now? Humans need a bigger mission in life than the ones we share with the animals to get us through these dark nights of the soul.

———

There are a thousand thousand reasons to live this life,
every one of them sufficient. . . . Wherever you turn
your eyes the world can shine like transfiguration.

DYING WORDS OF A PASTOR TO HIS SON,
IN MARILYNNE ROBINSON'S *GILEAD*

———

How does the church help a culture make it through successive bouts with 22? First, the church needs to own its stories of mental illness, depression, and temptation and open the storehouse of wisdom that comes tumbling out. Some of the greatest figures in history labored under the lash of depression and on the brink of 22. Even though bipolar disorder has only been recently named, bipolars for Christ might include Martin Luther and Charles Wesley, Isaac Newton, Ludwig van Beethoven, and Vincent Van Gogh[20] for starters.

One of Christianity's greatest hymnists, William Cowper (pronounced "Cooper," who lived from 1731–1800), was a deeply despairing and depressed human being. Yet he wrote some of the most famous and influential hymns in Christian history. At one time he was committed to an asylum after three suicide attempts. As a fourth one appeared imminent, a friend had the idea of entrusting to his care an orphaned baby leveret. Immediately Cowper assumed responsibility for its charge, and when the locals heard about his mental progress, they started bringing him other orphan rabbits to take care of.

For Cowper, the hare's ears were as masterful as his poems, and its amber eyes as penetrating as any of his metaphors. The more the hare brought Cowper outside his own creativity and into God's creativity, the better Cowper became. One day, he began writing again and "found" himself by "losing" himself in God's creativity.

> *Oh! for a closer walk with God,*
> *A calm and heav'nly frame;*
> *A light to shine upon the road*
> *That leads me to the Lamb!* [21]

Winston Churchill's constant struggle with his "Black Dog" moods were famous, but when he suffered political setbacks, he was frequently plunged into such severe depression that those closest to him feared he might take his own life. A noted British psychiatrist, after studying Churchill's character, concluded that it was through Churchill's struggles with the Black Dog that he acquired the iron will he needed to stand against Hitler when all seemed lost. "The psychiatrist put it this way: 'Only a man who had conquered despair in himself could have led a nation through its darkest hours.'"[22]

Second, the plague of 22s needs a theological rebuke. *Satan* is the English transliteration of the Hebrew word for "accuser" or "slanderer," which are both conveyed in our word *bully*. Satan is the great Bully, and bullying is one thing that creates the ferals, the forgottens, the out-of-bounds, the outsiders, the pariahs—all of whom are more susceptible to 22. Shunning, ostracizing, gossiping, defaming, accusing, slandering a pariah's name can all be ways of driving them to 22, that the world would be better off without them.[23] A 22 is the work of the accuser of the brethren. Where the thief comes only to steal, to kill, and to destroy, Jesus comes to bring whole life.[24]

If the Bully can get into your head and persuade you of (1) your unlovability (*I'm worthless*); (2) your helplessness (*I'm in over my head; I can't solve my problems*); (3) your poor distress tolerance (*I can't stand the way I feel; I can't take it anymore*); or (4) your burdensomeness (*Everyone would be better off if I were dead; the world is better off without me*),[25] then the Bully has got you where evil wants you.

Pop psychology says to tell people contemplating 22, "I love you, I want you to live, I will not judge you," which no doubt they all need to hear, and not just when they're thinking 22. Albert Schweitzer once suggested that a smile could stop a suicide. Think what an encouraging word, a pat on the back, a gentle grace note can do. If only we were to give every person we meet the benefit of the doubt and wonder about the contrast between the complex inner life that goes on inside their heads and presume that the halting, tongue-tied, imprecise snippets we manage to share with one another are reflections of a complex inner life.

Every person you meet today is hurting deep inside from something.
Go gentle into this good day.
LEONARD SWEET

But people contemplating 22 also need to hear the words of the sixth commandment: "Thou shalt not kill."[26] Samuel Johnson's *Dictionary of the English Language* (1755) condemns suicide as morally offensive in its very definition: "Self-murder; the horrid crime of destroying one's self." As part of his explanatory elaboration of this definition, Johnson adapts Samuel Richardson's heroine *Clarissa*'s (1748) views on voluntary death: "'To be cut off by the sword of injured friendship is the most dreadful of all deaths, next to suicide.'"

The Cathari ("Pure Ones") movement that flourished in France during the eleventh through fourteenth centuries was a rare exception to Christian orthodoxy regarding 22: They believed it was acceptable for a Cathar who had reached perfection to commit suicide to avoid backsliding from that state of purity.[27] But apart from that aberration, Christians have held a consistent position: Since God gives life, who else has the right to take it away? We are not our own. We do not belong to ourselves. So we guard the lives that do not belong to us but have been entrusted to us. Life cannot be ours to dispose of. Killing yourself is the ultimate failure of imagination and the final confession of hopelessness when God has said again and again, "There is hope in your future, says the LORD."[28] Hope makes the biggest difference between life and death.

In the midst of a culture that legalizes "assisted dying"[29] and insists on every individual's right to choose, even apart from the desires of the community, even Christianity has lost its edge against 22, historically a sharp one—and no doubt too sharp a stance in the past. A coroner's pronouncement of suicide (*felo de se*) resulted in forfeiture of the deceased's goods and property to the state, often leaving any surviving relatives destitute.

Religious as well as civil sanctions against suicide persisted in Britain and North America, and up until 1823 in the US, bodies of suicide victims could not be interred in consecrated ground, and the ritual humiliation of their corpses was not unheard of.[30] Suicide remained a crime in England until 1961, and it wasn't until 2017 that the Church of England lifted the ban on granting a full Christian funeral to someone who had 22'd.

Martin Luther did not resign to outer darkness those who took their own lives. John Donne called for "a perplexitie and flexibilitie" in the doctrine of self-homicide.[31]

David Foster Wallace, one of the great writers of our generation, famous for his outlandish footnotes, delivered a remarkable commencement address entitled "This Is Water" to the graduates of Kenyon College in 2005. Wallace shared with the graduates, "In the day-to-day trenches of adult life, there is actually no such thing as atheism. There is no such thing as not worshipping. Everybody worships. The only choice we get is what to worship."

Wallace warned the new graduates to be careful and intentional about the choices of what to worship, because some things can "eat you alive." If you choose to worship money and things, there will never be enough. If you choose to worship beauty and sexual allure, "you will always feel ugly. And when time and age start showing, you will die a million deaths. Worship power, you will end up feeling week and afraid, and you will need ever more power over others to numb you to your own fears. Worship your intellect, being seen as smart, you will end up feeling stupid, a fraud, always on the verge of being found out."

Wallace warned that these are the forms of worship "you just gradually slip into, day after day." He advised instead "simple awareness; awareness of what is so real and essential, so hidden in plain sight all around us." Ultimately, he suggested, "You get to decide what to worship."[32]

Sometimes we can't take our own advice. Three years after his commencement address, Wallace committed suicide after a lifelong struggle with depression.

"You can't praise a man for going to bed early," poet Robinson Jeffers (1887–1962) liked to say.[33] But you can't condemn a person for leaving the party early either. I believe that when children of God die by 22, Jesus will embrace them at the gate of heaven and say, "Son/Daughter, you found it a little too much for you, didn't you?" Fred Craddock sees the scenario a bit differently. He has God saying to the parents, by means of the church, "Thanks for all you've done for your son, your daughter. I'll take it from here."[34]

> WALKING IN FAITH

1. Why is it so hard for the church to own its stories of mental illness, depression, and temptation? Is shame the issue, or is our shame in this area rooted in our seeming lack of a theological answer?

2. What norms or mores within the church contribute to withdrawal from this issue?

3. On a practical level, how can each of us more effectively meet others where they are? How can we give every person the benefit of the doubt and respect the contrast between the complexity of their inner lives and the imprecise snippets they share with us?

4. How do legal trends such as assisted dying consciously or unconsciously influence the decisions of those who are considering suicide?

PRENATAL SCREENING AND "WRONGFUL LIFE"

Before I formed you in the womb I knew you.

JEREMIAH 1:5

FROM WHEN MY BOOK *Soul Tsunami* was written in 1999, the big question for couples has changed from how not to get pregnant to what are the ethical and best ways for pregnancy to occur.

Abortion has been such a volatile issue because it brings together the big three no one is supposed to talk about—sex, religion, and politics. As long as we do not inhabit a culture of life in which every child from the moment of conception is welcomed and cherished, and where women feel respected and treasured, abortion will continue to be an economic, social, and political as well as theological tinderbox, even though abortion rates in the US have dropped dramatically year by year since 2008 and have trended down since 1990.[1]

From the *Oracles of Astrampsychus*, we learn that a convenient way the ancient world dealt with those born weak or deformed or sick was infanticide.[2] The Romans practiced child abandonment routinely and ruthlessly. The prophet Ezekiel used child abandonment to describe Jerusalem in a prophecy: "On the day you were born, no one cared about you. Your umbilical cord was not cut, and you were never washed, rubbed with salt, and wrapped in cloth. No one had the slightest interest in you; no one pitied you or cared for you. On the day you were born, you were unwanted, dumped in a field and left to die."[3]

The Jews were different. "Jews think it criminal to kill any unwanted child," second-century Roman historian Tacitus wrote and Josephus confirmed.[4] This opposition to infanticide carried on among Jesus followers. Indeed, for most of Christian history, life was framed between the bookends of "the quick and the dead," where the "quick" or quickening was defined as the first fluttering movements of the fetus felt by the mother.[5]

You can have half a brick (or half an orange),
but you cannot have half a person.
PHILOSOPHER/ETHICIST TERESA IGLESIAS

But the simple belief in the sanctity of life and the dignity of all humans does not always yield simple answers. A new ethical front line is "wrongful birth" and "wrongful life." In "wrongful birth," prospective parents of a child with a disability— ostensibly whom the parents would have aborted had they received adequate medical information—can sue doctors for improper screening or counseling. In "wrongful life," a child with a disability (or those acting on the child's behalf) sues doctors and sometime parents for being alive.

Whether wrongful birth and wrongful life will be valid legal and moral categories in the future is yet to be determined, although it will be more pressing the more accurate genetic screening and prenatal diagnosis become in detecting birth defects. Already this culture's idea of "taking care" of Down syndrome is to invest in greater prenatal screening and abortion,[6] which have already wiped such children out of some countries such as Iceland, Denmark, and the UK.

Canadian feminist Wendy McElroy poses some questions that inevitably emerge from this minefield:

› Should the court system legally devalue the life of a disabled person?[7]
› Is it valid to equate a genetically produced disability with a medical injury?
› Should a lawyer representing a client be arguing that he or she should not be alive?
› Will doctors who remain in obstetrics advise discretionary abortions in self-protection?

› If wrongful birth and life cases proliferate, will doctors advise abortions even when risks are not probable?[8]

Most costly of all is the toll on the human spirit that comes when parents tell a child they wish he or she had never been born. Or when disabled children proceed legally against parents who loved them enough to bear them and care for them. Or the legal industry that will grow rich around the "wrongful birth" and "wrongful life" business. Or the untold numbers of children who will never enjoy the light of life because their lives are defined by others as "wrongful."

We are all disabled in some things, enabled in others. To edit disabilities out of the gene pool leaves all of us impoverished.[9] Any family with a relative who has Down syndrome knows they are disabled in some things but highly enabled in other things, like joy, trust, love, and mercy. Life would be lessened without them. Jesus takes his disabilities with him into eternity, and he sits at the right hand of the Father with wounded hands and feet. The risen Christ is a wounded Redeemer, a divine disablement. People with disabilities are made in the divine image too.

> WALKING IN FAITH

1. What does the term *wrongful life* reveal about a culture in terms of entitlement, the "victimhood competition," and the withholding of rights from the disabled?

2. How can the church better avoid the pitfalls of political and cultural polarization in confronting the trends where prenatal screening and "wrongful life" are concerned?

HOT SPRINGS INCAPACITATIONS

The mood and temper of the public in regard to the treatment of crime and criminals is one of the most unfailing tests of the civilisation of any country. A calm, dispassionate recognition of the rights of the accused, and even of the convicted criminal against the State: a constant heart searching of all charged with the deed of punishment; tireless efforts towards the discovery of regenerative processes; unfailing faith that there is a treasure, if you can find it, in the heart of every man. These are the symbols which in the treatment of crime and criminals mark and measure the stored up strength of a nation and are sign and proof of the living virtue in it.

WINSTON CHURCHILL

FUTURE RESIDENTS OF PLANET EARTH will look on our period as a particularly barbaric time, whether it be our treatment of the very old, the very young, the disabled, prisoners, the animals we eat . . . The ellipsis is a long one.

There are almost a billion disabled people in the world—that's almost 15 percent of the world's population, as many disabled people globally as Catholics. For some people, getting out of bed each morning is a life-affirming theological statement as strong as any that some of us will ever make. Jean Vanier, founder of L'Arche (The Ark), said that the disabled are our "teachers of tenderness" who free us from "the tyranny of normality."[1]

The Bible is full of disabled people, from Ezekiel to Paul.[2] In Jesus' day, epilepsy was called being "moonstruck" (Greek *selniazesthe*), as the ancients thought the shakes had something to do with the position of the moon.[3] In the ancient pirate code, a disabled pirate received an equal share to every other pirate. It will become more and more clear to all tribes and traditions what is not clear now to too many: Just as four disabled people saved a city from destruction,[4] so disabled people can help save our cities and our churches.

You can quibble but you can't quarrel with the biblical reality that all of us are equal in the eyes of the without-equal Holy One. That being the case, all of us ought to be equal in the eyes and laws of the world and the church.

> Words like *welcoming* or *inclusion* suggest those on the inside have the power to choose to accept those on the *outside*. This makes it sound like an act of charity to welcome those who are different or marginalized. However, it is not *our* place to welcome anyone because church is not a private club and we are not the gatekeepers. As soon as one new person comes through the doors, the community becomes a new community.[5]

> WALKING IN FAITH

1. In the future, our current use of terms such as *welcoming* and *inclusion* in speaking about the disabled, for example, will be seen differently from the way they are currently seen. How does "virtue signaling" in our discourse betray less admirable tendencies than the ones they are meant to convey?

11

RACE RELATIONS

IF ANTHROPOLOGISTS AND ARCHAEOLOGISTS ARE RIGHT, we are all descendants of an African Eve.[1] There are black Africans and brown Africans and red Africans and yellow Africans and white Africans. Race is the product of history and culture, not biology. So why is race a volcano in constant eruption?

The conversation on race has shifted from legal and political rights to business, economics, and education. There is now and will be a cultural reckoning with race and slavery. The question is whether or not that reckoning with slavery will lead to a reckoning with race.

We live in a world where blacks and whites see the same things very differently. We saw this with the trial of O. J. Simpson in the mid-1990s and the wide disparity of cheering and jeering that followed the jury's verdict. Nearly three out of four white people thought O. J. was guilty. More than three out of four black people thought O. J. was innocent.[2] Race relations have not changed much since then.

We see a similar dynamic in the differing responses to the Black Lives Matter movement. In the white community, there is the pushback of "All Lives Matter." Many in the black community respond with pointed sarcasm along the lines of "Why send a fire truck to a house that's burning down? Don't all houses matter?"[3]

Anger runs wild in white and black communities, as the mere mention of the cities Ferguson, Brooklyn, Baltimore, and Charleston make clear. To provoke an unvarnished, vernacular conversation on race in America is to venture into a volcano. But it is time to stop the mush in the mouth when people of different ethnicities sit across the table from one another. It is time to funnel down and tunnel into the depths of our nation's original sin and to do so in no-holds-barred, no-return-address conversations. The very future, not to mention the soul, of the nation depends on our willingness to pose jarring queries and jostling quandaries.

Almost all race conversations are not dialogues but duologues, in which everyone is talking but no one is listening.[4] What comes out of mouths in a duologue are projectiles laser-guided to their targets by unabashed political and moral correctitudes aimed to shut down, not open up conversation. No wonder black-white conversations are either hubs of hatred or hammocks of evasions and equivocations. This is as true for Christians as for non-Christians.

The only stable existence is a table existence.[5] Jesus saw all of life as an unending conversation over a vast table at which everyone is seated, even those with whom one disagrees. Jesus sits at the head of the table as the master questioner of history.

In fact, much of the Bible challenges us to ask the right questions rather than revealing to us the right answers. We begin life in a childish curl. We learn to unbend and stand ramrod straight, the body becoming an exclamation point. The older we get, the more we bend, our skeletons shrinking back into a question mark.

Such is the state of the conversation on race. Some of these questions and turns of thought are at the level of the childish curl, others the adultish mark. The best questions bring out not just convictions but also confusions so new understanding can be introduced.

Jesus didn't ask questions to get an answer so much as to provoke a restart. Perhaps race relations need restarts more than answers. Some questions we might wrestle well with together include

› Why is white always a metaphor for good and black always a metaphor for evil? Why is darkness a place of torment and temptation and lightness a place of purity and virtue?[6]

› Why are urban blight and racial divides so often blamed on white oppression and systemic injustice when cities are increasingly led by black mayors, black police chiefs, black attorney generals, black police officers fighting black-on-black crime? (For what it's worth, the question overlooks systemic and historical realities that contributed in significant ways to contemporary corruption and dysfunction.)

› When white people say "I don't see color," black people hear "You don't see me." When black people say "I see in all the colors of the rainbow," white people hear "You only see in one color." How should we see each other—colorfully or colorless?

› What can the church do to move the conversation from dart throwing to deep healing, from blaming to a place of bridge building? If everyone just keeps throwing darts, we only keep opening the wounds and making them worse.

› Where are our peacemakers and bridge builders? Who is raising up prophets of peace and relationality and dialogue? How might the church be a source of training prophets to bring people together not just in church circles but also in wider circles that matter to the culture?

What will make these questions an opening of a door to the future through which others can follow rather than the opening of a can of worms or Pandora's box?

First, Christians need to do more than build a bridge over the span that separates white and black worldviews. We must burn the bridge after crossing it.

Second, we need to forge a set of protocols for interracial dialogue, giving people of different races a tested framework that will enable the possibility of probing, honest dialogue without an abundance of hostility and with a deepening of respect. This will embolden and empower members of the black and white communities to actually try to extend a hand across the divide once each side is treated as a subject, not an object.

It is harder than you think to listen to others, to test claims against evidence, to compare different cultural sources of authority. Listening is not an innate trait or gift of nature. Listening is a talent to be cultivated with all its complexities and complicities. Listening involves an openness to voices other than one's own or listening to voices from other than one's own tribe.

In the late second century, the Greek philosopher Celsus, an antagonist of Christianity, observed that though Jews and Christians quarreled, they did not quarrel as loudly and as viciously as Christians quarreled with one another.[7] Followers of Jesus need to learn once again to have conversations with each other. Conversation partners need the freedom to look foolish and say foolish things across the table. Tables breed stories, and narrative is the healing balm of the wounds of the world. People are living storybooks, and anything that opens the covers is the path toward healing.[8]

For those bearing the monogram of the Messiah in their hearts, there are ten rules of engagement that apply to all honest engagements, whether they are about race, revival, or rug colors in the sanctuary:

1. No one has any right to argue with anyone until, to your satisfaction, they can state back to you the case you are making. Without that grounding, any debate is just two people shouting at each other.

2. Sometimes silence is the best form of engagement.[9] Haters need conversion, not conversation.[10]

3. Say no to negativity. Jesus is God's "Everlasting Yes!" as Paul liked to say.[11] Cringe from criticizing and complaining about each other. Martin Luther King Jr. did not say, "I have a complaint," "I have a beef," "I have a kvetch." He declared, "I have a dream."

4. No cheap shots or straw men. Don't play fast and loose with anyone's facts or feelings.

5. Abstain from playing the "reductio ad Hitlerum" card or pushing the button of the nuclear option "That's Nazism." When you declare someone a Hitler, you have ended all constructive conversation.

6. Learn to say "I have no dog in that fight" or "That's not my issue." Declare a fair catch when needed, and be quick to admit "Good point" or "You got me on that one."

7. Learn to lose gracefully. You can't win them all. You will lose some

fights you deserve to win, and you will win some fights you deserve to lose. Life is not fair.[12]

8. "The battle is not yours."[13] These five words rebuke all lordliness about our importance to God's mission. They comfort our sagging shoulders about how we're faring in advancing God's mission in the world, which will be victorious in the future with or without us.

9. Don't pick a fight. Be patient with each other, more commending than condemning. Why? If something said is of human construction, it will disappear. But if it comes from God, you cannot possibly win. In fact, you could find yourself fighting against God.

10. Don't worship divisiveness for purity's sake. Let there be no clefts in the church, except for one: "Rock of Ages, cleft for me, / Let me hide myself in Thee."

Any justice without the love of Christ surrounding it and repentance at the heart of it is counterfeit justice. Only Jesus is just and justifying. Our one constant prayer on the pilgrimage of life is a cry for mercy and forgiveness: "Forgive us our sins, as we forgive those who sin against us."[14]

History, as nearly no one seems to know, is not merely something to be read. . . .
The great force of history comes from the fact that we carry it within us,
are unconsciously controlled by it in many ways, and
history is literally present in all that we do.

JAMES BALDWIN,
"THE WHITE MAN'S GUILT"

British historian and socialist E. P. Thompson defined *presentism*—judging the past according to the values and virtues of the present—as "the enormous condescension of posterity."[15] Every age deserves to be judged on the basis of how well they pushed the boundaries and attacked the evils of their day, not ours. Of course, the discipline of historical context is never an excuse for evil. For example, only in the last couple of generations, for the first time in the history of the West, did people live without domestic servants. Yet might not one day our descendants look upon our dependence on low-wage labor for cheap clothing and entertainment as the use of slaves?

To be a disciple is to see life with gospel glasses. If the eye is sound, Matthew 6:22 says, the whole body is full of light. If the eyes of the church are more consistently on Jesus, our eyes will be more "sound" and our communities will be more colorful. The words of 2 Chronicles 20:12 must guide all conversations on race: "We do not know what to do, but our eyes are on you."

> WALKING IN FAITH

1. Race duologues are often less overt in the church than elsewhere. Is this due to the free flow of dialogue where race is concerned? Or is it symptomatic of a reticence to have the conversation at all? Explain.

2. What are the reasons for such reticence? What roles do shut-down tactics, stereotyping, and insults play?

3. How do our unwillingness to disagree with others and our need to make our disapproval known overtake our desire to understand the realities of race relations?

12

STEAMY INCARCERATIONS

THE UNITED STATES OF AMERICA IS THE WORLD CHAMPION of incarcerations. As of this writing, US prisons house nearly a quarter of the world's inmates.[1] There has never been in human history a prison system or criminal code the size of the current one. We incarcerate a greater percentage of our population than any other country, including Cuba, Russia, Iran, and even North Korea.

There are now more than forty thousand federal criminal offenses, not including state and local crimes. Every one of us could be prosecuted at any moment for something. And yet African Americans are incarcerated at a rate five times that of white people and make up more than a third of all incarcerated Americans.[2]

One of the surprises in recent scholarship has been that this place of barbarism is not the legacy of the "scientific racism" of the nineteenth and twentieth centuries but the progressive reformism that gained hold after World War II. Scientific racism said that certain races were inferior and prone to "crime, pauperism and sexual immorality." Included in these categories were Jews, Greeks, Spaniards, Italians, northern Mediterraneans, and Africans. But it has been the more recent wave of liberal experimentation—putting progressive principles into bureaucratic practice and engaging in social engineering within the justice system—that ultimately gave birth to the prison state.[3]

The best of intentions can have ill consequences. Through some Pulitzer Prize–winning research, former DC public defender James Forman Jr. has found that mass incarceration is in good measure the unintended result of war-on-crime policies to combat the drugs and violence plaguing urban communities.[4] Some scholars even argue that mass incarceration has created a racial caste system allowing for legal discrimination against people of color.[5]

The criminalization of drugs is a battlefront of the future. Drug crimes often get harsher punishments than violent assaults, rapes, and murders.[6] Addiction is not one of the seven deadly sins, nor does it violate the Ten Commandments. In fact, addiction is a reversible brain disease,[7] so the criminalization of drug use is a unique challenge to the logic of our modern justice system. Where is the church's moral outrage in the face of the obvious injustices in our criminal justice system? What are local churches doing to help communities reverse the curse that makes prison a statistical likelihood rather than an intervention of last resort?

It is better to let ten guilty persons to go free than that one innocent suffer.
"THE BLACKSTONE RATIO"
FROM JURIST WILLIAM BLACKSTONE (1765)

One of the best definitions of *prison* is from Bruce Anderson: "an expensive way of making bad men worse."[8] Ninety-five percent of all felony convictions now result from a guilty plea, which are generally negotiated on the basis of prosecutorial politics. Geofencing and electronic monitoring will gradually turn homes into prisons, replacing guards and bars with alarms and drones.

The death penalty has been justified this way: We kill those who kill, to show how awful killing is and to prevent others from killing. Read that again, please. In the era of Christendom, capital punishment was a religious ritual (replete with execution sermons) that brought the church and state together in support of death. This association is increasingly problematic, especially since it pairs the US in the world community with China, Iran, and Congo, the three other countries that most often execute their citizens. The abolition of the death penalty is already a fait accompli in international courts like the International Criminal Court, founded in 1998, where the current standard sets thirty years' imprisonment as the maximum penalty.

When you begin to let people who are "no good"
into your life, you are transformed.

JEAN VANIER

What is clear from a Christian perspective is that Jesus cared about prisoners and expected his followers to visit them, care for them, and pray for them.

I was naked and you didn't clothe me.

I was sick and you didn't care for me.

I was in prison and you didn't visit me.[9]

We are expressly told to treat every prisoner as if they were Jesus.[10] The author of Hebrews made Jesus' admonition explicit: "Remember those in prison as if you were together with them in prison, and those who are mistreated as if you yourselves were suffering."[11]

In the prison of his days,
Teach the free man how to praise

W. H. AUDEN,
"IN MEMORY OF W. B. YEATS"

"You will receive power when the Holy Spirit comes on you; and you will be my witnesses in Jerusalem, and in all Judea and Samaria, and to the ends of the earth."[12] These are Jesus' final words to his disciples. Scott Larson, president and cofounder of Straight Ahead Ministries, wonders how well we are doing with Samaria:

I think most churches do reasonably well in equipping members to reach their Jerusalem—those in close proximity like neighbors, coworkers, fellow soccer parents. And in Judea—people residing in other parts of the country or world, but who are mostly like us—relatives, fellow employees in other locations, or the guy in the seat next to you on a plane. And we engage lots around the ends of the earth these days, as record numbers of us head off to Haiti, Guatemala, or Africa on short-term mission trips.[13]

But when it comes to Samaria, the place of outcasts and outlaws, the "bad people" we lock up and lock out, we don't go there; which is why Larson asks the penetrating question, "Does your church have enough Samaritans?" Even prisoners need to be treated as humans: as people with problems, not as problems themselves. No human is a problem. No human is an animal. Animals live life. Humans lead life. Outside of prison, it's churches—if the gospel is being preached there—that should be home to the most outlaws.

In contrast to English historian Edward Gibbon's conviction that "few books of merit and importance have been composed either in a garret or a palace,"[14] some of the most momentous writings in history are prison literature. Four of Paul's letters were written in prison, as well as timeless literature from Revelation to *In the Belly of the Beast*, from *Pilgrim's Progress* to *Don Quixote*. Imprisoned authors such as Voltaire, Donne, Dostoevsky, Bonhoeffer, Lenin, Solzhenitsyn, Gandhi, King, and Mandela are just the more obvious examples. Albanian poet Visar Zhiti was released from prison with almost a hundred unwritten poems saved in his head. Albanian artist/writer Maks Velo spent eight years in a labor camp (for "deviating from the norms of socialist realism"), where he produced some of his most compelling work.[15]

Heavenly Father of us all, you alone can truly judge your creation. Help us to pray for all prisoners, no matter what their crimes may be, that they may find your grace, mercy and forgiveness. Amen.

A PRISONER'S PRAYER IN HOLLOWAY PRISON, ENGLAND

> WALKING IN FAITH

1. The post-World War II progressive reformism that has "improved" the United States criminal justice system has also criminalized some act or behavior for almost everyone, ensuring the punitive disposition of the penal system. How do our tough-on-crime stances reflect or fail to reflect a redemptive end?

2. Outside of prison, it's churches—if the gospel is being preached there—that should be home to the most outlaws. Is this the reality in our churches? Why or why not?

13

ECOLOGICAL EXTINCTIONS
AND HOTHOUSE HOME

We are our brother's keeper.
Not our brother's slanderer or enabler. Not his nitpicker or sycophant.
Not his foil, nor his foe, nor his thorn. We are not the beneficiary of clickbait
at his expense, nor the opportunist profiting from his weakness or error.
We are his keeper.

KAREN SWALLOW PRIOR,
TWITTER POST, JULY 29, 2018

JESUS IS NOT JUST LORD OF HISTORY; he is Lord of creation. In Christ is found the filling and fulfilling of the whole cosmos. A unitary Incarnation is the salvation of the universe. The more you believe in the Incarnation, the more you care about bees and trees. If you care for truth, you care for the earth. Herein lies one of the greatest theological vagrancies of the modern church.

Jesus' rising is eschatological as well as existential—the risen and rising Lord is the first sign of a "new creation" and the first sheaf of a future harvest embracing all creation. Twenty-first-century disciples of Jesus witness and participate in God's mission for universal reconciliation.

On June 18, 2015, Pope Francis did something unheard of for a pope: He issued an encyclical addressed not to other Catholics, but to humanity in general. Just as striking, the subject of the encyclical is not theology or ecclesiology but ecology. The pope, head of the world's largest religious body, acted not as the shepherd of the Catholic Church but as shepherd of planet Earth.

The good life is by definition an ecologically good life. The rainbow covenant God made with Noah includes animals,[1] and the redemption story of the Cross and tomb embraces all creation—humans, all creatures, and the earth itself.

Mitákuye oyás'i ("all are related") is a phrase from the Lakota language that conveys a worldview of interconnectedness held by the Lakota people of North America. It's a phrase that appears in almost mantra form in Lakota prayers, speeches, and everyday conversation. It is a way of saying that what happens to the particular impacts the universal. In English vernacular, we talk about the butterfly effect or the Songs of Trees, where the forest has its own dynamic intelligence based on a living network of interlinked relationship clusters that include, in David Haskell's words, "cells inside fir needles, bacteria clustered at root tips, insect antennae sniffing the air for plant chemicals, animals remembering their food caches, and fungi sensing their chemical milieu."[2]

In that day I will make a covenant for them
with the beasts of the field,
with the birds of the air,
and with the creeping things of the ground.
HOSEA 2:18, NKJV

"What were Easter Islanders saying as they cut down the last tree on their island?" Biogeographer Jared Diamond asks this in his book *Collapse*, a question that should haunt every human as they stare back at themselves in the mirror.[3]

Nothing stirs up the gospel gestapo ("discernment ministries") and heresy hunters more than when a Christian writes about infusing/suffusing the natural with a sense of holiness and infusing/suffusing the holy with a sense of the natural.[4] Why can't we elevate the status of animals (great apes, chimps, dolphins, etc.) without diminishing the uniqueness of humans? From a biological standpoint, what separates humans from other animals is our capacity for empathy, the expansion of the right frontal lobe. The roots of human consciousness are said to emerge out of empathetic responses.

When we try to pick out anything by itself,
we find it hitched to everything else in the Universe.
JOHN MUIR

Our failure as "keepers" is nowhere more evident than in an environment in serious peril. Ever since T. S. Eliot's "The Waste Land" (1922) and Rachel Carson's warning in *Silent Spring* (1962) of "the general warming-up" of the oceans, our poets and artists have pointed out the evidence all around us.[5]

Bernie Krause is a soundscape ecologist. He has been recording sounds from the wild and classifying sound signatures for more than fifty years. When he has gone back to compare and contrast the soundscapes he collected at the beginning of his scientific probes, fully 50 percent of his sound archive has gone silent.[6]

A 2010 study published in *Nature* revealed the comprehensive sweep of our ecological crisis. The study, which was led by Sweden's Johan Rockström and included US climate scientist James Hansen, identified nine "planetary boundaries" that are critical for human life on the planet: global freshwater use, chemical pollution, ocean acidification, land-use change, biodiversity (the extinction rate), ozone levels in the stratosphere, aerosol (or small particle) levels in the atmosphere, the nitrogen and phosphorus cycles that regulate soil fertility (and hence food production), and climate change.[7]

The study concluded that three of these critical planetary thresholds— climate, the nitrogen cycle, and biodiversity loss—had already been crossed. Land-use change, the phosphorus cycle, ocean acidification, and freshwater use are emerging problems that had not yet been breached but could be soon if nothing is done. The state of the ozone layer, which regulates the ultraviolet radiation from the sun hitting the earth, was the only good news. A global treaty to phase out ozone-depleting gases, such as chlorofluorocarbons, had made a difference.

The moral stakes of the global ecological crisis could not be higher for the future. Our very survival may depend on leaving our inherited pack patterns. Whereas our ancestors survived in the savannas by traveling, hunting, and feasting in packs, in the modern era following the pack can be life threatening, especially when the pack leaders are headed for an environmental cliff.[8] It is time for individuals to start thinking for themselves about what is best for the communal even when the communal thinks otherwise. Can we leave the crowd, the mob, the majority behind?

> That day when evening came, he said to his disciples, "Let us go over to the other side." Leaving the crowd behind, they took him along, just as he was, in the boat.[9]

The crowd is untruth.

SØREN KIERKEGAARD,
A DEDICATION TO THAT SINGLE INDIVIDUAL

It is now routinely suggested that global warming was a factor in the First Flood.[10] Most scientists fear that another great flood is coming. Already "acts of God" are commonplace, and "storms of the century" the norm.

When it comes to global warming, some say the problem is too big and do nothing. Others say there is no problem and do nothing, although these "others" are fewer since 2017 was the third warmest year on record and with 2018 on a similar treacherous trajectory. Will the church say that the problem is real and do something? Will the church announce that Jesus promises us life abundant, plentiful, bountiful? But will the church at the same time remind its members there is a difference between booty and bounty, plunder and plenty?

Half the world's electricity is still derived from burning coal. Whether we will act on carbon emissions in time to stave off ecological Armageddon (it is uncertain how much more heat the seas can be expected to absorb) will be the most defining issue of our day.[11] A decarbonized economy will be as good for capitalism as it will be for civilization itself.

We spray the fields and scatter
The poison on the ground

FROM UK POET LAUREATE SIR JOHN BETJEMAN'S
WITTY "HARVEST HYMN"

More than 99 percent of all the species that have ever lived have become extinct.[12] The bell tolls daily for another species gone extinct, and Christians respond with silence, shrugs, or at best the clichés of consolation. When you see your own people destroying the world, what is a Christian to do? What is a prophet to say? The cult of the invisible hand will not get us to the future without that invisible hand having gardening gloves. There are twenty thousand species of wild bees threatened with extinction by the four *P*s: poor nutrition, parasites, pesticides, pathogens. When humans see fields of green in savanna golf courses, playgrounds, or sports fields, we smile. When a bee sees the same landscape, it sees a desert with no flowers or food on which to survive. Every church needs to be a garden-church, every home a garden-home.

Part of the "extinction" taking place is not just one of biological species, chilling as that is, but also one of biological knowledge and natural experience.[13] The average educated and self-domesticated Westerner knows as much about nature as a Mangyan tribesperson is likely to know about computer software. When university students are asked to name all the trees they know, we can imagine an honors student responding, "Oak, pine, spruce . . . cherry . . . (giggle) evergreen. . . . Christmas tree—is that a kind of tree?" In contrast, some native cultures can name up to five hundred species of trees instantly and tell something about each one.

Noah didn't get to pick which animals to take and which ones to leave behind. He took them all—even that nasty little killer mosquito. The church's inability to articulate a compelling theology of creation and a coherent eschatology of the new creation helps explain the rise of pantheism, which in 1938 Cardinal John Henry Newman predicted as "the great deceit which awaits the age to come."[14]

Go, Francis, and repair my home.
THE CRUCIFIED ONE TO ST. FRANCIS

The priesthood of all believers is not just a call to be priests to one another. It is a call for us to be priests to the earth as well. In our origins story, God's prime directive to Gardener Adam and humans in general is twofold: *avad* and *shamar*, or "cultivate" and "care for." The noun *avodah*, of the verb *avad*, means "work," while the verb *shamar* connotes not just "care for" and "cherish" but "guard from harm" and "protect from peril." God created us to *avad* (cultivate) and *shamar* (care for) the earth, two words that appear together elsewhere in the Pentateuch only in reference to the priestly responsibilities of the Levites.[15]

Why is not every churchyard a garden and wildlife sanctuary, and every congregation an early warning signal of environmental danger? The ancients knew the healing power of gardens, and the Last Adam spent the worst, last night of his life in a garden. Gardens are one of the most multicultural and democratic places around.

A church that lives its prime directive will drive the future church into the local grounds in which God has placed it, there to discover the "rock from which [it has been] hewn, and . . . the hole of the pit from which [it was] dug."[16]

As trustees of God's creativity, we are called to make Planet Earth eco-poetry. *Poiesis* means "making," and *eco* means "household" or "dwelling place." The Incarnation is the apex of God's ecopoetry, but Creation was its inception and first expression. The "Let there be light" of creation that first illumined the universe was the same "I am the light of the world" light of incarnation that lit up the earth.[17]

---

*Let us pray: Eternal Father, at the very dawn of human history
you have given, through Noah, your protecting covenant to all animals
as well as to us. We intercede, therefore, for our friends the animals and
their welfare. Inspired by the Gospel message of mercy, given us by your
Divine Son, may all of us use our unique gifts of reason to protect
these less privileged creatures which share this planet with us.
We ask this through Christ our Lord. AMEN.*

THE VERITAS BOOK OF BLESSING PRAYERS

The world will be saved only if its infinite variety is conserved and culti-vated. Genetic uniformity leaves crops vulnerable to diseases. Local varieties not only adapt to local conditions and tastes but also carry on and raise the quality of life.

As maniacally as the Brothers Grimm's Rumpelstiltskin, we must learn to spin garbage into pure gold. Here are some smart wheels we can spin as we ecologize our lives:[18]

› Some science writers in the early twentieth century speculated that home windows would be solar panels, absorbing light during the day to emit light at night, replacing candles and electric lights. Where there's ample sunshine, solar power is a good option.

› Windmills, however, cannot be anything more than a temporary Band-Aid. Wind farms scar the landscape even worse than telephone poles and power lines, and they are an aviary holocaust.

› In terms of battery technology, Asians (Japanese, South Koreans, Chinese) are ten years ahead of the US, but all are decades behind what the technology can do with the right power.

› Petrol engines are highly efficient, but the demand for oil will peak
   in the next twenty years. Decarbonization and driving patterns will
   establish a new norm of electric vehicles (EVS), self-driving cars, car
   sharing, and drone vehicles.

› To find solutions to our environmental Armageddon, we will need
   to relook at nuclear power, large methane digesters, commercial LED
   lighting, building automation, bioplastics, industrial recycling, dis-
   trict heating, multistrata agroforestry, smart glass, high-speed-rail,
   intensive silvopasture, autonomous vehicles, solid-state wave energy,
   smart highways, hyperloops, and hydrogen-boron fusion.[19]

› We have resources aplenty to feed a richer and more populous planet
   by 2050, but we need to rationalize our supply systems: free trade
   in global commodity markets, enabling small farmers in poor countries to grow more food; agroecological approaches to farming; the
   restructuring of markets to support food security over commercial
   gains. The global food crisis often has as much to do with commodity
   speculation as it does with drought and climate issues.

› Urban agriculture will be a growth industry in the future, and the
   first evidences are already present in hydroponic greenhouses on the
   rooftops of buildings in New York and Chicago and vertical farms in
   other cities around the world.

› We are still in our infancy in terms of stewarding our scraps. The
   amount of meat discarded globally each year is equivalent to 11.6
   billion chickens, 270 million pigs, or 59 million cattle. We slaughter
   70 billion animals a year, a number projected to double by 2050.

› Serious recycling has only begun, and churches can play a major support role in helping people realize there is no "away" in "throwaway."

› Stop the dulling, deafening drumbeat of bad and trumpet the good
   wherever we can find it, like the giant pandas coming off the endangered
   species list in 2016 after decades of living on the brink of extinction.

VIPs (Very Important Pets)

If you want to explain to a post-Christian culture the nature of God's love,
or divine grace, you don't cite "a father's love" or even "a mother's love."
For God's love, you use the metaphor of a dog's love, which to this culture

means unconditional love, a love that embraces us even when we're at our worst, a love that rebounds even after our rejection and neglect.

It often happens that a man is more humanely related to
a cat or dog than to any human being.

HENRY DAVID THOREAU

The poet and hymnist William Cowper in many ways was born before his time. As mentioned earlier, he suffered from what we now call bipolar disorder and even attempted suicide on a number of occasions. What nursed Cowper back to health were therapy animals, starting with a rabbit and then a whole menagerie of "friends" that included guinea pigs, squirrels, ducks, hens, goats, sheep, and of course the omnipresent cats and dogs. He became a champion of animals, and his biographer George Melvyn Ella claims that Cowper was one of the first poets of the eighteenth century to advocate this familial relation toward animals.[20]

Twenty-first-century people will find it harder and harder to discriminate against anyone—not just based on skin color but also the kind of skin, be it fur, feathers, scales, or flesh. The dream of Jeremy Bentham will be more widely shared of a world where "humanity will extend its mantle over everything which breathes."[21] A new Earth Day will emerge out of Holy Saturday that will become a major liturgical celebration of the twenty-first century.[22]

This is more than a St. Francis "blessing of the animals." The phrase *pet owner* is already deemed offensive and in some places illegal (Boulder, Colorado). Almost half of all pet owners occasionally FaceTime their pets or talk to their pets on the phone. Almost one-third of pet owners have provisions in their wills for their pets.[23] There are currently more than a thousand insurance agents that specialize in pet insurance.

But beyond the elevation of pets in the lives and liturgies of humans, we are growing in our understanding of how animals can humanize us. Pigeons detect the earth's magnetic field and can distinguish between a Monet and a Picasso.[24] Octopuses and squids, as well as lobsters, crabs, and prawns, have a nervous system complex enough to feel pain. Empathy for animals has the capacity to make us more empathetic and thus to make us more ecologically responsible.

Most people treat their pets so well that, for these animals, going to heaven may be a step down. One of the questions every pastor will answer routinely in the course of their ministry is, "Will my pet go to heaven?" The Bible doesn't say so, but some of the greatest theologians in history (Martin Luther, John Wesley) were sure they would, based on the fact that God makes covenants with the creatures. God gave instruction for the care of animals in the laws of Moses and even allowed the law to be broken to save an animal in trouble. For many medieval Muslims, the debate was whether animals could go to paradise or hell, or just paradise. There is no debate about whether they would be joining humans somewhere.

Being raised in greener neighborhoods may have beneficial effects on brain development. Growing brains need green space for positive structural changes in the brain to occur, not to mention the needs of the spirit and the body. Every child's brain needs unsupervised time outside.[25] The closest to a jungle our kids ever get is jungle gyms, which they are frequenting less and less. Will our children be more curious and concerned about the makeup of the universe or the makeup of their own youniverse?

Love for our planetary home is hard, honest work. It can break the back. It can break the bank. But banks and backs have been broken for less significant causes. In the church, too few Christians want to save the world and too many want to save the saved. There is no future for either the world or the church in that.

> **WALKING IN FAITH**

1. If you care for truth, you care for the earth. Are your ideological predispositions at odds with the filling and fulfilling of the whole cosmos in Christ? Are they necessarily so?

2. How does our place as the capstone of God's creation free us to honor the rest of his creation without feeling constrained or diminished by such high regard?

3. How can we, the church, distinguish between booty and bounty, plunder and plenty, while also proclaiming the abundant life that Jesus promises?

14

SOLUTIONISM, DATAISM, SCIENTISM (SDS)

Scientists animated by the purpose of proving that they are purposeless constitute an interesting subject for study.

ALFRED NORTH WHITEHEAD,

THE FUNCTION OF REASON

THERE WAS ONE NATIONAL ELECTION when the president of the American Philosophical Society beat the president of the American Academy of Arts and Sciences. It was the presidential election of 1800, when Thomas Jefferson defeated John Adams.

Theology is the "queen of the sciences." Too many theologians have science envy, when it should be the other way around. There was an encounter between theologian and mathematician Isaac Barrow (1630–77), who contributed to the invention of calculus, and English poet John Wilmot (1647–80), the second Earl of Rochester. Wilmot resented theology and heralded reason. He greeted Barrow at court with honor: "Doctor, I am yours to my shoe-tie."

Barrow responded, "My lord, I am yours to the ground."

Wilmot met this deference with the one-up repartee, "Doctor, I am yours to the centre." Barrow came back with, "My lord, I am yours to the antipodes."

Not to be foiled by such a musty old piece of divinity, as he considered Barrow, Wilmot exclaimed, "Doctor, I am yours to the lowest pit of hell."

Barrow turned away and said over his shoulder, "*There*, my lord, I leave you."[1]

We need each other: theologians and scientists, people of faith and people of science. We need science's explanatory power. But the explanatory power of science cannot explain a lot: How about sheer existence? How about the origin of life? The more a culture of automation starts thinking like an automaton, the more it needs theology to remind it that humans are not robots but unrivaled mysteries of creation.

The problem is, we are not talking to each other except in isolated, professional circles. The blame is mostly ours, although voices like those of biologist Stephen Jay Gould justified the separation, contending that science and religion have little or nothing to say to each other.[2]

If Stephen Hawking said, "Philosophy is dead. Philosophy has not kept up with modern developments in science, particularly physics,"[3] imagine what he would say about theology. When is the last time you heard a sermon that brought in cognitive science, psychoneurolinguistics, epidemiology, biochemistry, even environmental science or anthropology? Okay—psychology?

Hayden Planetarium director Neil deGrasse Tyson, in his *Astrophysics for People in a Hurry*, promises that "you'll be culturally conversant in my field of expertise" by the end of the book.[4] If two hundred pages is all it takes, what's our excuse? If the marginalization of theology is to be slowed, the church of the future must raise up trusted guides to get us through the thickets of scientific thought and technology. Not Sherpas so much, who carry the weight for their companions, but scouts who go on ahead, get the lay of the land, report back what they see and read as the signs of the times.[5]

W. V. Quine, one of the twentieth century's leading philosophers, liked to say, "Science is refined common sense."[6] No more.

The fairest thing we can experience is the mysterious. It is the fundamental emotion which stands at the cradle of true art and true science.

ALBERT EINSTEIN,
THE WORLD AS I SEE IT

The irony is that, as theology has limited its definition of reality to the for-mal logic and logical systems of the philosophical, it ceases being theology and becomes science. As science has limited its definition of reality to the physical and the worldview of materialism, it ceases being science and becomes theology. Oliver Sacks confessed unashamedly how science became for him a substitute religion: "Evolutionary theory provided, for many of us, a sense of deep meaning and satisfaction that belief in a divine plan had never achieved."[7]

Theology can accept science without accepting everything that goes with it. The New Atheism masks a fundamental materialistic philosophy of life that needs to be constantly challenged. But will the church lift up a competing vision for the future other than solutionism and dataism? Solutionism is the belief that all problems can be solved through reason and technology. Dataism is the belief that the highest source of authority is algorithmic. Scientism is the belief that only scientific mentalities and methodologies are trustworthy and valid reconstructions of reality and that the scientific method applies to all arenas of life, whether philosophy, religion, or the social sciences.[8] In SDS (solutionism, dataism, scientism), our salvation lies in positivism, reductionism, naturalism, and materialism: the right algorithms, the right formulas—just add a little eye of newt and toe of frog.

Some problems are there to be handled, not licked. But the power of SDS is so strong that even if they're wrong, warns an Israeli historian trained at Jesus College, "it won't necessarily prevent Dataism from taking over the world."[9] What has brought us to this place of SDS supremacy?

When Charles Darwin arrived on the *Beagle* in December 1834 at the archipelago off south-central Chile called Chiloé, he went ashore on the island of San Pedro. As he put it in his journal, he found "a fox . . . of a kind said to be peculiar to the island, and very rare in it, and which is a new species." Human creatures were new to the fox. "He was so intently absorbed in watching the work of the officers, that I was able, by quietly walking up behind, to knock him on the head with my geological hammer."[10] Darwin's first response was to study something by killing it. He crushed the fox to death so he could dissect it. This is the essence of the "objective" scientific method behind SDS: To understand something, you don't stand under it; you stand over it and break it up.[11]

The temptations of reductionism can be seen in the uses to which functional brain imaging is put to use. Imaging technology of the brain in various emotional states has become so diagnostic and determinative that it can be viewed as the contemporary equivalent of the old "science" of phrenology.

But true knowledge comes not from a critical standpoint but from personal immersion.[12] Paper knowledge is one thing; personal knowledge is another. The world needs to hear the truth about the human:

You are more than an Amazon algorithm.
You are more than the neuroscientist's synaptic firings.
You are more than the biogeneticist's DNA.
You are more than the educator's IQ score.
You are more than the government's Social Security number.

Theology and science, faith and reason, literature and life fuse to form a rich tapestry of art, poems, novels, music, and sports. Where is a Christian faith that engages and excites the young? Right here.

The problem with theology today is not that it isn't rational enough but that it's not mystical enough. Mystical is not irrational but nonrational, superrational. The whole is greater than the sum of its parts. Your brain cannot produce consciousness or transcendence any more than your computer can write your sermons or your iPhone can compose the songs on your playlist. Each brain is unique and distinct, but we all can access a common consciousness and enter a zone of transcendence.

Hard science deals with soft questions. Soft theology deals with hard questions. The church must learn to master the imperious question, pose the hard question, and take measure of every move into the future.

Theology says something about everything, while other discourses often seek to say everything about something.

JOHN MILBANK

The printing press and paper, which had come into common use only in the fourteenth century, unleashed a sheaf of inventions in the sixteenth and seventeenth centuries, from flush toilets to pocket watches to bottled beer. And facts. Scientific "facts" were as much a modern invention as the nation-state or the denomination. Italian natural philosophers used the term *fact* in its modern meaning first in the 1570s, a usage that didn't gain intellectual currency and fluency in France and England until after 1660.[13]

Scientific "fact" has changed dramatically in the past.

Scientific "fact" will change drastically in the future.

Austrian philosopher of science Karl Popper's proposed "fallibilist" philosophy of science admitted from the start the mistake of thinking even our best scientific theories are true. Even as we celebrate them and use them, we must take them to be false in the long run, because the whole history of science is the overturning of one scientific theory after another.

Before 1543, it was scientific "fact" that the earth was at the center of the universe and that everything revolved around it.

Then Copernicus stepped in and said no, proving the scientific "fact" that the sun was at the center of the universe and the earth was nothing but a planet that revolved around the sun.

Then in the 1920s it became a scientific "fact" that Copernicus was not right about the sun being at the center of the universe, because the sun was actually in the suburbs of the Milky Way galactic disc, two-thirds of the way out toward the edge of the universe.

Then there was not just one galaxy in the universe; Edwin Hubble discovered Andromeda and demonstrated that there were most likely many more. By 2016 astronomers at NASA were speculating as many as 2 trillion.[14]

Then these galaxies were no longer thought to be in some kind of balance, but they were moving, and moving away from us, expanding as they went, and the further they were away from us, the faster they were going. The notion that the earth is whirling through space at thousands of miles an hour requires (then and now) an amount of faith and utter surrender of the mind that beggars any belief in a virgin birth or physical resurrection.

This meant it was now a scientific "fact" that 13.8 billion years ago there was a minute volume of atoms that had to explode. And on "a day without a yesterday" there was a Big Bang, a mysterious moment in which space and time began.

Then in the 1930s there was a new scientific "fact" that said something called *dark matter* was exerting a gravitational influence on the galaxies, stars, and gas clouds that can be seen, but still no one knows what that dark matter is.

Then in 1964 a new scientific "fact" emerged. Two American radio astronomers (Arno Penzias and Robert Wilson) discovered dark energy to go with dark matter—there were voids in space where nothing existed, and it must have been present in the initial Big Bang.

Then in 2000 it became a scientific "fact" that not only was the universe expanding away from a point of explosion, expanding against gravity, but it also wasn't slowing down, as one would expect. The rate of expansion is increasing, and the explosions are accelerating.

Comment is free, but facts are sacred.
BRITISH JOURNALIST C. P. SCOTT

An old academic joke distinguishes Anglo-American analytic philosophy, which asks about the moral implications of returning your library books late, from Continental philosophy, which asks what to do when the Nazis come. In the future, we must hold both questions together: one probing the precisions of our moral responsibilities, the other embracing the philosophical imperative to face the horrors of history and what science and technology might bring. It is up to the theologian to ask the most heretical question of our time: Is there something in the scientific method itself that consistently and persistently generates Holocausts and Hiroshimas?[15] What if true, deep understanding is less grasping and more gasping, less "holding on to that thought" and more beholding, less taking charge than being charged, less breaking it apart than bestowing a blessing?

The church needs to fall in love again with theology and relearn the art of theological reasoning. We need a fresh confidence in theology's capacity to meet and match the skeptical stances of positivistic and reductionistic scientism. G. K. Chesterton admitted to succumbing to the "romance of orthodoxy," or what the early church fathers, in their love for the fleshy images of the Song of Songs and the bosomy images of the Scriptures, might today have called the "sexiness" of Christianity. The intellectual allure of our sacred texts and canonical traditions can outcapture and outrapture the most glamorous sirens of the world.

The twenty-first century will be religious, or it will not be.
NOVELIST/STATESMAN ANDRÉ MALRAUX

What makes "smart" devices smart is that they're smart about you. They cater to your desires and sniff out your strengths. Algorithms—arguably the rhythm of the twenty-first century—are all about rational, directional, strength-based building blocks of information.

Algorithms are the skeletal support system of what makes smart phones, cars, homes. Algorithms are what make robots smart and AI intelligent. They are the aptitude behind every app we access. They get smart and then smarter by using "machine learning"—systems that continually rewrite themselves as they work. Machine-learning algorithm systems such as Siri, Cortana, and Google Maps offer you information based in part upon questions you have asked before. The systems learn to know what you most likely are interested in finding out or where you might be going.

The problem with this scenario for people of faith is that you cannot write any algorithm for the Holy Spirit. Algorithms are based upon predictability and reliability, upon rationality and repeatability, upon strengths and interests. That is absolutely not how the power of the Holy Spirit works in the lives of disciples. The Spirit is antialgorithmic because he is based on the unpredictable power of God's presence and our weakness.

Here's the closest you can come to an algorithm of the Spirit: Find out where you or your church are the weakest, where you are the most vulnerable, where you really have no natural gifts since that is precisely where God will use your weakness to bless others the most powerfully in and through you.

> WALKING IN FAITH

1. I (Mark Chironna) often tell my brothers and sisters in the faith that we are all called to be theologians. Are we all called to seminary? Probably not. But we *are* called to a holistic discourse in knowing God. The question is, In what ways do our perceptions of theology cause the word *theology* to intimidate or elude us? How are our responses similar to or different from that of people outside the church?

2. What fundamental beliefs undergird the adherence to solutionism, dataism, and scientism? What evidence of these beliefs is found inside the church?

3. Scientific fact continually changes; therefore, investing excessive trust in science is a recipe for uncertainty. Which areas of stress and unease in your life might be revealing an inordinate philosophical investment in scientific fact?

15

GENETIC ENGINEERING, ROBOTICS, ARTIFICIAL INTELLIGENCE, INFORMATION TECHNOLOGY, NANOTECHNOLOGY (GRAIN)

THERE ARE TWO HINGE MOMENTS in the history of books. First, the Roman invention of the codex—the binding of folded pages, which was the norm by the fifth century AD, replacing scrolls of papyrus. Second, the German invention of the printing press in the fifteenth century, which replaced illuminated manuscripts and handwritten books with a relatively new medium called *paper*, which became the basis for all media and shifted the very foundations of art.

Most Americans write hundreds if not thousands more words a day than they did ten or twenty years ago.

ANNE TRUBEK,
THE HISTORY AND UNCERTAIN FUTURE OF HANDWRITING

Followers of Jesus were famous for being among the first to use the codex. Gospels circulated in codex more than scrolls. Followers of Jesus were famous for being among the first to use the printing press, which has changed the face of Christianity for now more than five hundred years.

On the evening of October 29, 1969, the first data traveled between two nodes of the ARPANET, a key ancestor of the Internet. Even more important, this was one of the first big trials of a then-radical idea: networking computers to each other.

On the evening of October 29, 1969, Charley Kline and Bill Duvall, two young programmers from the West Coast, used special equipment built by BBN Technologies in Cambridge, Massachusetts, to connect their computers to each other. The first word on the Internet? They began to type "LOGIN," but the computer crashed after the letter "O." So the first word on the Internet was . . . "LO."[1]

Sometimes I think "LO" means the Internet is the beginning of a whole new beautiful world: "Lo! How a rose e'er blooming."

Sometimes I think "LO" means the Internet is the end of the world as we know it: "Lo! He comes with clouds descending."

Biotech is a baby Hercules that wants to kick the slats out of the crib.

BRUCE STERLING,
TOMORROW NOW

The first missionary in Japan landed there in 1549. The Japanese had no inkling who this creature was getting out of the boat. It had human form, but as an observer at the time wrote, "Might as well be a long-nosed goblin, or a long-necked demon. . . . Careful enquiry revealed that the creature was called a 'Padre.'"[2]

On April 29, 1770, Captain James Cook sailed his ship *Endeavour* into Botany Bay. The Australian aborigines on the shore paid his 106-foot ship no heed. It was unfamiliar to them and beyond their comprehension, and their denial was so strong that the ship became invisible and unnoticed. Not until a longboat was lowered into the water did anything register. Small boats were familiar, and they meant invasion, so all but two brave warriors fled.

The alien is beyond our acknowledgment. People can't see, or don't want to see, that which is beyond what they can understand. Blindness can now be reversed by implants in the brain, but people who have never seen are having trouble with the simplest of distinctions, like light and dark, because they have no framework for understanding the difference.

Part of the church's task in God's mission today is to bring to light what is hidden in our midst. The invisible is often more real than the visible. But we need the invisible to stay that way, because otherwise we have to deal with it. Faith does not give exclusive title or even inside track to "green pastures" and "still waters." In fact, faith is more likely to lead one into dark forests and deep blue seas, killing fields and troubled waters.

The latest industrial revolution is digital. "Everything that can be digital, will be"[3] is the new mantra evolving humanity as it brings together digital, biological, and smart networks; delivery drones; world brain; AR (augmented reality); VR (virtual reality); and GRAIN:

> Genetic engineering
> Robotics
> Artificial intelligence
> Information technology
> Nanotechnology

It will most likely be the artists and poets—not the scientists, sociologists, philosophers, or even ethicists—who grasp the significance of these new features of the Fourth Industrial Revolution.[4] It was not the futurists who first foresaw the immense impact on society of the home computer;[5] it was the artists who did, like novelist Ellen Ullman in 1994: "The computer is about to enter our lives like blood into the capillaries. Soon, everywhere we look, we will see pretty, idiot-proof interfaces designed to make us say, 'OK.'"[6]

But it is important that theologians and people of faith at least try to understand what is going on. The danger level is high. Genetic engineering, robotics, AI, IT, and nanotechnology come compassless, rudderless, and utterly heartless, and they come into a "my truth" culture totally unprepared to deal with normative questions. If "truth is individual," as photojournalist Molly Crabapple proudly claims in her unofficial capturing of the Occupy movement for her generation,[7] then GRAIN will quickly slip between the cracks (or chasms?) of morality.

The more GRAIN connects humans to one another and at the same time gives each human control over all aspects of life itself, the more willful and prideful the human species can become, and the more the whole is captive to the one broken link that would blow everything up.[8] In a highly connected world, we suffer from the misdeeds of a few as much as we benefit from the generous actions and affections of the many. Without a cruciform rudder, we lose our ability to find our way in the universe, a world now ruled by algorithms and GRAIN. Those who play god always pay a high price.

The digital revolution has been marching through society and dismantling or demolishing one institution after another. It will only continue its death march for those institutions that refuse to surrender their papers and insist on holding out for the past. Status quo means death; perpetual innovation and change is life. When the church resists change, it is a classic case of letting the dead bury the living.

Innovation is a social process and feeds on face-to-face interaction,[9] which makes human connection and collaboration more essential than ever before, not less. Moderns hated being beholden to anyone. But we are born beholden and we die beholden. Being "independent" was an artificial, unnatural, modern, temporary illusion. In the early church, there was no noncommunal living like there is today. *Communal church* or *church community* should be a tautology. What Jesus did was redefine the character and content, and reframe the composition, of community to include everyone.

Hence the danger of the language of "other" in referring to the marginal and outcast. For Jesus, there is no "other"—only "one another." There is only a path to the future when the "I" becomes "them" becomes "we," different but the same. As Virginia Woolf put it in *A Room of One's Own*, it is the "common life," and not "the little separate lives which we live as individuals," that is "the real life."[10]

The real face of postmodernity . . . is the face of the other.

DAVID TRACY,
"THEOLOGY AND THE MANY FACES OF POSTMODERNITY"

AR/VR (artificial reality/virtual reality) is already going from recreational use to corporate and personal use and transforming human life as we know it with body-enhancing, mind-altering advancements. Former Google and self-driving car guru Anthony Levandowski has already founded a church of the AI god, where humans can worship their robot masters.[11] Ray Kurzweil has long contended that once we implant a chip in our brains, we will be "godlike" and must function as gods. As we write these words, ten thousand people in the world are already "chipped" with digital implants in various parts of their bodies.[12]

New forms of religious community are springing from our interaction with computers.[13] There will be many new religions organized around worshiping this new connected intelligence,[14] new polytheistic AI religions that compete with the monotheistic IAm religions (e.g., Christianity).[15]

Regardless of whether or not it achieves "official" religious status, the new locus of religious faith for the culture will not be in Jerusalem; Mecca; Rome; or Springfield, Missouri. All will be replaced by Silicon Valley, the new kind of Vatican for the twenty-first century.[16]

An AI god will emerge by 2042 and write its own bible. Will you worship it?
CULT FICTION AUTHOR JOHN BRANDON

When we come to the rings of fire circling the GRAIN, we enter some of the craziest scenarios and biggest danger zones of the twenty-first century. Each one of these technologies has the potential to upend every aspect of human experience. The line between the grand and the ghastly has never been so thin. Atom bombs look like cap guns compared to runaway nanotech, genetic superpowers, malicious botnets, evil superintelligences, killer bacteria, antimatter holocausts, and unfriendly autopotent entities,[17] just to name a few.

Whenever we have tried to get the church to take each new wizardry of GRAIN seriously, people's eyes glaze over or they sneak out of the room. People don't want to hear about cyborgs, fermions, skyrmions, charm quarks, the Internet of things, and the like. But the ethical issues involved in GRAIN will make moral dilemmas such as double effect[18] look like child's play. Every dish on the GRAIN menu is a plate of fugu—a Japanese puffer fish delicacy that, if not properly prepared, contains a lethal poison.

Go with or against the GRAIN?

Each new research development that moves forward any or all of these technologies brings with it a risk of losing our humanity on the way to human perfection.[19]

All futurists plead guilty to premature promulgations. But we now need some premature moral promulgations to go with the premature prognostications, since in a world of GRAIN the line between the Wayward Way and the Godward Way is getting thinner and thinner.

English geneticist and biologist J. B. S. Haldane predicted something he called *ectogenesis*—the gestation of babies in artificial wombs. It seemed like bracing science fiction at the time, but Haldane was so confident of this new genetic technology that he assured everyone that the first ectogenetic child would be born in 1951.[20]

When someone from Appalachian culture says "Now, now," it doesn't mean "No" but means "Calm down, breathe deeply, and listen more care-fully." The culture and church need more "Now, now" times, both in general and specifically when living in a GRAIN culture.

Genome Era

The genome era has arrived. Genetic engineering enables us to delete and replace faulty genes, giving humans the false notion that we are all coded beings, and once we control the control, we can control everything. *Epigenetics* is a recognition that gene activity can be modified by one's environment, history, and experience and that genes do not predetermine who we are. Claims for the predictive value of genes to determine complex human behavior are evaporating.

In 1980, one of the most important judicial events of the twentieth century took place: *Diamond v. Chakrabarty*. By a 5–4 decision, the US Supreme Court allowed the patenting of microorganisms, or the patenting of life. In short, much of the living world is now within patent enclosure.

There is a Jewish legend about the sixteenth-century rabbi of Prague, Judah Loew ben Bezalel. In his desire to protect his community from potential annihilation by anti-Semites, he made a clay creature of huge strength and magic power to protect them: the Golem. One day, due to the neglect of its makers, the Golem ran amok, killing the very people it had been designed to protect.

Life patenting will be a major growth industry of the late twenty-first century, as humans will begin patenting human embryos, genes, cells, genetically engineered animals, etc. Genome-based medicine is not just the future but the present as well. The industrial factories of the future are the biofoundries of today that do the grunt work of biotechnology in their robot laboratories with their gene machines.

The whole genetic industry is only in its infancy, "mewling there in its crib, trying to find its toes. When it gets bigger, genetic engineering will radically expand our knowledge—especially our medical knowledge. However, it won't look or sound medical. It will break medicine open at the seams. It will reinvent its language and repurpose all its tools."[21] The problem is that the very same biotechnology that enables humans to vanquish viruses and bacteria also empowers humans to engineer even more deadly viruses and doomsday diseases.[22]

The New Biology is decommissioning Darwin, moving humans away from a strict naturalistic approach toward more holistic models of human enhancement. Genetics and cybernetics are revolutionizing our perception of how genes are turned on and off, especially how the mapped genome[23] can be edited to choice and to enhance the human condition. DNA editing, which puts humans in a position of altering the very genetic code of life, will bring huge benefits of eliminating diseases, enhancing intelligence, extending lives, empowering emotional restraints, and embellishing physical skills. A point will be reached when the human species, now posthuman, becomes the transhuman species, transforming all of human life and society.

At the same time, genetic engineering opens up a Pandora's box of issues, not to mention new life-forms that we ourselves have created. "Gene bombs" could eliminate malaria, but they could also release organisms into the environment that are out of control. Genetic splicing or cloning could resurrect extinct species, leading to de-extinction. But germ-line manipulation makes designer humans only a matter of time. Before you know it, we will be walking the streets with androids and genetically coded humans in their amplified (plastics) and augmented (digital) states.

When people find out about the CRISPR revolution already well underway, they will vacillate from volupté to vomit. CRISPR/Cas9 biotechnology is a gene-editing technology derived from bacteria that resequences genes to allow the virus to integrate itself into its host's DNA. CRISPR will make it seem like during the first-generation Frankenfoods scare and GM (genetically modified) transgenic-foods debate, the limbic regions of our brains were asleep, not glowing with conspiracy receptors. CRISPR allows humans to bend nature to our will and whim. With CRISPR we can rewrite any molecule of life in any way we desire.[24] The CRISPR process cleanses animal cells of unwanted viral passengers, thus enabling cross-species organ transplants. These molecular scissors that remove the risks of swapping disease when you swap tissues between species were only developed in 2012. In less than a decade, they will turn organ transplantation in particular, and biology in general, upside down in ways that will mystify the MEST (matter, energy, space, time).

Expect a huge "tech lash" to develop toward such extensions of personhood outside the human arena. Various camps of "human exceptionalists" are already forming, including the antitranshumanist Wesley J. Smith's Center for Human Exceptionalism, which contends against extending human boundaries almost as loudly as it contends for the intelligent design of the universe. Opposing this viewpoint are the Non-Anthropocentric Personhood people, those who see the potential for personhood in nonhumans, including, animals, robots, or uploaded minds, making them equally worthy of moral consideration as humans.

Robotics

Czech writer Karel Čapek invented the word *robots* in his 1920 play *R.U.R.* It comes from *robota*, meaning "drudgery." But the church got there before Čapek. In fact, the church was at the forefront of the robotics revolution by creating the first robot at a Catholic monastery (probably in Spain) in 1560. The robotic monk stood a foot high and was driven by a key-wound spring. It moved around, bowed in prayer, prayed silently . . . and still works to this day.[25]

Robots will be ubiquitous soon. They will start breeding, as computers are already doing, programming other computers. Already surgeons' new tools are not better knives but joysticks that control microrobots. Some surgeries, like appendix removals, will be done almost entirely by robodocs. Will you trust your life to a robot? In some ways, you already are, since every time you fly you are being driven by a computer programmed by other computers.

Robots and AI together will be beyond imagining, as robots learn and unlearn and surpass humans in both intellectual and emotional intelligence. Robots will go from being useful tools to indispensable companions on the journey of life. Some humans will even want to marry them.

Transhumans are superhumans who are sexier, stronger, and smarter. Transhumans are upgraded homo sapiens and will arrive by 2030 as brains begin to fuse with machines. Machines are already making us smarter and will move inside our brains soon. The challenge for the church will be this issue: No matter how cyborgian and digitally connected humans become, are they still the summit of authority in the universe under the sovereignty of God? Or will we submit to the authority of the cyborg?

As humans migrate to digital realms, including massively multiplayer online role-playing games (MMORPGs) such as *Second Life* and *World of Warcraft*, human identity also moves to and matures in virtual medium. Distributed personhood will need new legal protections to guarantee safe and swift online activity, and it will make all the more important the dance of the one and the many.

The future is a driverless, car-sharing, pedestrian, and pedaling future. Alternatives to ownership are boom businesses already: car clubs; ride-sharing; self-driving vehicles; and app-based taxi services like Uber, Lyft, and their Chinese counterpart DiDi. Car companies such as Ford and

GM are seeing the handwriting on the wall and retooling as "mobility companies."

Roland Barthes's comparison of cars to Gothic cathedrals resonates with everyone who's tasted the drug of sports car ownership and automotive rushes. Driverless cars lack soul and will end the romance with cars. The more we make cars utilitarian—safe, cheap, clean, quiet, and small—the less they capture our imaginations and the less hold they have over us. Long-term decline of driving among the young is already quantifiable.[26] If there is a new love affair with the auto, it will be with the back seat.

Cars will be missed as steam locomotives are missed. They created in their wake an exciting culture of mobility and nobility. But they terrorized the planet, tore up communities, polluted the air, blighted the landscape, and (according to the World Health Organization) killed 1.25 million of us each year with deadly abandon.[27]

AVs (autonomous vehicles) will steer the future, end auto-cratic culture,[28] and be a thousandfold improvement over human drivers. Robotaxi fleets running 24/7 will enable you to purchase rides in podlike vehicles without steering wheels or pedals. AVs may actually increase congestion on highways, but it will be driverless congestion, so you can be creative and productive, or just sleep, in the midst of gridlock. Paved roads may be reduced by as much as 50 percent, with the return of all that topsoil and a renaissance of urban farming and gardening. Cities will be returned to pedestrian-friendly places where parks and housing replace parking garages, gas stations, and boulevards. Handheld robots with human operators will do tasks like bricklaying, housecleaning, stonecutting, and house painting, and they will be able to argue with us about how much they've done and how well they've done it.[29]

We must learn to work with these new machines. If the church will only reboot into its true reason for being—relationships—this century of AI and robotics will be a great day for the church. The question to address is whether robots are tools to make life better or Trojan horses to reinvent life and become new life-forms.

People's biggest fear in this area is of a jobless future, since one industrial robot replaces six employees. Automation leads to joblessness. What do you do with unskilled workers? Autonomous cars could eliminate three hundred thousand driving jobs.[30] Silicon Valley is awash in sales of New Zealand real estate, described as "apocalypse insurance."

Yet one of the world's most roboticized nations, Japan, has only a 2.6 percent unemployment rate.[31] There are more than four hundred thousand

ATMs in the US, but the number of bank tellers rose between 2000 and 2010. While the average number of tellers per bank fell, the ATMs made branch offices so much cheaper to start that they opened more of them.[32] The 1950 census listed 271 occupations. By 2010 only one had been eliminated by automation: the elevator operator.[33]

Earlier thought about robotics was that it would make possible a universal leisure class—the robots would do all the work so humans could do whatever they wanted. Today robots aren't seen as liberators but as successors—we worry about their replacing us in the workforce (the very thing that appealed to us in a previous generation) and demanding civil rights until they ultimately supersede us. Automation can either make humans obsolete and "the useless class" or indispensable and invaluable. If you want to fit in, then a robot can replace you. If you want to stand out and fit together, then automation can help you be more unique and different and indispensable.

The most important question in twenty-first-century economics may well be what to do with all the superfluous people. What will conscious humans do, once we have highly intelligent non-conscious algorithms that can do almost everything better?

YUVAL HARARI,
HOMO DEUS

A greater worry than joblessness is outsourcing human judgment to machines. This is the argument of Tim Harford, who makes the case for the dangers of neatness and the value of experimentation, overlappings, and randomness in human decision-making.[34] In 2012, some Japanese students visiting Australia drove into the Pacific Ocean because of a glitch in their GPS system. Rather than question their technology, they had plowed on. They were fine; their car was not.[35] Worry less about robots taking our jobs, Harford warns, and more about them taking our judgment. Already the decision of whether your bank account will be charged a fee is made by a computer, not a human.

Tesla cofounder Elon Musk, Apple cofounder Steve Wozniak, and Stephen Hawking signed a 2015 letter urging a ban on autonomous weapons, warning about the "existential risk" of weaponized AI.[36] We've been watching humans battle weaponized robots forever in sci-fi films. Facial recognition software and drones already exist, with hundreds of churches already using facial recognition technology in worship.[37] Add to that biometric readings, robotics, and weapons and you have a picture of the future. As frightening as it appears, every generation thinks its integration of new technology is the end of the world as we know it. All these challenges are real but need not be apocalyptic.

The issues revolving around citizenship for robots aren't as pressing as the ethical ones. One of the most troubling and menacing features of the future is armed drones. The more autonomous the machine, the more moral commands will need to be coded into its system by roboethicists. The problem is, you can't hardwire ethics into computers, because ethical systems evolve over time. The genius of the US Constitution is that it is a learning document that allows for amendments that update and upgrade the original programming and don't cast in concrete the moral values of one generation that had blind spots for African Americans, Native Americans, women, etc. The key to teaching ethics to robots may well turn out to be, as every parent knows, to instill in them a sense of guilt.

But then, what if your robot is emotionally disturbed?

Artificial Intelligence

Artificial intelligence (AI), or what Kevin Kelly calls "cognifying information," will invade every aspect of our lives.[38] The age of AI is forcing us to rethink what it means to be human and to chart what is unique about human values and capacities. Some scientists, like Stephen Hawking and Martin Rees, have warned humanity that AI will most likely lead to catastrophe.[39] Elon Musk reminds us that because AI underpins a lot of the other GRAIN technologies, humans will have to augment themselves just to keep up with the machines. Larry Page, cofounder of Google, accuses those who want to restrain digitalism of being "specieist" and sees speciesism as the primary threat to cosmic evolution.[40] With Google's proliferation of ubiquitous listening devices into all our addresses and apparel, it is only a short distance now to the brain and the GRAIN human.

The idea of human/machine, born/made fusion is a terrifying one to everyone except science-fiction writers, technologists, and some philosophers. One author even suggests that Frankenstein has displaced Adam and Eve as the modern creation myth.[41]

But already smartphones give us superpowers with access to knowledge, wisdom, and abilities beyond anything nature gave us. Augmenting the human mind would be the ultimate superpower, the beginning of the cyborg age. The smartphone is already dead, and its final burial will spell the end of the machine age, when we carry machines with us (or they carry us), and the beginning of a cyborg age that bridges our bodies straight into the ebb and flow of the GRAIN.

The problem is that every augmentation brings with it an amputation. We gain something but we lose something too. Media and technology are not zero-sum games. When printed books first appeared in the 1470s in Augsburg, the wood engravers went on strike and stopped the presses. They thought they were going to lose their jobs. The truth of the matter was that they were more in demand than ever, so there was more work than ever. That was the blessing. The bane was that the work had become much more repetitive and less creative.

Some losses are good to go. We lost the slide rule when we gained the calculator. Maps are like slide rules. The more we rely on GPS, the less we can figure out for ourselves the directions to our destination. And the more we rely on machines, the more we lose our ability to find our way in the universe and map our coordinates with the heavens. The loss of human freedom and autonomy is not good to go. Some losses go at our peril.

To make AI autonomous will mark the biggest event in weaponization since nuclear weaponry. Autonomous machines will be making decisions about whether or not to kill humans without human checking. Already autonomous machines can identify humans—retinal scans—better than humans can identify humans, which in some ways makes enemy-friend split-second decisions more accurate. Or so the argument goes. MIT scientists have already created an evil AI by subjecting it to violent Reddit content.[42]

Smartphones are dead. They just don't know it yet.[43] Smartphones already have virtual assistants,[44] and technology will soon mediate all our senses, beginning with seeing and hearing.[45]

Wearable technology has been with us since watches and glasses, but soon wearables will biometrically store our passwords. Augmentation will take the body to the extremes, and AR (augmented reality) will erase the separation between the digital world and physical reality. As AR becomes the norm, or what you might call the new OS (operating system), it will lead to the disappearance of all mobile devices and screens.

Smartphones move to hands-free accessories like glasses, which will project detailed 3-D images straight into eyes and overlaid on the world around you. Smartglasses will soon be standard at workplaces and already are at use in businesses as diverse as warehouses, shipbuilding, and doctor's offices, where physicians look at a patient's records while looking at the patient instead of computer screens. Before you know it they will find their way into everyday life. People will get "modes" or "moded" to augment cerebral and corporeal processes, like we now get tattoos. These accessory wearables and prosthetics will in turn move to digital implants and tattoos, changing what it means to be human in that the physical and digital world become the same thing. Our theology of relationships must expand to include droids and robots.

The future is screenless in the seamless blend of RL (real life) and VR (virtual reality). But until then, screen time remains a mental, physical, and moral health issue. Screens are as addictive as alcohol and tobacco. A screen culture needs an ethic of images as much as a print culture needed an ethic of words. Every Gutenberg child learned the existence of "bad words." Are Google children learning the existence of "bad images"? We need an ethic where we discipline ourselves to filter what goes into our eyes, ears, mouths, and hands, especially in the face of the coarsening and raunchification of the culture.

Whether digital media renders its users more narcissistic, depressed, lonelier, and stressed than our ancestors is yet to be determined. It is significant that self-harm, eating disorders, body dysmorphia, anxiety attacks, and depression are on the rise in the US and UK. Maybe if we want to see tomorrow, we should look at the problems our kids are having today— hyperactivity, hypersensitivity, dyslexia, underactivity, obesity, undernourishment, fear, attention deficits, violence, anesthetization—and trace their sources as well as contrive resources to deal with them.

The crisis consists precisely in the fact that the old is dying and the new cannot be born; in this interregnum a great variety of morbid symptoms appear.
ANTONIO GRAMSCI

We post on social media. We don't live on social media. We don't live off social media. We post. We don't posit our existence from social media. We post. Every church is a postal carrier. The best postal carriers bring messages from heaven to earth, from inside the heart, deep in the mind, into the hands of others.

The augmented age will be populated with augmented selves. As of this writing, there are forty-nine AR companies, not including the huge investments in AR being made by Facebook and Apple. There are already fifty AR headsets in production, as well as glasses and wearables. AR is going into smart mirrors at Sephora and Nieman Marcus. AR is already being used in Google's Translate app, which employs computer vision, automatic translation, and a smartphone camera to show an image of the world that includes text.

Within the lifetime of our kids, the union of the born and the made will become seamless. Samsung, Netflix, and Facebook are all perfecting speech-to-text interfaces that translate thoughts directly from brain to computer. Neuralink, a company cofounded by Elon Musk, boasts a goal of building computers into our brains by way of a "neural lace" that lays on your brain and bridges it to a computer. It's the next step beyond even that blending of the digital and physical worlds, as human and machine become one.

Some neurotechnologies are already on the open market, not just in medical laboratories. In 2008, a woman in India was convicted of murder and sentenced to life on the basis of a brain scan that showed, according to the judge, "experiential knowledge" about the crime.[46] Ubiquitous brain-scanning tools, which open up the possibility of mental manipulation through neural technology, will bring to the fore a new civil/human rights movement: the right to brain privacy, the freedom from third parties reading your brain involuntarily.

AR and VR are kindred technologies but with opposite understandings of "reality." VR wants to plunge users into a "reality" that is artificial and unreal. AR wants to plunge users back into the real world supplemented by virtual layers of entertaining data and images. Whether it's AR or VR, the question is whether we will use technology to escape reality or to enrich it, as an end in itself or a means to an end, when the end is human relationship and activity. To make technology the end is the temptation of the future, the idolatry of the century.[47]

Before you know it, you may be saying "Aaah" to Alexa and seeking Echo's advice about your illnesses like you once did your doctor. Health diagnostics can be digitized, with wristwatches, toilets, or contact lenses gathering daily health data and sending it to AI doctors. AI will make medical diagnosis faster and more accurate. The accuracy rate for diagnosing skin cancers was 86.6 percent for dermatologists and 95 percent for computers, with fewer misdiagnoses.[48] Digital diagnosis will give people around the world access to medical assistance and offset the global shortage of 7.2 million health-care workers (as of 2017), a figure expected to double by 2035.

The problems with planned obsolescence increase in digital culture. Even vehicles like cars and tractors are so computerized, and outdated so quickly, that it's almost cheaper to get new ones than to fix the old ones. Indeed, barriers to mending are now built into the design. Expect a new "right" to emerge: the right of repairability.

We were told that VR (virtual reality) would be to our kids what the Internet was to us: a technology that would change everything. Push a button, and to your senses anything can feel like it's really happening—even though nothing is really happening. As we write this, VR has not lived up to its promise. It has still not made it into our living rooms and indeed has stalled, partly because it literally causes nausea and makes many vomit. Its technology causes what you see to lag behind what the brain expects, which causes the grogginess.[49]

Jaron Lanier, the computer scientist who popularized the term *virtual reality*, says this about his "baby": "Never has a medium been so potent for beauty and so vulnerable to creepiness."[50] With a novelist's eye for scenarios, Canadian author Tom Rachman poses some of the ethical issues in VR:

> What if you yourself murder someone in a VR game? From the outside, it would merely look like a person in headset and earphones. Inside, something hideous could be happening. Legal questions arise, too. Should crimes committed in VR be illegal? Before you say no, what about torture? Or sex crimes? What if the user has sexual relations with a VR version of a real person without their permission? This seems obscene. But is it a thought crime? An experience crime? Or no crime at all?[51]

The world of entertainment is not ruled by *Star Wars*, or Rihanna, but *Grand Theft Auto*. The video game industry is a $100-billion-a-year business, bigger than film and music put together. VR and AR will only make it bigger.

Games are no longer just play. Games constitute a whole philosophy of life.[52] Most importantly, video games are sources of complex storytelling, a storytelling that employs role-playing and game-learning. Every aspect of human life is being reshaped by the gaming paradigm.

For example, what captured the imagination of the world was not the steady stream of rich data produced by the Hubble Space Telescope. Rather, it was first the steady stream of images that were not hoarded by scientists but shared with the public. It inspired "citizen science," or crowd sourced, interplanetary space science missions, one of which was run out of an abandoned McDonald's on the campus of NASA's Ames Research Center in California, which used gaming platforms to connect volunteers to university-led science projects and online puzzle video games like *Foldit*, in which players determine the structures of real proteins. The results of team game playing have been so spectacular that some findings have been published in peer-reviewed journals.[53] Everyone plays games, but the games you play matter. The games remodel the gamers, and they not only enhance and enable our ambitions but also alter our desires.[54]

As of 2017, one free-to-play title—*Clash Royale*—brought in about $2.1 million a day from purchases like specialty armor, a mount for speed, etc. Most of these purchases come from just a few players, called "whales" because of their impact on the game. Since 0.2 percent of all players are responsible for 48 percent of all purchases,[55] the question becomes how to keep those whales happy and buying. One solution is to pay for other fish to stay in the ocean and play with them. A new job in the future will be a new kind of paid playmate. Game companies will pay money to poorer players to stay in the water and play with the whales.

The church must up its game to embrace the gamification of learning in general and discipleship in particular. Summer camp becomes not a boot camp in belief but a game camp in a living gospel.

IT (Information Technology) and IT (Internet of Things)
The Internet is now in the same category as water, plumbing, and electricity. It may soon be the number-one utility.

Think the Internet is the source of all evil—from "fake news" to terrorism? Socrates thought the shift from orality to textuality and the mastery of written languages would create those who "will appear to be omniscient and will generally know nothing."[56] Anyone who has ever been trolled is excused for thinking that Socrates may not have been so wrong after all. But the power of the web can be put in historical perspective: The master metaphor for the medieval age—chain of being. The master metaphor for the industrial age—machine. The master metaphor for the modern age—bodies politic. The master metaphor for the digital age—the web or network.

The success of a web-architected economy in meeting the hungers of the human heart are expressed in the rise of Amazon, Apple, Facebook, and Google. Together "the Four" have generated wealth beyond imagining ($2.3 trillion and counting). Some have called it "the greatest concentration of human and financial capital ever assembled."[57]

> Amazon appeals to our hunger for things.
> Google appeals to our hunger for knowledge.
> Facebook (and Twitter) appeals to our hunger for connections.
> Apple appeals to our hunger for beauty (and sex).

These four hungers are honorable. Or these four hungers can become the Four Horsemen of the Apocalypse.

Doubt the power of social media? On November 21, 2013, a Facebook post toppled the Ukrainian government.[58] When Facebook crashed during the summer of 2014 in some cities, many people called 911. Two billion people are allegedly active on Facebook at least once a month. That means any person or any church has the potential of directly and instantly communicating with 30 percent of the world's population at any moment. It is often said that Facebook is not for kids, only for their elders. But 80 percent of US teens have a profile there, even if their main postings are elsewhere.

Every church needs to be outward focused, exhibiting a unique online presence in their zip code. Every church needs in-house studios that can produce content for strong social networks and multimedia resources for both those inside and outside the church. This is where the young can make some of their greatest contributions to the body of Christ.

My Appalachian gramma had a saying: "If these walls could talk." These walls are already talking. In fact, soon everything will be talking, everything will be talking to everything else, and we will be talking to everything—from software to wetware. The collapse of the virtual and real will be so seamless that it will seem that even things know your thoughts because they will know you. It's called the Internet of things.

Digital first attached itself to text, then to music and videos, and now to things. The Internet of things[59] necessitates that security issues be design issues from the beginning, not value add-ons at the end. It also mandates at least three shifts in how ministry happens.

First, part of your ministry team is not just people; it's people, place, and prop. The word *incarnation* comes from Latin *carnus*, which means "flesh" and from which we get words like *carnal, carnival, carnivore, carnage,* and *carnation.* Give people carnations and carnivals or there will be carnage. Christian faith takes matter seriously; it is materialistic and wants to materialize in everyday life.

People need thingies. No pilgrimage ever ended without some sacred mementos or artifacts. Hence the tattoo phenomenon. When you sacramentalize the material with a "thingy" or "prop," it becomes an icon through which people can perceive divine realities and human raggedness more clearly.

Second, move from thinking "products" to "platforms," "resources" to "trampolines," tangibles to intangibles:

The largest cab service owns no vehicle (Uber).

The largest hotel chain owns no hotel (Airbnb).

The largest retailer owns no inventory (Alibaba).

The largest social media outlet generates no content (Facebook).

The largest app store develops almost no apps itself but "platforms" 2.2 million apps developed by others (Apple's App Store). Pastors must learn how to be curators of platforms that empower God's new humanity, gardeners caring for the caretakers of the tree of life.

The future is more about intangible than tangible investment, where intangible investment includes design, R & D, branding, and images. This is a radical shift from the modern church era's tangible investments in buildings, furniture, hymnals, offices, etc. Architecture is not the shape of a building but the substance of a message. The church of the future will be an intangibly rich economy that is highly scalable and has large spillover effects.[60]

Third, move from core to crowd. Cores are centralized, bureaucratized institutions that plan their way forward. Crowds are open-source, participatory structures that are always changing and making it up as they encounter new obstacles and opportunities. Immunity is found in community, not in individual dignity and vanity.

Make a fertile platform and invite the *imago Dei* creativity in. Wonder if the content wouldn't eclipse the container? Do you wonder what would happen if, instead of arguing with people, we invited them to platform or to table with us?

Nanotechnology

> *Not great deeds, but small deeds done with great love.*
> ATTRIBUTED TO ST. TERESA OF CALCUTTA

The quantum era has begun. *Nano* means "one billionth" or to go very small, minute, even microscopic. You can't get any smaller than the atomic level. They are now making computers out of atoms.

One of the hundred fastest computers in the world (1,600 teraflops) sits in a desk drawer on the fifth floor of an office building in Bristol, England. That's a huge computer in a nanotech world. Quantum computers are not made of the 0s and 1s of standard computers but the superpositions of bits that are both 0s and 1s so that these "qubits" are inescapably entangled with every other qubit. The result is a paradox: The nanotechnology of quantum doesn't scale down but up. It unlocks new worlds of possibilities in every arena of life. What we see is not how the world works; the quantum releases the real workings of the world.

Today we are in the realm of quantum computers where we were with the Internet in the 1990s: churning the crank of a Model T. But technology's future rests in quantum computation and quantum networks. Brace yourself for quantum-enhanced everything, from quantum cryptography to quantum accounting to quantum healing. Quantum anything is "better" anything.

Quantum computers makes the transistor look like Lincoln Logs. IBM has now gone public with one called Quantum Experience. It is hooked up to the Internet, where it will probably be located for the foreseeable future, because anything quantum is in need of intensive coddling and care.

> *More will mean worse.*
> SIR KINGSLEY AMIS

What makes quantum computers work so well? Two things, and maybe three: superposition, entanglement, and (maybe) probability amplitudes. In quantum superposition, bits (or qubits or qbits) can be stolen from alternate universes and used to configure data. What now takes the world's fastest supercomputer years to compute would take a quantum computer only seconds. In quantum computers, there are no limits, no horizons, leading some to posit the brain[61] or the universe itself[62] as a quantum computer.

The biggest surprise coming from quantum technology is that the counterintuitive can yield results of staggering precision. Quantum weirdness means that quantum technology will do weird things that we can't even predict and that the world will grow weirder and weirder. Stated differently, the world will grow more magical and mysterious, more unknown and uncertain. A human brain has 100 billion neurons. Within a few years of reading this book, your computer will have more transistors than the brain has neurons. No wonder the language of magic and mystery abounds on the frontiers of Silicon Valley when you're working on one product with tens of billions of transistors. No wonder all the millenarian hype that haloes information technology and turns everyone who writes about the Internet into quasi-religious visionaries.

The Christian of the future will be a mystic or he will not exist at all.

KARL RAHNER,
THE MYSTICAL WAY IN EVERYDAY LIFE

Both Muslim and Christian mystics like to use the gastric terms *sweet* and *sweetness* to describe their raptures in divine entanglement and super-position. The future will be getting sweeter and sweeter, with practicing mystics from every religious tradition and none. Nobody practiced mysticism before the twentieth century. There were mystics within religious traditions like Judaism, Islam, Hinduism, and Christianity who majored in various mystical features within those traditions. But the future will be filled with practical mystics who daily practice quantum mysticism from no religious tradition. The church needs to let shine two lights it has hidden in bigger and denser bushels of critique, control, and contentious verbiage. Those two lights are the same word with one letter of difference: the *mystery* and *mystory* of faith.

A quantum world will also bring with it people whose "mystory" exists in quantum realms of indefinability from a theological standpoint. Even Jesus-focused people—too mystical for the rationalists; too rational for the orthodox; too orthodox for the progressives; too progressive for the conservatives; too conservative for the academics; too academic for the charismatics; too charismatic for the evangelicals.

Because of nanotechnology, where you basically downsize to upgrade, there is a new openness to the small, the human scale. The power of small numbers, the power of one, has never been greater.[63] Every small is a great gift from God. This is the culture that will live up to the promise that "small is beautiful," which boomer culture failed to do.

I am done with great things and big plans, great institutions and big success. I am against bigness and greatness in all their forms, and with the invisible molecular moral forces that work from individual to individual, stealing in through the crannies of the world like so many soft rootlets, or like the capillary oozing of water, and yet rending the hardest monuments of man's pride, if you give them time.

WILLIAM JAMES,
LETTER TO MRS. HENRY WHITMAN, JUNE 7, 1899

Modernity's infatuation with big is over, as the bruises and damages of Big Government, Big Business, Big Labor, Big Church are still tender to the touch. This is the biggest obstacle to the globalized empire of bigness: the hunger for small-unit self-sufficiency and small communities that can be economically viable through telework and telemedicine. Some of us were always drawn to the smallest room of any house. This culture has made that smallest room its home.

St. David of Wales (500–589) spoke these dying words to his monks: "Be joyful, keep the faith, and do the little things."[64] God is large in life's littles. The little things are what reveal our love for the one who loved us first[65] and bind people into a community of faith, love, and service. The little levers are what crack open a universe of possibilities. God uses most mightily not those who possess "big" gifts and claims on the Spirit of truth, but those who surrender their littles to the Spirit's special claim on them.

Life is a great bundle of little things.

OLIVER WENDELL HOLMES,
THE PROFESSOR AT THE BREAKFAST-TABLE

The Cloud

To go back to the beginning is to go forward to the future. It is more important than ever to break bread with the dead. In a GRAINy world, we need the guidance and guarding of the past as we enter this future.

The Cloud is where the ancestral voices are heard and where the memory of the tribe is stored. For the church, the Cloud led through the wilderness, hovered over the ark, filled the Temple at its dedication, and covered three of the disciples at the Transfiguration.

The path to true originality loops back to origins. How can one be original in one's trajectory without first living inside a great tradition? Only God forms and reforms out of nothing. The rest of us have to improvise out of something.[66] No one thinks for themselves. The only things new under the sun are our attempts to make it appear so.

The wisdom of the Cloud is not some apocatastasis, or restoration to the original condition. This kind of "originality" is only plagiarism. The wisdom of the Cloud is an anamnesis, a "remembrance" or "memorial reenactment," like a medical record that keeps reminding us of who we are, where our uniqueness of DNA resides, and the story of how we got to where we are today. In anamnesis, you use your origins story as a means to think about challenges you are facing.

If we are to move missionally, relationally, and incarnationally into this GRAINy future, we will be returning to our origins story on an almost daily basis. Genesis becomes a fulcrum for faithful thought and forward movement. The Genesis gift is the ultimate in regifting: taking some of the most challenging moral and ethical issues of our day and filtering them through and subjecting them to the tincture of our original DNA.

Arguably the greatest living storyteller of our day, Philip Pullman, is a devout atheist whose trilogies proclaim the death of God and in the La Belle Sauvage trilogy portrays the Magisterium, or church, as the evil empire. No wonder Pullman takes on J. R. R. Tolkien whenever he can, comparing himself to George Eliot. At the same time, Pullman admits that the Genesis story of Adam and Eve is "the central story of our lives, the story that more than any other tells us what it means to be human."[67]

Genesis saved Harley-Davidson in the early 1980s.[68] On the brink of bankruptcy, Harley-Davidson didn't go back to the drawing board. They went back to their genesis, their strategic narrative, the rock from whence they were hewn.[69] They reconceived themselves out of their original DNA and asked themselves what the angel asked Hagar: "Where have you come from, and where are you going?"[70] True originality is trusting the story enough to reconceptualize out of the original, strategic narrative.[71]

God is younger than all else.

AUGUSTINE OF HIPPO (NOW ALGERIA)

What Protestants used to dismiss as the "trappings" of the church's strategic narrative—the smells, bells, chants, stained glass, rosary beads, narrative arcs, and art—are the rocket fuel for imagining new futures.

A future church has Jacob for its patron saint, since authentic revitalization involves wrestling with the precedent and power of the original creation. This may be the oldest and hardest trick in the book— making the old new again. Any genetic engineering done to make the church more compliant with GRAIN culture must be done by going back to our Genesis. If we ignore the original narrative and norms that birthed us, we are doomed.

In the hit television hit series *Mad Men*, Don Draper, a creative director for an advertising agency, walks away from a client and with these words dismisses him as a waste of time: "Jesus either lives in your heart or he doesn't." This is the original impulse that birthed the church, and it needs to rebirth a church of the future. The church today has a case of multiple personalities, flitting from one unsettled identity to another. Many of those identities have little or nothing to do with Jesus. Does Jesus still live in the heart of his church?

We've got to get ourselves
Back to the garden.

JONI MITCHELL,
"WOODSTOCK"

> WALKING IN FAITH

1. How is the belief that "all truth is individual" a force multiplier for the compasslessness of genetic engineering, robotics, artificial intelligence, IT, and nanotechnology?

2. Much of the living world is patented. We are moving toward the patenting of human embryos, perhaps in the late twenty-first century. What do you foresee as the impact of such changes? How do they evidence progression or regression?

3. How will the "breeding" of transhumans impact the divinely appointed role and placement of humans in creation? (Explore the possibilities.)

16

GENERATIONS AND
THE SILVER RUSH

HUMANS HAVE YET TO KNOW what the human can become. "We may be the last generation to die."[1] So begins the first chapter of Alvin Silverstein's controversial book *Conquest of Death*. Ridiculed and mocked in 1979, today such claims to immortality, along with "recipes for immortality," are now routinely found in scientific journals and the writings of a growing army of transhumanists marching to the future in their augmented dreams.[2]

In 1917, the average life expectancy for a British woman was fifty, and for a British man, forty-five. In 2013–15, the most common ages of death were eighty-nine for women and eighty-five for men.[3] Longevity may be the triumph of the twenty-first century. But we must never confuse longevity with life. There is more to life than not dying, and there is a price to be paid for longevity. One in six of us will be taken down, slowly, by dementia—a disease that is no respecter of class, intelligence, creativity, or achievement. When our language begins to fail us, what will rescue our humanity and preserve our dignity? Music, dance, and art. We begin life as artists; we end life as artists. Our "medium" is our life; the world is our easel. Our brush is not something exterior but interior—our dreams, imagination, creativity. The church of the future must see us all as artists and showcase our artistry. The first thing that ought to come to our minds when we think of lifespans that go decades past the centenary is not *declining years* or *dementia* but golden years of highest creativity, biggest impact, and greatest achievement.

––––––––––

Death destroys a man, but the idea of death saves him.

E. M. FORSTER,
HOWARDS END

––––––––––

One of my closest personal friends was born in 1897 and died in 2003.[4] What kept her so young, so long, was that she kept randomizing her life with fresh faces, fresh ideas, fresh books, fresh flowers and plants, and fresh places. She lived in three centuries, an actuarial likelihood for many children born between 1980 and 2000. The church is forming and norming faith in twenty-second-century children. How do you think we are doing? How many Die Progress Units will they experience in their lifetimes? Aging is increasingly regarded as a disease, treatable with drugs, diets, therapies, and procedures leading to outright eradication. Fitness is the new faith, and health foods and spinning (indoor cycling) the new sacraments.

The separation of the body from rituals of parting is one of the most pronounced changes in the history of death memorialization. In the competition between burying and burning, burning now has the ascendancy.[5] But the future most likely belongs to "green funerals" and composted bodies, which do not involve wrapping in chemicals and concrete or releasing into the air carbon and mercury. Event planners are proving more popular than funeral directors, and pastors have allowed and sometimes encouraged funeral liturgies to be ousted by "celebrations of life," which makes the pastoral role less and less relevant.

In the history of the church, the funeral liturgy is a blessed-are-those-who-mourn time of remembrance of the dead and prayer for the living, as well as a witness to resurrection and life. Bereavement was a time when pastors helped people deal with some of the most powerful emotions known to the human species—fear, grief, abandonment, loss, love. People need to mourn, even more than animals.

Maybe we should learn something from our friends with the second largest brains of all ocean mammals. In the summer of 2018, a world united in heartache as they watched a grieving female orca named Tahlequah (J35) caress and carry the carcass of her newborn lifeless calf for seventeen days, one day for every month of gestation. She dove constantly to nudge the corpse to the surface to prevent it from slipping away into the depths. She conducted this mourning tour over a thousand miles of ocean, working through a mother's loss in her rituals of wailing and sorrow.[6]

Old age is a massacre.

PHILIP ROTH,
EVERYMAN

Life therapy has now replaced death therapy. Only recently has "bereavement" become less about the dead and grief over their loss than dealing with the living and life therapy for the survivors.[7] Soon livestreaming of funerals will be standard, and memorial and "life celebration" videos will be as common as wedding photographs and videos.

The old genre *Ars moriendi* (art of dying) is being replaced by the lost art of immortality. Ritual visits to health clubs and medical-industrial sanctuaries have replaced trips to church.[8] The capricious Grim Reaper is being chained and tamed, only let out to wield his blade in as short and structured a sweep as science will permit. Laws that legalize assisted dying for those with six months or fewer to live will be volcanic vents that open up on every front and will require the full range of the church's theological resources on values of Christian faith and culture.

Indefinite life spans may be as little as thirty years away. Boomers can expect to spend more time in retirement than they did in the workplace. To treat them according to their age is the kiss of death for older people. Anyone in the tourist business can testify to the increasing number of people using AARP discounts and requesting cribs in their hotel rooms. The stress on the social fabric of exploding numbers of aging parents in China has even forced the government to pass laws penalizing by fines and jail those who fail to visit aging parents and care for their physical and spiritual needs.[9]

Not only do I reject the torment of a medicalized death, but I refuse to accept a medicalized life, and my determination only deepens with age.

BARBARA EHRENREICH,
NATURAL CAUSES: LIFE, DEATH AND THE ILLUSION OF CONTROL

As of this writing, you might say people over fifty consider old age to arrive at ninety. People under fifty consider old age to arrive at seventy. People over ninety ignore calendars. They think they're the same age as you. No senior thinks that others look at them the way they actually have become but as if they were the age of the other facing them. For those in it, elderhood is ageless.[10]

Centenarians are the fastest-growing percentage of the population. In fifteen years at most, there will be more elderly in the US than children, and in Japan, Depend incontinence products already outsell diapers. Aging boomers will not go quietly like earlier generations, out of sight and out of mind. The new norm of life expectancy may soon become 120 due to the following physical, biological, and chemical augmentations:

> physical augmentations such as wearable tech and exosuits;
> lifestreaming lenses that will improve vision and make Facebook as antique as a girdle book;
> neural and brain microchips;
> biological augmentations like CRISPR gene-editing technologies that make IVF advances look like child's play;
> 3-D printers with living cells that render organ transplants obsolete;
> nootropic supplements (smart drugs and brain enhancers) as routinely distributed as aspirin is today;
> neurostimulation devices; and
> BMIs (the slow progress of Brain-Machine Interfaces, first demonstrated in 1969, will warp-speed forward).

Thanks to science and technology, it is less precise to talk about the "aging" of the population than the "younging" of the population. And the elders who are "youngins'" are the church's greatest untapped resources.[11] Many people are living so long that their social deaths are preceding their physical deaths by months and even years. This is bringing to the fore a whole new form of loss and bereavement for pastoral care: mourning over the departed who are still here. This is also bringing issues of euthanasia to the fore, with some governments already unwilling to pay for life-extending treatments but willing to pay for life-ending drugs. A third of all dollars spent by Medicare are spent during the last year of life, much of it on aggressive medical interventions that do not extend life but do extend agony and suffering.

The time will come in your life, it will almost certainly come, when the voice
of God will thunder at you from a cloud, "From this day forth
thou shalt not be able to put on thine own socks."

JOHN MORTIMER,
THE SUMMER OF A DORMOUSE

One of the most distinguishing features between Christians and pagans in the future will be contrasting attitudes toward suffering. No one finds pain and suffering glamorous nor edifying, although some Christians in the past have been guilty of romanticizing them with such silliness as replacing "grief" in the third line of Dostoyevsky's quatrain with "pain":

The darker the night,
The brighter the stars.
The deeper the grief,
The closer is God.[12]

But whereas the world tries to eliminate or ignore suffering through abortion and euthanasia, Christians confront it, not to condone or celebrate it, but to find ways for suffering to be consecrated, reconceived, and repurposed in the light of God's mission in the world. Christians will also be attacked for staying with the afflicted until the end, always looking for ways for suffering to be made redemptive through faith and prayer.

Medieval monastic communities were famous for being those who moved in when everyone else moved out. When plague or disease or disaster ravaged a community, even when the church had abandoned it, the monks moved in to take care of the weak, the abandoned, the helpless, and the aged. Monastic disciplines of separation and silence are not means of escape from the world but means of training for higher forms of engagement in the world.

In some ways, age has never been a meaningful category, except for ageist mockings and belittlings—from Yeats's "When you are old and grey and full of sleep"[13] to T-shirt poetry like "Done Listening to Old White Men." But age has always been a matter of psychographics rather than demographics, with some of the "youngest" people out there being some of the "oldest," and vice versa. When we talk about master players and game changers in the world and in the church, biological age becomes irrelevant. Discipleship "age" is everything. There are people both in and out of the Scriptures, such as "Moses, Jesus, Muhammad, and Buddha, all traditionally understood to have been in their thirties"—the equivalent of our Third Age (from the sixties to the nineties)—"when they moved to their foundational leadership roles."[14]

Still not believing in age I wake
to find myself older than I can understand.

W. S. MERWIN,
"NO BELIEVER"

What does become front and focus is the issue of what is human. Who will say yes to augmentation, and who will remain "pure"? What about those who can't afford augmentation? Will a new "racial" divide arise between the augmented and nonaugmented? Will those who can afford technological enhancements to their DNA become altered to the point they no longer are able to breed with nonenhanced humans? Will we start praying for the helpless, the hapless, and the bionic-armless?

If you get close enough, you can't find any painting in any gallery that doesn't contain a spiderweb of cracks. With aging comes craquelure. The paradox is that the cracks and decomposition are the precise signs of the composition's authenticity and value. The craquelure is also what releases stress in the canvas, preserving its flexibility for the future and enhancing its value.

U2's Bono found the worth of craquelure in the aging of Frank Sinatra's voice. Bono compares Frank Sinatra's singing "My Way" early in his career to when Sinatra was seventy-eight: "Sinatra's voice is improved by age, by years spent fermenting in cracked and whiskeyed oak barrels. As a communicator, hitting the notes is only part of the story."[15]

Contrary to stereotype, recent studies reveal that a person's creativity can increase with age well into the eighties.[16] Creativity peaks with the age of your spirit, not your body, and packs a punch at every age. There's an inherent devaluing in craquelure in the move toward augmentation that the church can speak prophetically to, since for Christians God's power is made perfect in our weaknesses. But the unaugmented will increasingly require mercy ministry and even refuge. So there's also the remedial angle: How will the church care for those whom biotech has left behind? The presence of white hair in a church should lift our hands in praise for the goodness of God's grace.

A knight was a knight for life, or for as long as he could hold a sword.

God's calling on every one of us has no expiration date. How we choose to spend our calling in whatever season of life is a decision for which we all will have to give an account.

———

He was twenty-four years old! Soon he'd be twenty-eight.
In a few more minutes he'd be thirty-five, then fifty. Five zero.
How had that happened? He was eighty! He could feel his vascular
system and brain clogging with paste, he was drooling . . .

YOUTHFUL PROTAGONIST IN *TWILIGHT OF THE SUPERHEROES,*
BY DEBORAH EISENBERG

———

The division between the very old and the very young may also be one of the most fractious fault lines of the future.

If you are of or above a certain age, you'll recall that when it came to going to church as a kid, or going to school, or going to meet grandparents, or even going to the mall, you were to dress appropriate to the nature of your destination. You, of course, couldn't have cared less. Pajamas or shorts or sweatpants would have been fine for each one of them. But a child learns over time to tailor one's outfits to the settings.

When we became teenagers, we weaned ourselves away from our parents' preferences and experimented with our own tastes. We dressed according to what we judged would make us look the best in given settings. Sometimes we'd push the edges of the appropriate so that we could be seen better by those who were there. We all wanted to be noticed.

In a Twitter-Google-Instagram-Facebook culture, our default context is online. The default for dress is what will make us look best in the selfies we take and what will bring us the most online notice, the most likes and comments. One only cares about the real-life context as a frame for the online image. In other words, one approaches everything with one thing in mind: Is it Instagram worthy? Is it Facebook friendly? Is it Twitter tweetable? This new online default is one of the sources of our severe identity crisis and alienation, leading to all sorts of dissociative disorders, including dissociative amnesia, derealization disorder, and dissociative identity disorder. What parent would set their children loose and unsupervised at night in Times Square with its 360,000 visitors a day? And yet we give children cell phones earlier and earlier, letting them wander unsupervised across digital superhighways and through the back alleys of the Internet with its 3.2 billion visitors a day.

Worship is not Instagram worthy. By its very nature, worship is God worthy, and it celebrates not an individual but the community of worship. So, is worship to become Instagram friendly or an Instagram-free zone? Do we need environments in our church for people to take their social media–moment pics? Culture-compatible does not mean culture-compliant. Just to add more electronics to worship doesn't add more electricity to worship. The power is in connection, not circuitry. And the connections between the very old and the very young are some of the strongest powerhouse connections of the future.

Childless women get it. And men when they retire;
It's as if there had to be some outlet
For their foiled creative fire.

W. H. AUDEN ON CANCER,
"MISS GEE"

> **WALKING IN FAITH**

1. In the micro sense, Christians often seek to ignore or eliminate their own suffering due to the fairly common misperception that Christians are chosen to escape suffering. In what ways does this avoidance deprive us of growth? How does it short-circuit our empathy and emotional availability to others?

2. In the context of becoming fully human, how might a holistic Christian view of suffering and maturity contribute to creativity within a church community?

17

RAPIDIFICATION

When I fail, as I must, I can only recall the desert monk who told his disciple, "Brother, the monastic life is this: I rise up, and I fall down, I rise up and I fall down. I rise up and I fall down."

KATHLEEN NORRIS,

ACEDIA AND ME

THE SOCIAL AND CULTURAL LANDSCAPE is changing at a faster velocity than ever before. What about the religious landscape? Is it changing? Should it change? If so, how much? Change can be good or bad.

Because we suspect some of our twenty-second-century kids may live to be 170, here is what the church was talking about nearly two hundred years ago. In the Methodist tribe, one of the biggest issues consuming local churches was "promiscuous seating" at church, by which they meant the radical notion that families (including children) could sit together in worship instead of having separate seating for women and children on one side of the church and men on the other. In 1847, this change was causing splits in churches, inciting charges of heresy, tearing apart communities, and causing civil war in families, and it wasn't "resolved" until the 1852 general conference.[1] One wonders how many of our holy hullabaloos today will look just as ridiculous 100 or 150 or 170 years from now as this holy hullabaloo back then. But there are some historical changes that could help us today if they were changed back.

People think the world's getting worse. . . . What's actually happening is our information about what's wrong in the world is getting better.

COMPUTER SCIENTIST/FUTURIST RAY KURZWEIL

Want to insult someone in the fifteenth or sixteenth centuries? Call them "perfect." "Free from errors" (*senza errori*) is how Giorgio Vasari, the inventor of art history and biographer of Renaissance artists, described the paintings of Andrea del Sarto, a colleague of Michelangelo, da Vinci, and Raphael. This was not a compliment but a put-down, a "damning . . . with faint praise"[2] for not aspiring to new heights and for "a timidity of spirit" that failed to push boundaries.

If you're going to reach for the stars, expect a lot of dirt and darkness in your future. Errors and mistakes are necessary ingredients in all creativity and innovation. When they're missing, it's a sign of trouble, not virtue.[3] In 1996, Joni Mitchell released a compilation album called *Hits*, along with a companion album called *Misses*. We are all marbled mixes of misses and hits, wrongs and rights, sinners and saints.

This isn't the information age. This is the disinformation age. This is the overinformation age. In one single second, more information is produced than you could absorb for the whole of your life. Pope Francis referred to this dynamic as "rapidification."[4] In one day, more books and articles are published than you could ever read.[5] Technology is accelerating the pace of change into exponential dimensions never seen before.[6]

The onset of change, or more accurately the onslaught of accelerating change, throws commonly held notions and time frames out the window. The half-life of any subject, whether biology, engineering, or computer science, is getting shorter and shorter, meaning one's information base can be wrong in a hurry, and to say someone is "experienced" may be an impairment more than an asset.[7]

Maybe we ought to be talking about the *motern world*[8] rather than the *modern world*. *Modern* is based on *modo*, which means "just now." But the word *moto* means "in motion" or "keep moving." The only way to hit a moving target is to get ahead of it. In the modern world, you could carpe diem. In the motern world, you can only carpe mañana.[9]

Rapidification should make us all more humble, contrite, and open to learning. In some of the wisest words about the nature of religion in the last hundred years, the leading Jewish theologian of the twentieth century, Abraham Joshua Heschel, put it this way:

> It is customary to blame secular science and anti-religious
> philosophy for the eclipse of religion in modern society. It would
> be more honest to blame religion for its own defeats. Religion
> declined not because it was refuted, but because it became

irrelevant, dull, oppressive, insipid. When faith is completely replaced by creed, worship by discipline, love by habit; when the crisis of today is ignored because of the splendor of the past; when faith becomes an heirloom rather than a living fountain; when religion speaks only in the name of authority rather than with the voice of compassion—its message becomes meaningless.[10]

Or as Pope Francis said, "When somebody has an answer for every question, it is a sign that they are not on the right road."[11] God overflows all containers, including our two-pound boxes of brains. To say that divine revelation is perfected in Jesus is not to say that anyone enjoys perfect knowledge of that divine revelation. Perfect knowledge of that perfect revelation will only be fully revealed at the end of time. Besides, it has been known to happen that humans sometimes hear God wrong.

Wrongology

All that we do
Is touched with ocean, yet we remain
On the shore of what we know.

RICHARD WILBUR,
"FOR DUDLEY"

Thomas Aquinas said, "The utmost of human knowledge of God is to know that we cannot know God."[12] Knowledge unites us to God, but as Aquinas says that we are "united to Him as to one entirely unknown."[13] If your view of God is not open to emendation, expansion, and reconsideration, then your theological understanding is idolatrous.

Information doubles in the world about every seventy-two days. More than two thousand new websites go online each day. A minimum of two thousand books are published worldwide each day, and forty-one thousand updates are posted every second. All this available information is taking its toll on the human psyche and spirit. Is too much information as dangerous as too little? Maybe a shortening attention span is not so much a reflection of handicap as it is of our expertise in drinking from a data fire hose and our developing ability to cut a wide swath through a vast data stream rushing past us.

In George Bernard Shaw's most hard-hitting three-act play, *Major Barbara*, Undershaft says, "You have learnt something. That always feels at first as if you had lost something."[14] Every learning entails a loss of learning, an unlearning, a shedding, even if that learning loss is ignorance. Every day the news forces us to engage in the uncomfortable but salutary task of abandoning some habitual assumptions.

Technology is moving too fast for our moral, social, and political systems to keep up with or make sense of. Our greatest vulnerability in an age of exploding, exponential information is not a failure to learn but a failure to unlearn.

It is no longer possible to learn a skill that can last for a lifetime. Learning itself is the ultimate skill of the future. Learning is now the new mandatory profession behind every profession. Everyone must now learn a living to survive.

The lawyer who stops learning is a fraud, guilty of malfeasance.

The doctor who stops learning is a hoax, guilty of malpractice.

The pastor who stops learning is a miscreant, guilty of unholiness.

The Christian who stops learning is a betrayer, traitor to the name *disciple* (*mathētē* in Greek, which means "learners" or "students").

It was said of the first Christians that they devoted themselves to prayer and study.[15] Even Peter grew in his theological understanding, at first rejecting Jesus' definition of Messiahship but then, after the Resurrection, giving up his dream of a Power Messiah and embracing Jesus as the Suffering Messiah.[16]

Welcome to Church: Your Bridge to the 1970s

The awakening of creativity and innovation among followers of Jesus, and the need for church to be a culture of change and innovation, cannot be overplayed. Through the twentieth century, the church proved itself more interested in restructuring than rebooting—more strategic in planning and implementing control than preparing for multiple scenarios and exploratory innovations.

The problem with innovation and experimentation is that we will often get things wrong, say wrong things, and have to deal with things gone wrong. So the need for compassion and patience is higher than we currently find acceptable. Whatever "side" you're on, people on the "other side" can be mistaken and not malign, wrong and not wicked, errant and not evil, naive and not nasty. At the same time, history is littered with catastrophic ideas once thought to be panaceas—like corporal punishment to cure undisciplined behavior, capital punishment to deter crime, lobotomies to avert mental illness, tobacco to cure what ails you, and hospitalization or "rest homes" for children with disabilities.[17] Stakes are high, and so our standards must be higher still. But the church of the future must have a high toleration threshold and forgiving spirit for waywardness and wrongness.

Perhaps because the church once went through a Donatist schism (fourth through sixth centuries), the church is proving to be not as "Puritan" as a posttruth culture. The more society is said to be losing its moral compass, the more Puritan (or better, Victorian or Philistine) the society becomes.[18] It shuts up and closes down conversation. So-called free societies can police opinion even better than the KGB or MSS, as Chinese students coming to the US are quick to find out on college campuses. Increasingly, writers like Philip Roth, Norman Mailer, Saul Bellow, and Ernest Hemingway are being removed from reading lists as purveyors of sexism. Harper Lee and Mark Twain have been censored for their use of racist language in dialogue even though such language was the patois of their day.

This is Stalinism, not Puritanism. If we are only going to read those writers who got it all right, it will be a very small reading canon. Imagine how different the story of the Western world would be without John Wesley, William Wilberforce, Hannah More, Elizabeth Fry, William and Catherine Booth, or Florence Nightingale. Now add your own favorites. Every single one of them got some things wrong—very wrong, embarrassingly wrong. But that doesn't mean we can't celebrate their contributions.

Thomas Aquinas may be one of the greatest theologians in the history of Christianity, but no seminary would hire him today. He was gravely wrong about some things (for example, his belief that women lack sufficient rationality to teach and provide moral guidance to their children). Every generation "knows" things that future generations will condemn; bad beliefs and fallible "facts" are part of history's march toward knowledge, wisdom, and truth. All knowledge, in fact, is a falsehood waiting to happen—except knowledge of Jesus.

The right to be wrong is essential to being human. But it's more right, even the essence of righteousness, to repent and confess when you're wrong. There is little value to being right without redemption.

Propensity to error is not a hallmark of our human misery but a highwater mark of human creativity and imagination. Benjamin Franklin loved to tell stories about how wrong he was about some things more than to boast about his inventions and discoveries. When Ludwig van Beethoven was dying, he reminisced with friends about his life and concluded that if he had to pick from all his life experiences, if he had to give up all the memories but one kind, he would keep his failures, because his failures and disappointments taught him more than his successes and triumphs. If we only learn from and listen to people who have gotten it all right, we will live in silence.

The church of the future needs to embrace a theology of failure[19] that does not punish risk but rewards falling down and getting back up again. Jesus gave us a sacrament of dirt—shaking the dust off our feet[20]—to accompany the sacraments of bread, wine, and water. For reasons of failure or fallaciousness, when we are stuck and afraid to "move on," it's time to take the sacrament of dirt. When stuck with those who are not receiving you, or stuck in bad overtures, think of all those in the future who are awaiting you and wondering where you are; think of all those new overtures that the future needs, and keep moving. Our messes and misses can become missives of miracles if we confess and turn them over to God.

If you ever drop your keys into a river of molten lava,
let 'em go, because man, they're gone.

JACK HANDEY

> WALKING IN FAITH

1. With the half-life of any subject getting shorter and shorter, the shelf life of your information base is evaporating. Being experienced might be less of an asset than you once thought. What is the upside of this dynamic, and how could it change your view of the future and of future possibilities?

2. Culture-wide, our shortening attention span is our way of drinking from a fire hose of data. Cutting a swath through the torrent and extracting wisely from it is a skill set that affects our ability to become all we are called to be. How can fine-tuning this skill serve in fulfilling your assigned measure of rule?

3. In what specific ways can the church respond to the future by embracing a theology of failure that, instead of punishing risk, rewards falling down and getting back up again?

PART THREE

Hot Church

18

REPRODUCTION CRISIS

Yes, Jesus loves me. . . .
Please come and tell me so.

UNKNOWN

TWO BIOLOGISTS DEFINE CULTURE THIS WAY: "Culture . . . is behavior or information with two primary attributes: it is socially learned and it is shared within a social community."[1] There it is: A culture requires an identity that is "socially learned" and "shared." In other words, identity requires discipleship and evangelism, the two biggest failures of the contemporary church and the two biggest imperatives of the future church.

Organ Failure

If our first command is "Be fruitful,"[2] and Jesus gave us the litmus test of "You will know them by their fruits,"[3] our fruits are dreadful if not rotten and need reseeding and rerooting in original Jesus soil.

The greatest chasm is not between different religions but between religious faith and skeptical scientism/secularism.[4] US respondents say they are at ease with people of different religions at a rate of 85 to 90 percent. In fact, religious faith is on the rise. As of 2016, 75 percent of humanity profess some religious faith. That figure is set to rise to 80 percent in twenty-five years.[5] Sociologist of religion Grace Davie has named this approach to belief "vicarious religion," a better way of formulating the current situation than the pet one of "believing without belonging" or "spiritual but not religious" (SBNR).[6]

While statistics prove declining religious activity, they also document no decline in interest in religion and religious faith. The one thing you can count on in the twenty-first century is the return of religion, although that "religion" comes in new forms like golf, games, Glenmorangie, playlists, and politics. Even atheism is now a religion, with its own houses of "worship," priests, liturgies, and anthems. John Lennon's "Imagine" may in fact be atheism's high-water mark.[7]

Religious faith is increasing, but religious affiliation is decreasing. The greatest development of the twenty-first century so far is the rapid departure of establishment religion from our shared life in neighborhoods and nations. Even "professionals" in the world of religion try to downplay their "religious" standing. The evangelical archbishop of Canterbury, Justin Welby, asks that people not refer to him as a Protestant.[8]

Nones, Dones, Comes, Somes

The fastest-growing "religious" movement in the country are the "nones."[9] Evangelism and apologetics will increasingly take place in a cultural climate of rising *nones* and dones, receding comes and somes. Jesus loves all of them.

Nones include atheists, agnostics, and those who say they believe "nothing in particular." Nones want no part of religion in general or Christianity in particular. Many nones have replaced the much-hated "organized religion" with organized atheism. The atheization of Western culture looks to only pick up its pace.

All proofs or disproofs that we tender
Of His existence are returned
Unopened to the sender.

W. H. AUDEN,
"FRIDAY'S CHILD"

Dones are those who claim a been-there-done-that relationship with the church and are often its greatest critics. They wore out the T-shirt and will never put it on again. Nobody has told them (or they remain unconvinced) that the cure for bad religion is not no religion but good religion.

Comes are faithful attenders, those who make religion a part of their everyday life and go to services on a regular basis.

Somes are episodic attenders, those who faithfully appear on holy days like Christmas Eve, Easter, baptisms, weddings, and funerals, or those who claim to be "spiritual but not religious."

We used to hear "I'm spiritual but not religious" as the positive yearnings of people looking for deeper experiences of faith that they weren't finding in specific religious traditions. But "spiritual but not religious" can be one of the most condescending and colonialist statements anyone can utter.[10]

What that phrase has come to mean is that you arrogate to your individual advantage those juicy portions of religious traditions you find appetizing and brush aside the remainder as unprofitable and unworthy of your palate. SBNR is an act of goddifying self at worst and consumerist tourism at best, as one wanders the aisles of the supermarket of religions and picks out this and that as mementos of one's visit and as stray morsels one may want to consume without respect for their origin or commitment to their context. SBNR treats religions as brands to be consumed, not belief systems to be understood or faith traditions to be honored.

As Laurie Hays Coffman writes, wouldn't we all like a religion that has

No requirements, only promises?
No expectations, only freedom?
No sacrifices, only blessings?
No people hard to love, only me?
No stooping nor dying, only rising?
No structures, only success?
No discipleship, only decisions?
No cross, only crown?[11]

To follow Jesus is not a solitary, scratch spirituality. We are following in the footsteps of ancestors, starting with the apostles. We are living out a connection that extends in space and time and, because of us, expands into the future. We critique the community of faith as a lover's spat from within, taking on and taking down those silly, archaic legacies that hamper faith and those defective and damaging inheritances that traditions often get very wrong and that, when passed on without change, can actually hurt humanity.

Ninety percent of USAmericans say they believe in God. Not long ago, however, that figure was 99 percent.[12] Even though a whiff of respect still hangs around steeples in some places, in the future the church will increasingly be seen as a foreign, scary place, and the culture will look on the church with sneers, a snicker up every sleeve, and with an eye for pretentiousness, fraudulence, and hypocrisy that is sharper than ever.

Twenty-second-century culture, and Christians themselves, will tire of scholars and even preachers who know everything about the Christian life except how to enjoy it. Plato said that philosophy was a way of learning how to die. Jesus said that following the Way is learning how to die well and live well.

It will not be easy in the future for disciples to be postal carriers of God's gospel love letters. Like the Pony Express riders of the nineteenth century, we will learn to use multiple media to get the message across (riders changed horses every ten to fifteen miles). We will need to learn to evangelize in teams (riders passed the bags in relay race fashion every seventy-five to one hundred miles). We will face dangers of context (rain, sleet, snow, hail) and attacks from surprising places (buffalo stampedes). We will be mugged and robbed and hijacked, thrown off course and separated from our mission as surely as today's filtered world enables people to control what gets to them and keep away what they don't want to see. Pony Express riders developed better guises for getting around obstructions, and evangelists today need story filtration to move through the mesh of obstacles and onslaughts. Some letter carriers died delivering the mail then; some will die delivering the mail in the future.

————————

Messenger of Sympathy and Love
Servant of Parted Friends
Consoler of the Lonely
Bond of the Scattered Family
Enlarger of the Common Life
Carrier of News and Knowledge
Instrument of Trade and Industry
Promoter of Mutual Acquaintance
Of Peace and of Goodwill Among Men and Nations

CHARLES W. ELIOT, "THE LETTER," INSCRIBED ON THE OUTSIDE
WALL OF THE NATIONAL POSTAL MUSEUM IN WASHINGTON, DC

————————

That is why the ultimate apologetics for the future is a rapture aesthetic that promises not to rapture you out of the world but to meet Jesus in every person and place you go. Volcanic culture is rapture ready: Some are survivalists or apocalypticists who are waiting for the end, but even more are wanting not to be saved *from* the world but saved *for* the world, taken into the world with new purpose and passion.

Jesus wants to bring us a rapture experience—the rapture of being fully alive, the rapture of Jesus' taking up residence inside each of us and becoming part of who we are. Jesus did not come to deliver us from our humanity but to recover and discover our true humanity. Jesus did not come into the world to get us out of the world or help us escape the world but to enter it, embrace it, and engage it more deeply and divinely. Jesus was always evoking the world we are in and making it better, not escaping from the world and alienating us from it.

Authentic evangelism nudges people to be captivated and enraptured by Christ, not conquered for Christ or won to Christ.

Christianity is not primarily a religion of the Book, as Islam and the evangelical fundamentalists understand it, or even of the Jewish Law. . . . Strictly speaking, it isn't a religion at all. . . . In many crucial and excruciating ways, it is an anti-religion, a critique of all the human forms of faith from a prophetic perspective which recognises that religions generally decay into religiosity, that icons deteriorate into idols, and that aesthetic ritual degenerates into ritual anaesthesia. It urges agile vigilance against all human gods, especially the gods of reputation and status.

IRISH POET AIDAN MATHEWS,
FASTING AND FEASTING

Christianity is less a religious system or belief system than a set of faith relationships that bring meaning to life—with God, ourselves, one another, creation.[13] Faith means never having to go anywhere Jesus isn't. Faith is the assurance and trust that you will never go anywhere in life that is godless, where God has not already been or will someday depart from.[14] Discipleship is not assenting to a belief system, operating out of some ethical norms, or subscribing to a political agenda. Discipleship is recognizing, receiving, releasing, and reproducing Jesus.

A volcanic culture calls out for an eruptive faith with the fire and fury of the first century still swirling about it. Every bush is burning, but faith invites people to gather around the fire to get warm, not burned. Too much of the old apologetics has lit fires that burned people—a fight club more than a campfire, singeing their souls with our fumes and plume-high posturings. Jesus himself gave us the proof of the gospel that we needed to make hearts burn: "Your love for one another will prove to the world that you are my disciples."[15]

There are those who see the "mystical" as the quest for that moment of transcendent bliss, experiences of transitory enlightenment, the climbing pursuit of mountaintop moments of ecstasy and encounters with God.

Then there are those who see the mystical as an ongoing indwelling of the Spirit, who brings Jesus to life in us as we share his resurrection life and the Spirit becomes articulate in us. In this sense, the highest act of human reason is the rational acknowledgment that mystery exists, a mystery that is alive and active. The excitement of living the mystery of faith is that it is the very essence of mystery to keep pumping out surprises and sudden revelations. But the leap of faith is not a melt into mysticism or a landing onto rock-hard certainty, but a journey of trust into the misty, mysterious land of hope and love.

A genuine atheist is one who simply does not see that there is any problem or mystery here, one who is content to ask questions within the world, but cannot see that the world itself raises a question.

HERBERT McCABE,
GOD MATTERS

The former is the mystical life. The latter is the mysterium life, a fluid condition of permanent transfiguration[16] where the mystery becomes mystory. Welcome to the new apologetics.

> WALKING IN FAITH

1. A standing argument of the "nones" is one that also corrupts the church: the disdain for "religion" (in quotes for a reason). The sentiment may be rooted in the emptiness of mere form, but the cynicism attached has become resistant to what true religion is: one's bonding to God. How, if at all, has this misunderstanding of religion touched your family? Your faith community?

2. What barriers have you encountered as a carrier of God's gospel love letters? How can you get around the filters and other obstructions along your "route"? What compels you to deliver anyway?

THE DECLINE AND FALL
OF SEMINARIES

I am not a teacher, but an awakener.

ROBERT FROST

IN THE MEDIEVAL WORLD, thinking about God was done in a monastery where it was bathed in a liturgical setting amid devotional practices. In the modern world, thinking about God is done in a university where liturgical formation is replaced by academic formation marked by a disputational spirit and critical practices. Whether seminaries are under the university umbrella or freestanding, the university model of disputation and deconstruction reigns.

The issue is not that seminaries are "too academic." The issue is that seminaries need new academics, a new model of academe that will make sense of what is going on around us based on what went on in the past, explore what the impact of change has been before and will be now, and suggest preparations that will enable the church to adapt. Just as the culture needs public intellectuals, the church needs public theologians who will write in the vernacular and not cast out the colloquial. Theologians often wear it as a badge of honor not to "suffer fools gladly,"[1] but Jesus suffered fools daily and embraced lepers warmly.

The seminaries are at a critical crossroads. Their lecture-drill-test semester-based model of learning, whether in classrooms or online, is a holdover from Germany's sixteenth-century innovations of gymnasium learning and Gutenberg technology. Declining denominations still require seminary degrees for future ministers (if they are to attain their union cards), but seminaries are no longer the portal for ministry, nor their graduates the candidates of choice for much of the dynamic portion of US Protestantism. The Internet has become the global platform for the exchange of knowledge among people, and seminary faculty have been some of the staunchest defenders of Gutenberg culture and the holiest holdouts from TGIF (Twitter-Google-Instagram-Facebook) culture.[2] Maybe it is time for local churches to resume their traditional roles of being major educational forces in both the church and the world.

A church of the clergy, by the clergy, and for the clergy
is not where our future lies.
FATHER PETER DAY

The best church has something of the seminary in it, and the best seminary has something of the church in it. Seminaries used to be the places where the church did its best thinking. Faculty were encouraged and rewarded to cross the barbed wire barriers that separated academic disciplines. Some seminaries even functioned as R & D centers for the church.

In the quest for academic prestige and scholarly glory, seminaries are now more accountable to the academy and its guilds than to the church and its ministries, to religious studies methodology than to theological studies and ecclesiology. Instead of seeing orthodoxy as an inspired consensus arrived at over centuries of arguments and debates about how to best describe the mysteries of revelation, the very concept of orthodoxy is suspect, because orthodoxies are "imperially imposed." When a faculty member's personal subscription to the Apostles' and Nicene Creeds becomes academically radioactive in seminaries that are being given millions of dollars a year by denominations to prepare pastors for its churches, it is time to issue a yellow alert.

To some degree, of course, all faculty bear the triple burden of vocations to the life of the church, the academy, and the wider culture. But increasingly, seminary faculty have thrown off the burdens of the church for those of the university and the politics component of culture, and they are as committed to scientific and nonreligious versions of providence as our predecessors were to theological ones. Having failed to find substantial readers in the church, theologians withdrew into the echo chambers of the academies and there found secure homes writing for one another. Even when the language is still there, the love for the church is often missing.

With that shifting of focus away from the church and toward the academy, seminaries have become virtually indistinguishable from colleges and universities (without the obligatory obsequious rites of church bashing and Christ smearing). If you arrive in seminary with a faith in Jesus, the religious studies fixation gradually breaks it down until it decomposes into theories and critiques and problematics, leaving a body full of intellectual energy but drained of blood and bare of beauty. William Muehl, in his 1984–5 Beecher Lectures at Yale, quoted a colleague: "Taken together the faculty of this seminary has destroyed more churches than the Luftwaffe."[3] The problem is that we tell the joke with pride, not embarrassment.

Declining denominations have been faithful to seminaries, requiring future ministers to have seminary degrees and investing millions of dollars a year in each seminary. But the seminaries themselves have often turned their backs on the church and romanced the university. Once the seminary curriculum preserved the veneer of church vernacular, even if its heart lay in the arms of the academy. But many now don't even bother with the lambskin covering. A graduate school of religion and a school of theology have become virtually indistinguishable, and the academy's crackdown on raising up leaders for the church is gathering steam.

The training of clergy in the future will be a reconceptualization of the apprentice model, based in the local church. The word *seminary* literally means "seedbed"—seedbed for learning and faith formation. For a century now, seminary learning has been based on the accreditation of an institution. The ultimate accreditation, however, is "Can you do it, and how well?" In the future, seminary learning will be based on credentialing of a person, not the accrediting of an institution. And the primary locus for "seminary" learning will be the local church, who will partner more with credentialing bodies than with accrediting institutions. Every church must become a school for discipleship, educating ministers and missionaries and prophets.

A seminary is by definition a community of inquiry and formation that learns how to teach others to lose yourself in Christ.[4] In Russia there is a pet saying that conveys the impact of Aleksandr Pushkin on Russian culture: "Pushkin is our everything." A seminary is where you go to learn to exegete the statement "Jesus is our everything."

They have taken away my Lord,
and I know not where they have laid him.

EPITAPH ON HEADSTONE FOR SEMINARIES

In the future, the church must find ways to let Jesus out of academic prison. The core curriculum for all theological education and human formation needs to be . . . Jesus. All studies have one object: to know Christ and make Christ known. This is the end of all learning and eloquence. In Christ, we experience the full panoply and promise of human existence.[5]

> WALKING IN FAITH

1. The church needs public theologians who will write in the vernacular. When they do, the door of theology swings open, inviting one and all to enter the conversation and enliven the church through truth. How then do we challenge the church's tendency toward (1) elitism where theology is concerned, and (2) the denigration of theology as the enemy of faith?

2. A cult—a group that shields its people from dissent and dissenters—may be considered a "safe place" by its members, but it is not a learning community. When a house of worship becomes an echo chamber, the gospel is reduced to a comfortable set of opinions. If you are a church leader, are you requiring pastoral and other staff members to enter the educational fray and have their mind-sets challenged? Why or why not?

19

SACRALIZATION AND IDOLS

A philosophy that does not include the possibility of soothsaying from coffee grounds and cannot explicate it cannot be a true philosophy.

WALTER BENJAMIN

THE WORLD IS NOT BECOMING MORE SECULARIZED. The world is becoming more sacralized. In fact, a better name for "postmodern" would be "postsecular."

The society-wide repudiation of faith has not led to a society becoming more secular. We are living in an age where the gods are not so much *ex machina* as they are *in flagrante*.

It is time to declare secularization theory dead. We now inhabit a postsecular, profoundly sacral culture. Harvard sociologist Peter Berger (1929–2017) finally admitted that his forty years of predicting the gradual demise of religion (secularization) was mistaken. In fact, he observed that the twenty-first century would remain "furiously religious" (with the possible exception of Europe).[1] European elites and North American intellectuals seem to be the last people to recognize this shift.[2]

I don't believe in God, but I miss Him.

JULIAN BARNES,
NOTHING TO BE FRIGHTENED OF

To talk about the "religious" and the "secular" is a recent invention of language anyway, at least not before the sixteenth century. But there is no understanding of the social-scientific process called *secularization* (in either its grandest or most limited forms) that brings us to the place we are now where people are turning their homes and bodies into sacred cathedrals through incense-heavy fragrances in the form of body gels, colognes, air sprays, and incense sticks, few of which sell for under $100.[3] Sacred smells and sounds now house the soul and sublime the spirit, and it takes a sacred journey or pilgrimage to get us out of our sacred spaces.

As an explanatory thesis of what is going on in culture today, secularization fails on all fronts.

The faster we flee from God, the more numerous the homeless religious sensibilities out there frantically looking for a place to land in the culture.[4] God now has many names, even when the name *God* is never spoken. Who are the heirs to religion's vacant throne? You can see our sacralizations and pluritheisms everywhere you look, from kneeling at the altar to selfhood, the theater of body art, or the terrarium of nature.

The Kardashians are exponents of a physiological paganism,
which cultivates the body rather than the spirit or—God forbid—the mind.

PETER CONRAD,
MYTHOMANIA

Here are some of the most obvious ones, each one with its sacred texts and canonical traditions:

› *Blue-Dome Cathedrals:* In West Virginia and other mountain cultures, there are some high and holy days that dare not be desecrated. The opening of deer-hunting season, which may be the most sacred, registers some of the highest records of religious practice. The worship of Gaia will continue to grow: No idol is good, but better to make an idol of a tree than an idol of a bank—at least God created the tree. It will be more important than ever to remember how Christianity is a GOOD religion (Get Out Of Doors).[5]

› *The Cathedral Market:* Wall Street worship leads to marketolatry. Moses broke the Ten Commandments tablets when he saw people worshiping the golden calf. We break the Ten Commandments themselves in pursuit of the golden calf—bull markets and the golden goose. Money is god. Economy is religion. Understanding the market is theology. But just because something is bought and sold in the market does not mean it has value. Price is not the primary or even elementary indicator of value.

› *The Cathedral Mall:* More and more people are careening through time with no inner life at all, thanks to the mind-sapping inanity of consumerism. Consumer culture rips off our wallets as it rips apart our souls.

› *Cathedral of Sports:* Sports is becoming more and more a religion, and for most of the planet, FIFA World Cup is world communion. People even wear vestments to worship, and the clothes the celebrants wear are carefully chosen and designed.

› *Cathedrals of Experience:* Experience is itself a religion for this culture. The sacralization of experiences exists everywhere from food to tourism to worship itself.

› *The Cathedral Celeb:* Celebrity worship is its own religion, with disciples known as *fans* and with a few devotees who are more like apostles, also known as *stans*. A celebrity culture worships the golden calf of personality and cares little for personhood. *Personality* is a social construct. *Personhood* is a state of being. Celebrity worship may be the most mind-sapping inanity of all our sacralizations.

› *The Corporate Cathedral:* Steve Jobs dubbed the iPhone "the Jesus phone" and was quite aware of his status as a tech messiah. Some people called him a "crazed shaman"; others, a "Benedictine monk" or "savior." Jobs loved to show up at Apple Christmas parties in his black-shirted clerical garb and episcopal condescension. When the first Apple computer was put on the market, the selling price was $666.66, and the very name chosen—Apple—was a semi-ironic statement that it was as much a cult as a company. In his absolutist insistence on perfection of design and function, Jobs was looking for devout disciples more than loyal customers.[6]

› *The Cathedral Kitchen:* Food is now a sacred experience, with high priests ("celebrity chefs"), denominations, rituals, and sanctuary kitchens. It may be the new golden idol that does the most damage in the long run. Contrary to the sixteenth-century German saying "Sugar spoils no dish," sugar ravages health and may make a diabetes crisis the worst medical health issue of the twenty-first century.

Expect new, exciting flavors coming from the world of coffee and chocolate, given the newly discovered genetic diversity of their yeasts compared with vineyard-yeast strains. Sugar will be defined as an uppers drug at best, a poison at worst. What tobacco was to the twentieth century, sugar will be to the twenty-first century. At the start of the twentieth century, diabetes was virtually unknown in China. At the start of the twenty-first century, more than 10 percent of the Chinese population is suffering from it.[7]

› *The Cathedral of Self:* "Selfies" are appropriately named. Generation Self-Made (boosters) gave birth to Gen Self-Help (boomers) gave birth to Gen Self-Esteem (busters) gave birth to Gen Selfie (millennials) gave birth to Gen Self-Righteousness (postmillennials). Even the language of personal discovery and spiritual growth has become a mask for gratifying one's own desires. All his life Jesus himself did what we all must do: He died to self and lived in God. He set the self on the shelf, showing not so much self-confidence as God-confidence, not as much self-centeredness as God-centeredness.

› *Cathedral of Sound:* There are 13,000 Spotify playlists with titles that contain both the words *sacred* and *choral*, with 600,000 containing one or the other.

The true return of religion . . . is the one that does away with the barriers, which we hold to be impermeable, between religion and everything else.

RENÉ GIRARD

If the language of the future is less one of "supernatural," then it behooves the church to claim the words *transcendence* and *transcendent* before the culture snatches it. The "something" Jesus invites people to see "in you" is not so much something "within you" as something "beyond you." The more the sacralization of the psychological, the more we must resist the psychologization of the sacred. The role of the sacred is less to solve problems than to open up new doors to new possibilities.

The sacred helps humans hear God and one another properly. To be human is to hear into connection the tantalizing world of the flesh with the transcending world of the spirit. Jesus is "the Human One," the one who brings back humanity's original superpowers. When Jesus makes us superhuman and superpowered, we don't even have to wear long underwear.

Não ter deus e um deus tabém.
[Not to have a God is to have a God.]

PORTUGUESE POET AND PHOTOGRAPHER FERNANDO PESSOA

The sacralization of life means this culture can't resist whatever has the capacity to transport and enchant. But when everything becomes sacralized, nothing is sacral, which makes sacraments all the more essential to the future life of faith. The ultimate sacrament? Your attention and presence. Your very presence, the nuggets of all-there-ness you give to someone, are bouquets of flowers, boxes of chocolate, communion wafers of sacramental life.

> WALKING IN FAITH

1. Describe the ironies, in your view, of the manifestations of sacral culture described in the text. What draws even professed "secularists" to the sacral?

2. If the role of the sacred is less to solve problems than to open up new doors to new possibilities, how do we recognize those doors, and how can they be missed?

20

HELL, HEAVEN, AFTERLIFE

OVER THE PAST COUPLE OF DECADES, the religious world has been consumed with the afterlife—both by those (especially children) who claimed to have been there and returned and by those who claim to know what exists and what doesn't in the sweet by-and-by. Such probings will only get more fierce and prickly in the future. This will be brought to the fore by technology, especially with the advent of cyborgs and brain downloads and by pastoral care issues associated with an increasing demand for pet funerals.

The psalmist once asked, "Where can I flee from Your presence?" His first answer is predictable and soothing: "If I ascend into heaven, You are there." His second answer is as surprising and startling today as it was then, so much so that it trails off unanswered in midsentence in some Hebrew manuscripts: "If I make my bed in hell, behold, You are there."[1] If hell is defined as the place of the dead where God is not,[2] how can God be where God is not? Once again we are reminded that God's ways are not our ways, God's thoughts not our thoughts.

But the deepest truth of the psalmist is twofold. First, you can't have a heaven without a hell, just like you can't have good without evil. Second, no place is beyond God's healing presence and power. The only real question about hell is this: Will it be empty?

Will anybody be there? If so, who?

I go to seek a Great Perhaps.

REPUTED LAST WORDS OF RABELAIS

In three of the largest Muslim nations in the world—Indonesia, Turkey, and Saudi Arabia—61 percent of Muslims say, "My faith is the only true path to salvation, liberation, or paradise." Only 19 percent of Christians in Europe and the US say the same.[3]

Welcome to the future.

Rupert Shortt notes the delicious irony that "fewer people in the Western world believe in God these days than at any point in history, and even fewer believe in hell," while at the same time "glimpses of hell are everywhere—in war, pornography and self-harm, to name just a few. And children are far more likely to encounter images of these hells than ever before. For even if they are not seeing horror and pornography on their smartphones, their friends are and it is becoming playground banter."[4]

Almost every world religion has the problem of what to do about hell. But for Christianity it is a peculiarly contentious problem.[5] First of all, Jesus founded his church at the "gates of hell"[6] and sent his disciples thenceforth on a go-to-hell mission. Every disciple was commissioned not to go to the best and the brightest but to the worst and the wronged—and there raise and raze hell.

The question of hell confronted the church early on. Some theologians like Origen elaborated the doctrine of *apokatastasis* to include universal restoration and reunion of all peoples in heaven.[7] This is probably the default position of many USAmerican Christians, although it is most likely conveyed in the form of a wink and a nod. The universalist position is based on the presumption that what makes heaven *heaven* is its universality. Every last person on the planet—Nero, Caligula, Attila the Hun, Genghis Khan, Hirohito, Hitler, Himmler, Pol Pot, Charles Manson included—must be present and accounted for. Jesus, however, suggested that what makes heaven *heaven* is not the guest list but the guest of honor—the bridegroom being feted at the feast.

There is also the extinctionist perspective: When you die, you become extinct. Saul Bellow, in *Ravelstein*, admitted that atheists who insist on ultimate extinction do so with more than a bit of bravado. "Nobody can and nobody does accept this. We just *talk* tough."[8]

Hell is what ultimately preserves human freedom. "Where the Spirit of the Lord is, there is freedom."[9] Without hell, how are we free? Because of the reality of human freedom, the seventeenth-century English poet John Milton conceived of hell as a real possibility. Milton imagined Satan saying, "Better to reign in Hell, than serve in Heaven."[10]

Russian philosopher Nikolai Berdyaev saw this better than anyone.

He believed in preserving each man's right to hell, each person's right to decline God's invitation, to exclude oneself, to prefer to spend eternity with oneself, loving oneself, than with God and loving God.[11] From page one of the Bible onward, we are free to go to hell, if that is our choice. G. K. Chesterton argued something similar: Hell is "God's greatest compliment to humanity," the gift of the ability to refuse the gift and Giver.

Soren Sweet has a saying about Orcas Island, where she spent the first eighteen years of her life: "It's paradise, if you can stand it." Dallas Willard portrayed this feature of being able to "stand it" as the open sesame to the Pearly Gates: "I am thoroughly convinced that God will let everyone into heaven who, in his considered opinion, can stand it. But 'standing it' may prove to be a more difficult matter than those who take their view of heaven from popular movies or popular preaching may think. The fires in heaven may be hotter than those in the other place."[12]

I sometimes wonder if hell might be as simple as not being able to "stand" heaven. It remains for those who don't believe in hell to explain what to do with those people who don't want to be happy and glad. Some people enjoy misery and discomfort. The seventeenth-century mystic Emanuel Swedenborg defended hell, not as a place to which one is condemned to go by the divine, but a place some people are drawn to by their own personal preferences, a realm we choose to take refuge in to escape being free, being responsible, being enlightened.[13] Some people are addicted to suffering and misery for all sorts of crazy reasons and don't really *want* to get out of the mess they're in. Episcopal priest/author/chef Robert Capon (1925–2013) put it like this: "Now heaven is entirely populated with sinners saved by grace . . . and hell is entirely populated with sinners saved by grace."[14] Heaven is the state of being in love, a space of expansion. Hell is the state of being in self-love, a space of enclosure.[15]

Forever round the Mercy-seat
The guiding lights of love shall burn;
But what if, habit-bound, thy feet
Shall lack the will to turn?

QUAKER JOHN WHITTIER

It is hard to see a life lived in dedication to the eradication of God's image in humanity, or the obliteration of humanity itself, to escape any judgment in eternity. Are there no consequences for our actions, no matter how evil or depraved or abusive? Is life not Truth and/or Consequences? The sealed moral universe of secular ethics, where right and good are things we make up as we go along, cannot be broken without the eschatological claims of an ultimate judgment of moral action. Besides, even the best party has a bouncer, because if the selfish, godless, heartless, remorseless, and ruthless didn't get bounced, they would spoil it.

The future will not be kind to those it hears hoping for hell. Even if Christians believe in hell, how could they do otherwise but hope that no one is there? If Christians want people there to support our theology, then we are idiots. If Christians want people there because we're vindictive, then we're monsters. How can it be a Christian "hope" that anyone—in exchange for either a horrible or even mediocre seventy or eighty or ninety years on earth—would receive an eternity separated from God?

Love is God's last word. But some people are hard of hearing.

> WALKING IN FAITH

1. We are free to go to hell. I (Mark Chironna) believe that hell is God's provision for those who reject his invitation to the family. Is the granting of a person's choice unfair, as many in the broader culture believe? Why or why not?

2. How do you interpret the statement "God will let everyone into heaven who, in his considered opinion, can stand it"? How might "the fires of heaven . . . be hotter than those in the other place"?

3. What do you make of Swedenborg's description of hell as a place some people are drawn to by their own personal preferences? In what everyday ways do we unconsciously refuse to take refuge so that we might escape being free, responsible, or enlightened?

21

#CHURCHTOO

JOHN ROBINSON (1576–1625) WAS PASTOR TO THE PILGRIMS and inspired the *Mayflower* expedition. He never made it to the New World himself, dying in Holland. But he instructed the first Pilgrims in the biblical warrant for active roles for women in religious affairs. "Immediately, and extraordinarily, and miraculously inspired," he instructed women to "speak without restraint" during a church meeting. In fact, if men didn't have the courage to speak the truth to the church in public, women should move to the front. "Yea, in a case extraordinary, namely where no man will, I see not but a woman may reprove the church, rather than suffer it to go on in apparent wickedness."[1]

A social revolution is about to blow its top. It has been seething and simmering, gathering power and strength from deep underground sources that periodically erupt and prophesy the power of this volcano. But this volcano will erupt with such force and power that it will in some ways define the twenty-first century. If it turns into a war of the genders, no one wins.[2]

"Women hold up half the sky," Mao Tse-tung reportedly said while harassing peasant girls and dismissing single women at twenty-five as "*sheng nu*" ("leftover woman"), a social custom still prevalent today.[3] If women hold up half the sky, they ought to be paid equal wages with men for doing their half.[4] Equality for women has been taking giant strides, with even Saudi Arabia extending voting rights to women in 2015 (though only in local elections).

Barriers to women now are in the economic, cultural, and religious arenas, although social and cultural stigmas still remain. No one is busier or works harder in the twenty-first century than the average working woman who is married with children. Not her husband. Not her single counterpart. Not her housewife counterpart. Some things for women have even gotten worse.

———————

We like our wives to be yogurts, plain yogurts—so that we can flavor them as we'd like. My fiancée is a plain yogurt. She's low maintenance and doesn't really have her own ideas. I like her because she's easy to manage.

A THIRTY-FIVE-YEAR-OLD CHINESE INVESTMENT BANKER,
QUOTED IN ROSEANN LAKE,
LEFTOVER IN CHINA

———————

In every stage of education, girls frequently outperform boys.[5] But among the top ten major tech companies, women make up less than 30 percent of the workforce. In technical roles, this number drops to under 20 percent.[6]

The women's movement is a bursting backlash against patriarchy and subjugation that will leave no institution untouched or untoppled. What had been kept hidden is now being revealed, and the "revealing" is revolting: More women have been murdered as a result of domestic violence between 9/11 and 2012 than all of the victims of 9/11 and American soldiers killed during that time, combined.[7]

Women can be anything they want to be. They can be as haughty as men. They can be scientists and presidents and generals. After all, the founder of the Salvation Army, William Booth, was fond of saying, "Some of my best men are women."

In this century, it will be conceivable for women to aspire to be pope. The next pope will likely find a way or be forced to find no revealed mandates rejecting the priestly ordination of women.[8] Celibacy will almost assuredly be lifted in this century. It will increasingly be harder and seem more bad-tempered, even mean, for any church leader not to see that equality and mutuality of male and female is biblically correct and a win-win for the church.

Women were at the foot of the cross and the front of the tomb. It was a woman who first preached the Resurrection. Women felt they could approach Jesus and that Jesus heard them. It was women who, with their brother Lazarus, were Jesus' best friends. Like no one else in the ancient world, Jesus elevated women, not by imbuing them with a degrading sense of their own victimhood, but by treating them with respect and honoring their unlimited potential as daughters of the King and tutors of truth.

Joan Taylor, a historian of Jesus and professor of Christian origins and Second Temple Judaism at King's College London, believes that Mary Magdalene had the Magdala name given to her, not because she was from Magdala ("tower"), but because Jesus loved giving people nicknames (Peter = "Rock"; James and John = "sons of thunder"). He called her Mary Magdala because she was a tower of discipleship.[9]

It is quite remarkable, considering the apostle Paul's culture, how many women he lists as coworkers in the spread of the gospel:

> Nympha
> Apphia
> Junia
> Phoebe
> Priscilla
> Euodia
> Syntyche
> Mary
> Tryphena
> Tryphosa
> Lydia
> Chloe
> Lois
> Eunice

A catacomb fresco (San Gennaro) in Naples, Italy, portrays Cerula, a woman holding the four Gospels flanked by flames. Significantly, she is not wearing a stole but something that looks like a donut-shaped shawl over her paenula, a cloak which after 382 CE was the official garb of Roman senators and other important public officials. No one has yet fully decoded what the images on this upper garment are or symbolize. Crucially, she is surrounded by open volumes of all four Gospels, suggesting that she had real influence and responsibility, since bishops, and bishops only, had open Gospel books placed over their heads during their ordination rituals. The flames of the Holy Spirit come out of the Gospels, symbolizing the Spirit's role to inspire the bishops in their preaching.[10]

Some of the most exciting scholarly research on the women who followed Jesus and the role of women in the early Jesus movement will be coming out in the next couple of decades. It promises to revolutionize our understanding of the early Christian movement and provide us with wisdom on how to deal with a future where . . .

› Asian Christianity already has more women preachers than men preachers. This fact is all the more remarkable given that Asian esteem of boy babies is so high: As of 2005, the number of "missing" girls and women in Asia (a result of preselection of boys over girls in Asian childbirth and the malnutrition of girl children) stood at 163 million, more than the female population of USAmerica.[11]

› Sharia property laws limit women's inheritance to half that of men.

› More and more nations will be outlawing female genital mutilation, even as these practices are increasingly performed on girls.

› The perilous circumstances of "glass cliffs"[12] allow women to break "glass ceilings," but such breakthroughs bear greater risks of failure and censure than they did for their male predecessors.

In the words of colleague David McDonald, "A female perspective on Jesus wouldn't simply demonize men or elevate women; a truly female telling of Christ's life would supply new insights concerning Christ himself. Because women have more to offer than their gender."[13]

If you want to explore the past, spend a day with Danielle Steele, where female romance literature has one theme: Women come out on top by taking control of men and reducing them to the roles of lover, husband, father, and provider.

If you want to get a foretaste of the future, especially when women's imagination and creativity are allowed free rein and unfettered access without the constraints of the status-signaling games played among men, just spend an hour experiencing Beyoncé's 2016 visual album *Lemonade*. It is an intricately woven tapestry of music videos offset by chapter titles like "Intuition," "Denial," "Apathy," "Emptiness," and, ultimately, "Resurrection," all connected by a voiceover from Beyoncé reading the poet Warsan Shire. It deserves iconic status beyond black women for its exploration of vulnerability, suffering, sacrifice, and pain.

Just as Hagar discovered she could not live without the Well of Water when she encountered Yahweh, and just as the Samaritan woman discovered she could not live without the Well of Water when she encountered Jesus at Jacob's Well, so men and women both need to cross over into each other's territory and learn together to dwell in the Well with mutual respect and regard.

> WALKING IN FAITH

1. As a backlash against patriarchy and subjugation, the broader women's movement is erupting with new strength in a season of profound disillusionment. In what ways might disillusionment be remedied as barriers and injustices are brought down? What new forms of disillusionment might surface?

2. What artificial gender barriers remain in the church? How do you explain the prominence of women preachers in the Asian church in light of the profound Asian preference for boy babies and the "disappearance" of many millions of Asian girls?

22

POLITICAL RELIGION

We are children of our age,
it's a political age.

All day long, all through the night,
all affairs—yours, ours, theirs—
are political affairs.

WISLAWA SZYMBORSKA,
"CHILDREN OF OUR AGE"

POLITICS IS THE NUMBER-ONE religion of USAmerica.

We write this as political atheists: people who worship at the altar of no party. In one of the great reversals of the twenty-first century, young evangelicals are largely progressive and liberal, while older evangelicals are largely political conservatives. For King Jesus, it is not enough to rail at how life is going, or wail about how awful the world is getting, if you aren't derailing evil and trailblazing good. To be Kingdom-engaged means an enlarged heart, a heightened imagination, a managed mind, and a damaged ambition for revenge.

We declare three citizenships: Firstly and primarily, we are members of the body of Christ and citizen of the Kingdom of God. Secondarily, we are citizens of our country. Thirdly, we are citizens of the world.

Politics works like scissors. When the axis of one blade moves high, the other moves low, and in the scissoring, everything gets cut to shreds. Party politics has gotten to the point where each side constitutes an *ism* and the hostility between the two political cartels sounds like the Crips and the Bloods. This antagonism even extends to our churches (that is, if one "party" has not driven out the other so that our churches are as segregated politically as they are racially). In Jesus' day, the intramural fight could even get more intense than this. But you hear little of that in Jesus' message. Jesus rejected the offer of political power from Satan,[1] and he disappointed the masses who thought he would be a political Messiah and who put him to death for a political crime he did not commit.

You can't speak truth to power if you're prophesying a party line.

MARK CHIRONNA

When you hear the phrase *all-powerful God*, what kind of power first comes to mind? If it's other than love, it's not the God of Jesus. God's power is the power of love, the greatest force for change and might for right in the universe. The world's power is in wealth and weaponry, political armature and bureaucratic armaments. Jesus' power is disarmed with its strength in weakness and wounds, its potency in vulnerability and honesty.

Disciples need to be *hot*—with a passion for Christ, our calling, and the church. Disciples need to be *cold*—with a calm, steady, impassive sense of poise and responsibility in the face of political and social upheavals.

Volcanic culture politicizes *red-hot* everything it touches. In fact, the story of modernity is in some ways the dissolution of Christian faith as religion and the emergence of politics as religion.[2]

Poets talk about poetry.

Physicists talk about physics.

Physicians talk about medicine.

Politicians talk about politics.

Christians should talk about Christ.

So, why do we so often talk about politics?

The politicization of religion is the danger of our day. The only thing worse you can do to a faith than to turn it into a philosophy is to turn it into a politics. When pastors start sounding like candidates for office, we get nervous. Faith that is prophetic must challenge, not channel, politics.

Personal harm is at the heart of politics.

PETER STOTHARD,
THE SENECANS: FOUR MEN AND MARGARET THATCHER

Politics has not always been what it is today—the art and science of personal harm and destruction. The ancient Greeks used the word *political* to mean more than voting in an election. *Politics* referred to all interactions with other people—from the home to the temple, from the neighborhood to the nation to the world. It was another way of talking about the art of relationships. So in this sense, the Jesus gospel was at heart deeply "political" because it had everything to do with relationships.

The Greek philosophers believed the qualities necessary for sound "political" leadership in pursuit of the common good were the relational virtues of prudence, courage, honesty, justice, and temperance (moderation). Our politicians bald-facedly profess and practice pragmatic "virtues" of dishonesty, dissembling, feigning, and protection of their own kind. In politics today, there is no "good," much less "common good," that transcends the interests of class or party or ideology.

Modern politics has become, at best, what philosopher Robert Nozick calls "argumentative bludgeoning."[3] At the heart of politics beats camouflage, which is a prettified term for lying: It is a job requirement for a politician to be able to lie in good faith.

There are three political parties in the United States:
Republicans, Democrats, and Methodists.

ULYSSES S. GRANT

Politics is the struggle for power, the struggle of power with power. Out of the struggle emerges government, which is the ordering and confiding of power. When Thomas Aquinas reflected on relations between state and church, he postulated that even if humanity had not fallen, even if it were a perfect society, we would still need the structures of state to organize the way we live together and work together. The danger of power—"Power corrupts" (Lord Acton)—is that power distorts our vision of ourselves vis-à-vis others and God. Prayer is the antidote to power's corruption.

The twentieth century is a glass-case exhibit of the immense suffering that can come from politics: Franco's concentration camps, Stalin's Gulag, Mao's Laogai system, Kim Il-Sung's labor and indoctrination camps, and worst of all, Hitler's Germany. The prewar camps of the 1930s, places like Dachau, Sachsenhausen, Buchenwald, Flossenbürg, and Ravensbrück, were not extermination camps. They were set up to imprison and subdue political opponents and social outcasts, anyone the politicians didn't want. Extermination camps were set up in 1941 onward, when Nazis began to murder Europe's Jews in Sobibor, Majdanek, and Treblinka. Studies of the

German guards at these camps reveal that they were not psychopaths but ordinary persons who had become deeply politicized.[4] And deeply politicized people lose their humanity when they live by the principle that the end justifies the means; hence Jewish German philosopher Walter Benjamin's aphorism that fascism is the aestheticization of politics and his call for a new politics of aesthetics.[5]

Politics is the entertainment division of the military-industrial complex.

FRANK ZAPPA

When politics becomes faith, or a religion becomes politics, we have confused ends with means and lost both. A long time ago, Anabaptist theologian and pacifist Vernard Eller (1927–2007) wrote *Christian Anarchy* (1987), which taught us that you absolutize the end but relativize the means.[6] You don't assert theological authority for a means, only for an end. For example, peace is an end. Peace is absolute. But the means to peace, the forms of peacemaking, needs to be relativized. There are those who are pacifists. There are those who see "just war" as the means, or armed negotiation. People in the military see themselves as peacemakers. There are various means to a peaceful world. Similarly, the notion that every child of God deserves health care is an end. How best to get to a world where every child of God has adequate health care is a matter of means. To fight about ends is a very different battle than to fight about means. Followers of the Alpha and Omega, the One who is the Beginning and the End, should not get lost in the wilderness of means. The church of Jesus Christ should have generals and pacifists, capitalists and socialists, sitting beside one another in pursuit of the same ends: peace and justice.

Ancient politics absolutized ends and relativized means. Modern politics absolutizes means and relativizes ends, since to the relativized mind of our times one end is as good as another (except of course for certain ideological ends).

POLITICS, n. A strife of interests masquerading as a contest of principles.
The conduct of public affairs for private advantage.

AMBROSE BIERCE,
THE DEVIL'S DICTIONARY

Pope Francis's comment in 2013, "Who am I to judge?" registered one of the highest-ever scores on the religious Richter scale. It will go down as one of the most influential and deciding statements of the first quarter of the twenty-first century. For such a provocative declaration, it really is a simple, basic, biblical proposition: It is God alone who judges us, and Scripture which guides our judgments.

No one was a stauncher socialist than theologian Paul Tillich, but no one believed more firmly than he did in the Protestant Principle—famous for reminding the church that all its theologies, all its activities, all its politics stand under the judgment of the Cross. This conviction made him humble about his politics: They were relative and should never be absolutized.[7]

Why must our means be relativized? Our templates can quickly become temples, ends to be worshiped and protected. The church is as prone as the culture to making shrines of means, to making temples of templates.

The "greasy pole"[8] of politics can be used by anyone for political gain under the aegis of "God's politics." At its worst, Christianity can easily become a political platform of the left or the right with a tinge of religiosity.

The linking of religious fervor with political passion is always suspect and increasingly unnerving. When politics greases the wheels of theology, the wheels usually come off. Statecraft is the domain of the kingdoms of this world, where Machiavelli reigns, the Malcolm X/Saul Alinsky "by any means necessary" governs, and the pursuit of power justifies any means.

We are stardust brought to life, then empowered
by the universe to figure itself out.

NEIL DeGRASSE TYSON,
ASTROPHYSICS FOR PEOPLE IN A HURRY

The proper stance of the church vis-à-vis the state is an attitude of resistance to power. Christianity is, by its very nature, subversive of every status quo. (Subversive but not seditious, however. Nero was the tyrant of his day, and the city of seven hills a hellscape, yet Paul appealed to Nero in Rome.[9])

Where does Jesus say in the Bible, "I will send you politicians to do my work for you"? Jesus told us to look around in our back alleys and side streets, and in those places, to be Jesus for the people in front of us, to tend the dying and mend the living. Jesus told us to dig deep into our own pockets to help those in need, not pick-pocket others. The church's business is not playing politics, appeasing or sucking up to the political elitist machine, but instead undermining them, challenging them, and only using them when necessary. The Way is a way out of the rat race, in politics as well as in economics. If God is a political being whose politics corresponds to our own politics, then God demands no more of us than our politics require.

The Jesus "party" was the party that resisted politics in both synagogue and state, the nonpolitics party, the party that fundamentally critiqued politics and was allergic to political culture. Christians follow a Lamb that was slain, not a donkey or an elephant or even an eagle.

The strongest poison ever known
Came from Caesar's laurel crown.

WILLIAM BLAKE,
"AUGURIES OF INNOCENCE"

The church has always forged alliances with unholy power and might, starting with Paul and Nero. When evangelicals found themselves working with Enlightenment rationalists, Jedidiah Morse gave this warning in his Fast Day Sermon of May 1798: "Let us beware . . . of blending [the] end with the means. Because atheism and licentiousness are employed as instruments, by divine providence, to subvert and overthrow popery and despotism, it does not follow that atheism and licentiousness are in themselves good things, and worthy of our approbation."[10]

If the church is being the church, it is always forging alliances with unholy instruments. And it will need to be a part of more unholy alliances in the future than in the past.

The central conservative truth is that it is culture, not politics,
that determines the success of society. The central liberal truth
is that politics can change a culture and save it from itself.

DANIEL PATRICK MOYNIHAN

If there is one metanarrative in the First Testament, it is that all Goliaths who glory in their superiority of weaponry, wealth, wisdom, and ways of life fall down. All the superpowers of the Bible—the Egyptians, the Assyrians, the Chaldeans, the Medes and Persians—perish in the ashes of their achievements.

Before John Betjeman (1906–84) was Poet Laureate of the United Kingdom (from 1972 until his death), he received a request from the head of religious programming at the BBC Home Service to write poems on current affairs from a Christian point of view. He refused and wrote a poem in 1955 about the suggestion instead, bringing into question the notion that there was only one Christian point of view on every issue of the day.

The Reverend Martin Wilson wrote
To me a most disturbing note
Demanding of me Christian views
On current matters in the news. . . .

The poem then goes on to celebrate the quietness before the arrival of daily newspapers, with their "dreadful reports":

Riots in Cyprus, trouble in Greece,
Russia, it seems, is keen on peace.
A Christian comment on the news?
Dear Martin Wilson, I refuse.[11]

Christian involvement in politics is of course appropriate. But it's not a sacred obligation for everyone, and some people might prefer other conduits of prophetic witness and channels for goodness, beauty, and truth. Only some Christians have the freedom to be politically active in their home countries. Nevertheless there is always a civic responsibility to do something to make your home better.

Evil must be fought, but no political strategy will ever eradicate evil until the day of divine harvest. So we enter the political arena with audacity and modesty: humble hearts, compassion for the burdens of governance, and audacious trust in both the moral seriousness of our concerns and the power of suffering love to transcend political power. All the while we recall that every meddle in politics ends up a muddle, or a form of mud wrestling. What Winston Churchill is said to have declared about the political arena applies even more today: When going through hell, keep going.

> WALKING IN FAITH

1. All isms are schisms; political schisms have left many churches as segregated politically as they are racially. Where will this trend lead? Will political divisions bolster the racial divide indefinitely, or will they precipitate the church's desegregation?

2. You can't speak truth to power if you're prophesying a party line. In what practical ways is the taking of political stands cooling our passion for Christ and neutering our missional role?

23

PARADOX: PURGATORY
OR PARADISE?

Wind extinguishes a candle and energizes fire.
NASSIM NICHOLAS TALEB,
ANTIFRAGILE

MODERN CHRISTIANS HAVE TENDED TO OVERLOOK the importance of time and place. Ray Oldenburg, in *The Great Good Place*, calls understanding and diagnosing the experience of place "environmental psychology."[1] We have often failed to read the Bible in its context of time and place, not to mention failed as "environmental psychologists" to read our own times and places. For example, Jesus said none of his followers should walk by a neighbor in need. But Jesus lived and moved in small villages and communities, when a big city had maybe as many as ten thousand people. If we put Jesus' dictum into practice today in Seattle or Orlando, we'd only go a block a day.

In volcanic time and place, everyday life is arrhythmic. The beats skip and swing rapidly between one swelling extreme to another in Well Curve fashion, with the Bell Curve middles falling out and those hugging to it dropping through the cracks. There is a reason why nothing looks like it should, everything appears back to front, and things seem upside down: They are. What is an atom? A wave—and a particle. What is an atom made of? Hadrons, bosons, fermions, quarks, leptons, protons, electronic muons, gluons, and neutrinos—the building blocks of life. Each elementary particle is accompanied by a known or hypothetical opposite; even life comes in surround sound.

The twenty-first century is not a neat and tidy world of either/or, nor a safe world of blended gray, but a protean, pluriform, colorfully panoramic, Promethean world of both/and, and/also, and either/or. Opposite things are happening in our world at the same time, and they are not contradictory. Right now, throughout Africa (especially South Africa), people are stepping out of hunger and poverty and into type 2 diabetes. In Brazil, it is not uncommon for teenage girls to be both obese and anemic. The more we eat, the sicker we get.

We live in a world ruled by butterflies and gorillas: The butterfly effect is where small inputs can have massive consequences, where a butterfly flapping its wings in Seoul can create a snowstorm in Seattle. The eight-hundred-pound gorilla is the unspoken but unbeatable presence of a colossal entity that must be reckoned with.

The modern world was a guide through the grayness. Today's world is a ride on a rainbow. The modern world looked at life from the center. Today's world looks at life from the peripheries, the edges, the margins—and from those who live there. The center is seen as boring and colonial. Except in reference to Muslims, *moderate* is a bad word. Candidates for public office proclaim themselves not "moderates" but "extreme moderates." The church is theologically marooned either in the sixties or in the sixteenth century.

The truth is not in the middle, and not in one extreme, but in both extremes.
CHARLES SIMEON OF CAMBRIDGE

If truth be told, Truth is less found in the parametric instability of the middle of the pendulum swing than in the parabolic harmonious oscillation of the limits of the pendulum's amplitude.

> The more we live in a digital age, the more we will discover and reinvent the analogue medium.

> The more the flawless precision of our technology, the more enamored we are by things that are flawed, imprecise, and natural.[2]

> The more social media improvises and optimizes transparency, the more the "right to be forgotten" or to erase your data footprint will be fought for as a basic human right.

> The more human fixation is increasingly the individual youniverse, the more we focus on the cosmic universe, a phenomenon one French sociologist has awkwardly named "individuo-globalism."[3]

> The more we are driven by self-interest, the more our drives and desires are derived from the herd, groupthink, mass instincts, mob mentality.

A mob is usually a creature of very mysterious existence, particularly in a large city. Where it comes from and wither it goes, few men can tell. Assembling and dispersing with equal suddenness, it is as difficult to follow to its various sources as the sea itself; nor does the parallel stop here, for the ocean is not more fickle and uncertain, more terrible when roused, more unreasonable, or more cruel.

CHARLES DICKENS ON THE 1780 GORDON RIOTS IN LONDON

There is a creative region in each of us that can only survive by remaining private and hidden. Unfortunately, privacy is no longer a right. Privacy has been privatized into something that you purchase or trade or sell. The biggest names and most famous people of the future will be those who lived under the cloud of anonymity, known for being unknown. But why would anyone want to live so that no one notices you're alive? Consider graffiti artist Banksy, the first international artist of the Internet and famous for being anonymous.[4] Banksy is an anticapitalist capitalist laughing all the way to the bank.[5]

If I talked I would become like any other comedian.

CHARLIE CHAPLIN,
MY AUTOBIOGRAPHY

It used to be that the kiss of success was to claim what you were doing was intended for the general public (GE, GM, General Foods, General Dynamics, General Mills, General Nutrition, General Conference, General Assembly, General Store). Now to be labeled "generic" is a kiss of death. Far from trying to conquer or rescue the middle ground, the middle is now toxic.[6] All middles are in trouble, including the middle class, which is shrinking dramatically.

Angry voices are the loudest on social media. Technology emboldens those willing to take the most extreme positions, be they demagogues, satirists, or terrorists.

The world is getting more bipolar. A growing minority of "anywheres" are highly educated, professionally permeable, socially elastic, and geographically mobile, juxtaposed against a majority of "somewheres" who are rooted in family, respectful of place, and wed to permanence and consistency.[7] Languages are becoming more universal and standardized, with English, Mandarin, and Spanish the current world languages, and languages are becoming more regional, with dialects (e.g., Glaswegian Scots) making a comeback.

The life of faith in a volcanic culture is both easy and hard, simple and complex, wide and narrow, roundabout and ramrod straight. It's not enough for the church to call out the contradictions and paradoxes. It must explore them, incarnate itself in them, and bring them together in harmony and health. As our faith gets more simple ("Unless you are converted and become as little children"[8]), our theology should be getting more complex. Dig beyond the surface of any Jesus contradiction or inconsistency, and you will explode a depth revelation or be transported by a transfiguring metamorphosis. In my theology, I am building a cathedral, my own version of a Gothic cathedral, with lots of chambers and sepulchres and balustrades and balconies. But in my faith I am walking the cathedral garden (garth) with Jesus.

When we try to pick out anything by itself, we find it hitched to everything else in the universe.

JOHN MUIR,
MY FIRST SUMMER IN THE SIERRA

Christianity is a byword for the bipolar. The Cross is the sum of all that is evil. The Cross is the sum of all that is good. The Cross tells of the horrors evil can do. The Cross tells of the holiness love can do. A sacramental sense of life makes you look twice at everything, seeing the world eucharistically through the double lens of the visible and the invisible.

Jesus, Lamb and Lion, fully human and fully divine, comes in surround sound. If you only hear one thing, you're probably not hearing Jesus.[9] Theologians like to refer to this as a *coincidentia oppositorum*, a Latin Neoplatonic phrase meaning a "coincidence of opposites," first attributed to the fifteenth-century German polymath Nicholas of Cusa.[10] But in the

Hebrew and Christian traditions, it is less of a coincidence than a concatenation, a unity or dance of opposites.[11] Christianity's version of bipolar leaves the paradox intact and forces the imagination to move past contradiction into mystery. To survive in the future, every disciple of Jesus ought to consider printing on their calling card "mystery mongerer, paradox peddler."

One of the most puzzling but paradisiacal paradoxes of the Christian religion is the double-ring affirmation that the future has already been accomplished in the present. In the Eucharist, we "remember our future." To "remember" (*anamnesis*) here means more than not to forget the future, or to remember to brush your teeth, or to catalyze the present for the future. To remember our future is to bring the future into the present more than the past. For our story is one of a future already accomplished in the past, which we celebrate and platform in the present. If you don't "get" paradox, it's hard to "get" the gospel of Jesus.

Two of the most widely quoted literary words are E. M. Forster's "Only connect." Almost always quoted out of context, nobody seems interested in what Forster wanted to connect: the two opposites of prose and passion (or poetry). Here are his words: "Only connect! That was her whole sermon. Only connect the prose and the passion, and both will be exalted, and human love will be seen at its height. Live in fragments no longer. Only connect, and the beast and the monk, robbed of the isolation that is life to either, will die."[12]

"Only connect" doesn't refer to reaching out to the "other," or showing empathy to others, but originally was Forster's shorthand definition of the ultimate connection: joining the opposing sides of every human being, the saint and sinner, the "monk" and "beast," so that love might move from mere functioning to flourishing and flowering.

Perhaps the most demanding and pressing double ring of our day is global-local dynamic. Everything is becoming more globalized and at the same time more localized, even tribalized. This kind of world is not one that should spook us, for in some ways it is our natural habit and normal state. How can you be a disciple of Jesus and not have a global vision? "For God so loved the world. . ." Jesus introduced into history the revolutionary notion that what bound people together was not blood but an individual's freedom of the will to love, forgive, and serve. Personal identity had no limits other than those self-imposed. Sometimes it is hard to see the history-making genius of a tradition for the sins and griefs of that tradition.

A human life, I think, should be well rooted in some spot of a native land, where it may get the love of tender kinship for the face of the earth, for the labours men go forth to, for the sounds and accents that haunt it, for whatever will give that early home a familiar unmistakable difference amidst the future widening of knowledge. . . . The best introduction to astronomy is to think of the nightly heavens as a little lot of stars belonging to one's own homestead.

GEORGE ELIOT,
DANIEL DERONDA

At the same time, how can you be a disciple of Jesus and not love your zip code enough to cry over it, as Jesus did over Jerusalem?[13] God "so loved the world," but he came to a specific place and time in a Semitic idiom. Jesus was the Savior of the world, but he embodied the Torah in the Sermon on the Mount, God's blueprint for creation. Unlike some people, who do not deign to stoop to the particulars, God got down and dirty in the particular. To be a Messiah and man for all time, Jesus first had to be a Messiah and man of his time.

Truth is absolute, but it's relative to time and place. Absolute Truth is true in relative ways. The absolute can only be experienced through the relative, the universal through the particular, but God cannot be limited to the relative or the particular.[14]

All people should be loved equally. But you cannot do good to all people equally, so you should take particular thought for those who, as if by lot, happen to be particularly close to you in terms of place, time, or any other circumstances.

AUGUSTINE

If you want to think "formula" for the future, think this: *Particularize in order to universalize.* The way to the universal is through the particular. In fact, the more authentically particular you become, the more universal your voice, because there is nothing more resonant than an authentic, particularized voice. Provenance is how you authenticate something.

The world does not need a more universal universalism but a more particular universalism, a universalism that emerges out of our particularities. The world does not need any more people who love everyone in general so much that they love no one in particular very much. Winston Churchill is loved everywhere around the world because he believed in British superiority in everything. "Success" in the future is not in your numbers but in having the resonance of an authentic, artisanal voice.

It was the custom of the ancient church to name bishops after places, a habit that tagged those territories as marked fields for the Holy Spirit and mission posts for people serving in and outside their borders. Locations were important because it was important to orient the missions properly. Every bishop carried a named place as part of his title. You could not go around or get around a bishop's context. Hence the dedication of churches usually included "orienting" rituals that positioned them theologically toward the east and the horizons surrounding it. You can't have a placeless particularity. Even saints come from particular places (Tarsus, Padua, Lisieux, Canterbury, Clairvaux, Bingen, Assisi), from which to go to the universal.

No one today is better than Wendell Berry at what poet and visual artist William Blake (1757–1827) described as the ability "to see a World in a Grain of Sand / And a Heaven in a Wild Flower / Hold Infinity in the palm of your hand / And Eternity in an hour."[15] A film on Berry's life stole his mantra "Look and see" as its title. Wendell and his wife, Tanya, taught their two kids to look and see around them and to look and see the world through the lens of rural Kentucky. The rest of the world reads Berry's books and sees itself through that same look-and-see lens.

When I walk around a gallery, I see many works of art. Some I like, some I dislike, some I think I understand, and some leave me cold. Yet in each case the artist has expressed something utterly unique and special that only he or she fully knows and loves. When I walk along the street and look into the eyes of the people I meet, may I have the grace to remember that I am walking through God's own art gallery.

MARGARET SILF, *2012: A BOOK OF GRACE-FILLED DAYS*

Particularize to universalize is the essence of an incarnational faith, one that integrates Christian life within the local culture in such a way that it enriches the entire body of Christ. In each church, in each person, Christ is born anew. The Jesus story begins again. The Incarnation is inseparably linked to the *parousia*, a word that translates from the Greek as "presence." Jesus' Parousia, his presence, his arrival, his coming is announced in his incarnation in every person and in every place. There is one Jesus but many

Christs (hence the word *Christian*, which means "little Christ"). Disciples are not copiers of Christ but continuing incarnations of Jesus' life and love.

The inorganic world of the mechanical, mathematical, digital cries out for the organic world of the senses (smells, bells, chants). The more the artificial, the more the artisanal. The more the algorithmic, the more the artistic. This is why artisan church wins out in the future over asphalt church, the no-parking churches over the all-parking churches, the artisanal church over the franchise church. When everywhere you look on the landscape you see cliffs and sinkholes and bottomless pits and erupting environments, the attraction of tradition's ongoing solid stability is understandable. And the more local and real the tradition, the better. The essence of artisanal faith over a franchise faith? In artisanal faith, you think with your hands and feet, not with committees or resolutions or good intentions.

A poet's hope: to be,
like some valley cheese,
local, but prized elsewhere.

W. H. AUDEN,
"SHORTS II"

Everything must have a terroir, especially a church. *Terroir* is that one-of-a-kind taste that can only be imparted by a particular combination of factors unique to one place and time. In the case of fine wine, terroir includes a distinctive, localized, specific combination of factors, including soil, climate, and sunlight, that give grapes a distinctive character. The harmony with one's habit is the essence of the artisanal and its key marker.

Flattening out regional tone, tiptoeing around local toughness and roughness, settling for the least offensive and bland narrative with the glass and glitz: All these are rotting remnants and unpleasant aftertastes of the stale, samey modern and its conformist suburbs.

Appalachian culture has long disparaged food that was what all grammas called "boughten." To eat "brought and bought" food was an invasion of the home with alien presences. To be sure, food supplies will get more global, more imported, more affordable, more processed, as transgene agriculture feeds the world. At the same time, food will become more local, homegrown, hand spun, artisanal. We may even find that God has given each area of the world (except for cities) sufficient food in the air, land, and sea to feed its own indigenous population.

Whether your church is mega, mini, or multi, it will need to bring back the artisans who hand-make their creations and give each a terroir. The evolution of the megachurch will be the multichurch, which both hypercentralizes and decentralizes at the same time.

My work as a teacher and writer has been to discover
glimmers of the Absolute in every particular.

CHET RAYMO,
WHEN GOD IS GONE, EVERYTHING IS HOLY

Terroir is the proof in the artisanal pudding. Where did the pohole grow that's in your Hawaiian salad? Did you cut your breadfruit with an ulu? The premier tequila maker today, Mexico's Patrón, makes its magic in small batches using a wheel carved out of volcanic rock to lacerate the blue agave plant and squeeze juice from the maguey pulp. You know it's Patrón tequila if you can taste the volcano. Bar culture has gone from big nightclubs to cocktail lounges to neighborhood bars, tap rooms, and craft cocktails.

You know it's Jesus if an individual and communal follower of Jesus is painting their own original and unique portrait of Christ with their life. It is our ultimate act of creativity: to image God in each one of our lives lived in community. We learn from the past and from our peers the true meaning of originality.

Christianity is wrongly thought of as Western, but it has an Eastern lung and a Western lung. When I look at a two-lunged Christianity—the global whole of the faith—the church is my great source of hope and my great source of despair. Two opposite things can be true at the same time, although to shout and scream all at once takes a bit of practice.

> WALKING IN FAITH

1. Which small inputs are having massive consequences within the church in the way, metaphorically speaking, that the flapping of a butterfly's wings in Seoul can create a blizzard in Seattle (Butterfly Effect)? And what eight-hundred-pound gorillas must be reckoned with?

2. How does the church explore contradictions and paradoxes in a volcanic culture? What lies beyond the seeming inconsistencies and why does a more complex theology match a more childlike faith?

SALT, LIGHT, AND THE SIMPLEX CHURCH

Christian truth is symphonic.

HANS URS VON BALTHASAR, *TRUTH IS SYMPHONIC*

APART FROM ONE ANOTHER, sodium and chloride are toxic. Put them together, and they become salt. The future is heavily seasoned with salt— a cocktail of complexity and simplicity.

Everything in the world is getting more complicated and complex by the minute. Everything in the world is getting more simple and elemental by the minute.

Every study of creativity highlights the juxtaposition of difference as the key ingredient in birthing innovation and imagination. One reason why Christianity has proven to be one of the most creative and generative of all religious traditions is precisely because its native habitat is one of harmonious parabolic oscillation.

Christianity . . . forms the richest expression of culture in history, even though you're unlikely to find even a mention of it on many a Cultural Studies course.

RUPERT SHORTT,
"HOW CHRISTIANITY INVENTED MODERNITY"

When a football team goes into a slump, it's not the time for the coach to introduce more sophisticated and complex patterns into the playbook. Every football team that makes it into the NFL playoffs is not there because they have innovated complex plays and sophisticated scoring methods but because they have mastered the basics of the game: blocking, tackling, throwing, catching, running.

The twenty-first century will be a time for a back-to-basics church: praying, Bible reading and study, evangelism, discipleship. Only then will we be able to be, as David McDonald lays out in *Then. Now. Next.*—his manifesto for the future—a church "that pounces joyfully on new opportunities, confident in her ability to make mid-course corrections; a church that prototypes, iterates and improvises as we progress in step with the Spirit."[1]

No writer should ever be afraid of complex sentences, even in an egalitarian age of "accessibility." Complex thoughts often require complex sentences. In defense of his sometimes complex, or what some would call "labored," writing style, Gerard Manley Hopkins said that there were "excellences higher than clearness at a first reading."[2] All writing need not be a substitute for milk and cookies or wedding cakes.

> *To make one's living out of the vividness of one's opinions*
> *is often to purchase impact at the price of subtlety.*
> KENNETH MINOGUE

The height of patronizing is the condescension of fake egalitarianism. The notion that people who cannot speak or write eloquence cannot be touched by eloquence is the arrogance of the intellect. We can all be shaken, stirred, or raptured by language that we cannot ourselves utter. The knowledge or love of the good, the true, the beautiful is not limited to those who can create or understand the good, the true, the beautiful.

A simplex church brings opposites like the simple and the complex together into one. In a world of Fox/CNN, each side fueling the fires of its base, the need is greater than ever for the trialectics of faith, a simplex church that occupies the overlap of both extremes and points to the Third Way of Jesus.

The more you get absorbed in a topic, the more you get dragged deeper into it. At the same time, the more you get dragged deeper into the subject, the more you realize how much you need to come up for air and enjoy the surface and the simplicity of floating on the surface, where the water shimmers and tinsels and where you receive the inspiration to take those deep breaths and go down again.

The church is called to be a people of the "down-and-outers," the bottom-up, down-and-dirty people who follow in the footsteps of the first disciples, the party of the miscast, the religiously disenfranchised, the politically disadvantaged.

One must still have chaos inside oneself
to be able to give birth to a dancing star.
FRIEDRICH NIETZSCHE

> **WALKING IN FAITH**

1. How is getting back to basics in the church complementary to the complexity of what is good, true, and beautiful?

24

CONCIENCE

*I think we should talk more about our empathy deficit—
the ability to put ourselves in someone else's shoes; to see the world
through the eyes of those who are different from us.*

BARACK OBAMA, XAVIER UNIVERSITY COMMENCEMENT
ADDRESS, AUGUST 11, 2006

THIS CULTURE IS IN A MORAL FREE-FOR-ALL.

The church is in a Christological free fall.

Anarchy is the breeding ground for tyranny.

Since religion has given up its role as the guardian of morality in Western societies, what has replaced it? Conscience. God made us to not be able to look straight into the eye of human depravity without blinking. That blink is the human conscience, bristling at sin. Does this culture still blink?

The etymology of *conscience* combines *com* and *scire*, which connote knowledge shared with another, a "knowing with." The key question is "knowing with" whom? With God? With oneself? If the latter, then Shakespeare put it best in Richard's soliloquy in the final act of *Richard III*: "My conscience hath a thousand several tongues."

The "crisis of conscience" in Western culture is not that there is none but that conscience has come to mean the self-reflexivity of "How do you feel?" more than "What does that inner knowing of the divine say?" More "What does social media say?" than "Follow your moral code." More "empathize" than "listen." A culture of privileged service and self-transcendence has been replaced by a culture of self-awareness and self-gratification. Woe

227

betide an anything-goes future when geek science weds Greek philosophy, since the words *rational* and *rationale* are only one explanatory *e* apart.

This is one reason why the more the culture collapses its moral sensibilities, churning out media monsters of mendacity, the more puritan, hypocritical, and morally uptight society becomes. At the same time ABC announced that the Miss America pageant would give up its swimsuit competition, a new season of ABC's *The Bachelorette* opened up where you can expect to see almost-naked bodies and hot-tub sex with multiple partners. Society insists everyone has the right to do whatever they want with their bodies at any time and with any person, with satisfaction and pleasure the sole criteria—and then become outraged when someone does just what the culture is telling everyone to do? With reality TV shows *Naked Attraction* (2016–) and *Love Island* (2015–) existing alongside the banning of mistletoe at office Christmas parties, we live in a confused culture that is getting more libertarian and more puritanical at the same time.

No right, no wrong, no rules for me. I'm free!

ELSA, "LET IT GO,"
IN DISNEY'S *FROZEN*

A culture of relativism doesn't produce moral dementia, laxity, or libertinage. It produces moral hypothermia. Just because you have no morals doesn't mean you don't have lots of scruples and scandals. Hence we live in a culture that turns messy moral dilemmas and complicated ethical issues into Manichaean debates, where it boils down to good and evil and you're on one side or the other in righteous rigidity.[1] A soap-opera sense of justice is the most sophistication we can muster in our addiction to a never-ending succession of moral melodramas vacant of moral discernment. Worse than an egoist is a moralist. At least the egoist is focused on what's best for themselves; a moralist is confident they know what's best for you. Moralism is not the Jesus gospel but the "another gospel" of Galatians 1:6-7: moralism based not on normative values but on personalized feelings and individualized empathy. Ethics and morality have little meaning outside of affinity alliances.

Volcanic culture has thrown ethics and morality out the window and wants to put in their place empathy—feel what you feel, experience what you experience, and then move on from there. This even has scientific status with the research of Joshua Greene, professor of psychology at Harvard

University, who has specialized in studying human moral decision-making. He concludes that regardless of what ethicists might claim, our moral judgments come straight out of that Stone Age vestige of the brain called the *amygdala*.[2] In other words, all our ethics is but a rationalization of emotional reactions and reflexes.

Ironically, even academic philosophers don't believe this. A 2009 survey of thousands of philosophers who teach in colleges and universities discovered that two-thirds were cognitivists (there is right and wrong) and 58 percent realists (moral values have independent existence outside the mind). Or in the words of British philosopher Julian Baggini, who reports on the study, "It seems that after churches, philosophy departments are one of the last bastions of the belief that morality involves actual facts that can be known."[3]

Empathy is based on emotion. Not only are emotions easily choreographed, but emotions of identification and internalization can also drain your energies and exhaust your spirit to the point where it does not help make the world a better place. Because you are putting yourself in the other person's shoes, empathy is inevitably one-sided, partisan, and irrational. From the start, its adhesive attachment foils efforts to move strategically into the future.

Meanwhile, all empathy falls short. One can never fully know what another person thinks or feels, and we resent it when others think they do—even though we are gratified and blessed by their efforts.

Yale University psychologist Paul Bloom advocates cognitive versus emotional empathy, what he calls *rational compassion*,[4] or what elsewhere we have called *intimatedistance.* The pitfall of intimacy is that you need sufficient closeness to identify with the person or problem; but you need distance so that you don't fall down into the same abyss with them and so you can be in a position to help them out of the pit. Emotion needs to be tempered with reason as well as the broader context of our moral decision-making.

As mentioned, novelist E. M. Forster is known for his *Howards End* phrase "Only connect." But British literary critic Frank Kermode (1919–2010), in his Clark Lectures (2007) at Trinity College, argued that Forster's most important dictum was not "Only connect" but this one: The transcendence of art is based "on an integrity in man's nature which is deeper than moral integrity."[5] In each one of us, there is an "integrity of transcendence" that resonates in the human spirit in every situation. There is always a right thing to do even though that right thing is not untainted with wrong and even though there is no sure-fire formula specifying the right thing for the next time. A mixed blessing is a blessing nonetheless. But we need to learn to trust that integrity of transcendence, which awakens within us an echo of recognition, a romance of resonance, a receptivity of familiarity, a tug of truth. In other words, a conscience.

I care very little if I am judged by you or by any human court; indeed,
I do not even judge myself. My conscience is clear, but that
does not make me innocent. It is the Lord who judges me.

THE APOSTLE PAUL,
I CORINTHIANS 4:3-4

Christians might talk about it differently. No matter how "saintly" the person, we all "see through a glass dimly."[6] We claim no immaculate perceptions. The lifelong process of sanctification is to use our little bottles of Windex and clean the dirt from that pane of glass as vigorously as we can. But the best we will ever do is to know in part. So we will always know some things wrong. Professor Charles Nielsen of Colgate Rochester Divinity School, an early church historian and Reformed theologian, used to say to his seminary students, "Class, you can count on this from me: Eighty percent of my theology is right, twenty percent is wrong. I just don't know which is which."

If a pastor or teacher says something that, when you hear it, your spirit immediately recognizes as truth, then you are taking it from the same source as that pastor or teacher is taking it from—the Holy Spirit. Truth is recognition, the resonance of a resident integrity of transcendence. Maybe when someone says something, your spirit feels convicted that you've already known deep inside what they're saying, but you've been burying it or have been afraid to bring it to light. Maybe your spirit is still struggling with the reality or the enormity of what is being said, but you have this deep inner sense that truth is being spoken even though you don't like it. Either way, *Nullius in verba*: "Don't take it from me." Only take it from the Holy Spirit.

But what if you hear something and your spirit immediately recoils and says, "That's just wrong. That's not right. I don't believe that at all!"? If that deep inner voice is telling you that something is awry, and it clashes with the resident integrity of transcendence inside you, then once again, *Nullius in verba*: "Don't take it from me." Only take it from the Holy Spirit. What you're hearing could be that pastor's or teacher's 20 percent. Even the venerable Royal Society didn't get it all right. Jonathan Swift mocked Isaac Newton and the Royal Society for wasting time and money on scientific pursuits and projects such as the extraction of sunbeams from cucumbers.[7]

Humans don't mind hardship, in fact they thrive on it; what they mind is not feeling necessary. Modern society has perfected the art of making people not feel necessary.

SEBASTIAN JUNGER,
TRIBE: ON HOMECOMING AND BELONGING

Of course, that could also be *your* 20 percent. Which is why, either in resonance or recoil, we need to be in conversation and community with one another to make sure the Holy Braid is being plaited correctly with all three ingredients present and checking each other: Holy Spirit, Scripture, Jesus. When we get something wrong, it's usually because one of the plaits in the Holy Braid is not connected properly.

To listen to your conscience is to listen to your body, or more precisely, the divine speaking through your body. If the seat of reason is in the head, and the seat of emotion is in the heart, then the seat of the Spirit is in the organ that connects the two to one another: the spinal cord. The stirrings of the Spirit that form the surest basis of conscience are registered in the gut and the spine. Russian novelist and poet Vladimir Nabokov (1899–1977) put it this way in relation to artistic delight: "That little shiver behind is quite certainly the highest form of emotion that humanity has attained when evolving pure art and pure science."[8]

The gut first registers a queasiness or slight nausea about something, sending up early warning signals, which the spinal cord then turns to shivers or shudders. Let the spine bring the guts to mind and heart. You know everything is connected in the Spirit and the signals are clear ("My conscience is clear") by the shiver or the shudder.

Mister Rogers' Neighborhood will be judged as one of the most profound programs in the history of television. An ordained Presbyterian minister, Fred McFeely Rogers (1928–2003) wrote every episode, every song, every scenario; pulled the strings of every puppet; and responded personally to every letter he got from kids all over the world. Rev. Rogers never talked about God or Jesus but produced arguably the most sophisticated religious program ever on television. It was a show that taught kids in simple terms how to be human in a complex and uncertain world, and how to treat others—even those who were different in body and color, demeanor and speech—with respect, kindness, and grace. In the dictum of E. M. Forster, of an "integrity of transcendence" illuminated *Mister Rogers' Neighborhood*, and it needs to illuminate our new global neighborhood.

> WALKING IN FAITH

1. How does a culture of self-authenticity and self-awareness support or undermine the reality that human beings are created in the image and likeness of God? How does this affect human function and fulfillment?

2. Our volcanic culture has thrown ethics to the curb and replaced it with empathy or some representation of empathy. What aspects of the intended outcome of empathy are lost or distorted when ethics and morality are diminished? Where do you see this loss or distortion demonstrated in society?

25

NUMBERS AND NARRATIVES

Stories can create the wonder that turns strangers into sisters and brothers.
SIKH POET AND CIVIL RIGHTS ACTIVIST VALARIE KAUR,
TED TALK

"NUMBERS DON'T LIE." You've heard that expression. Don't believe it for one second. They lie all the time. By creating us in his image, God gave humans a divine dignity. In a world increasingly ruled by algorithms, humanity must never be reduced to mere numbers or digits or units.

But people care for a story—there's the truth.
ELIZABETH BARRETT BROWNING TO A FRIEND

In the Bible, the majority always rules wrong. Truth is not a democracy. Change and the future come from the margins, the minority, the Two-to-Three Principle ("where two or three gather"),[1] or what scientists now call *critical mass*. But you can't get anywhere with biblical appeals to an algorithmic culture. In a world of numbers, narratives are everything.

The plural of anecdote is data.
ROGER NOLL

Narratives that come with provenance, narratives that are personalized and customized as anecdotes, can carry the weight of the world. The word *anecdote* originally meant "something unpublished." It carried a cachet of confidentiality and scandal. Whiffs of amateurism and unsophistication still hang around the word *anecdote*, and to an increasingly lesser degree, the word *story*. But not for long. The world is changed not by force of numbers, but by emporiums of light; plantings of seeds; pinches of salt; and stories of truth, beauty, and goodness. The classic confessions of faith are priceless, but the best confessions of faith are stories of God's saving action in our own histories and in the histories of others we know.[2]

Sing in me, oh Muse, and through me tell the story.

CLOSING WORDS OF BOB DYLAN'S NOBEL LECTURE (2016),
QUOTING OPENING WORDS OF HOMER'S
EPIC "ODYSSEY" (750 BC)

In a world that says "Trust the algorithms," the church must say back "Trust the story" and "Trust the Spirit." *Why do you show respect and compassion for animals?* Our generating story tells us so. *Why do you know it's not right to clone humans?* Our generating story tells us so. Trust the story.

But before anyone can trust anything, they must know what it is they're trusting. Everyone should know their origins stories. Can you tell your genesis story? Have you taught your children theirs? How well do we know the biblical Genesis story of how everything began? How many Christians themselves read the Bible not to enter the story, but to excavate the words? What is missing is a foundational fluency in the stories of the Bible. Even a watercooler fluency in the biblical story would help.

New ways of thinking sneak behind well-fortified lines of logic when they are embedded in stories. Only narratives are stealthy enough to get past all the "watchful dragons" (as C. S. Lewis might say) protecting the status quo. Jesus' metaphors conduct reconnaissance missions behind the lines of every culture and each new generation.

The heart of culturomics, including politics, is now significs, symbolics, metaphorics, and sonics—encompassing life into story structures, sign rubrics, metaphor frameworks, and soundtracks. Even concerts now are storytelling events, where the stage is not a platform for noise alone but mostly for narratives.

A long time ago, Edward Said stated that Israelis and Palestinians would never be able to begin to imagine a shared future until they were able to craft a single intertwined narrative of their pasts.[3]

Truth embodied in a tale shall enter in at lowly doors.

ALFRED, LORD TENNYSON,
IN MEMORIAM

One of the worst conditions any individual or institution can be in is the absent-story syndrome. Humans cannot live without story, so if we aren't living our own stories, we'll be living at the mercy of someone else's story.

Stories are the bloodstream of the body of Christ. The future depends on making every church body's circulatory system more healthy and on oxygenating its blood with biblical narratives.

If story is the lifeblood of the body, propositions are the skeleton, and you can't stand up and walk without a skeleton. But propositions and principles come from the stories, not stories from the propositions. Besides, if truth were nothing more than propositions and principles, the Bible would be one long list of dos and don'ts, and we'd be done with it. If God chose story and metaphor to reveal who he is, why do we think using propositions and points is so much better?

Stories are not some kind of narrative hook to enter the pillared temple of words in the form of principles, points, and philosophy. Stories are the temple itself. It's not so much that a spoonful of story makes the medicine go down. The story *is* the medicine. The most natural shape that human thought can take is a metaphor that spins a story. Metaphor is the mortar of the mind, a mind that thinks in stories. That's why humans are a storytelling species. Wherever humans go, we leave behind bread-crumb trails of stories.

Jesus, the Bread of Life, was the greatest storyteller who ever lived. The better the storytelling, the more Jesus is in the church. Metaphor is metamorphosis.

In an important but little-known book entitled *Engaging Unbelief*, Curtis Chang explores the schematic commonalities between Augustine's *City of God* (AD 400s) and Thomas Aquinas's *Summa contra Gentiles* (AD 1260), as each theologian confronts the epochal threat of his generation.[4] Chang outlines their apologetic strategy as follows:

1. Enter the challenger's story.
2. Retell the challenger's story.
3. Capture the story in the wider story of Christianity by exposing the challenging story's "tragic flaw" or inadequacy.

To be sure, Augustine and Aquinas faced different threats. Augustine confronted a culture turning hostile to Christianity and Aquinas negotiated the rapid expansion of Islam. But both utilized this same method of apologetics.

Of course, Chang does not leave us with history alone; he then shows how Christians can confront the challenges of our day the same way. To seize the future, we don't ask people what they want or need; we hear their hungers and hurts in stories and songs. We don't find a need and fill it; we find a story and sing it—but only if we know our own story and trust the grand narrative, the lordly libretto of the Bible.

Maybe there's a land where you have to sing
to explain anything.

WILLIAM STAFFORD,
"A COURSE IN CREATIVE WRITING"

The semiotic matrix of the future is as follows:

1. *Storify, not versify:* While chapter and verse were added to the Bible as helpful tools for finding the story, they have become instruments for losing the story and finding points instead. "Verses turn stories into propositions, which help lawyers (like John Calvin)," one of my doctoral students, Len Wilson, likes to say. Of course, Moses didn't come down from the mountain with Ten Stories or Ten Metaphors. There is a time for narrations and a time for declarations, a time for metaphors and a time for "Thus saith the Lord."

2. *Make the story a movie in your mind:* After we master the metaphorical continent that is the Bible, we must turn that story into cinematic form so that we "see" it in our minds' eye. The ancient rabbis exhorted Jews studying the Torah to "turn it over, turn it over, because everything is inside of it."

3. *Trust the story.* Israel Joshua Singer advised his more famous younger brother, Isaac, to avoid *zugerts* like they were the Ten Plagues. *Zugerts* means "explanations" or "expositions" or "nonvisual interpretations." Isaac Bashevis Singer took his older brother's advice and won the Nobel Prize for Literature (1978).

   Faith is not "to live as if the story were true." Faith is to stake your whole life on the belief the story *is* true. We have been taught to trust the words of the Bible as inspired and authoritative. It is time to trust the metaphors and stories of the Bible as inspired and authoritative as well. Indeed, in a world where every commercial is inviting us to trust our lives to this story or that story, the only story worth trusting your life to is the Jesus Story.

4. *Receive the story first; theologize last.* Let the story work on you before you work on a story. Don't theologize until you let the story put your soul through a workout of mind, body, and spirit. Few things in life are as precious, or as fragile, as a true story. Your life is a painting. Ten years from now, when you look at that same painting, you are a whole new painting. But it is still you. Likewise, every time you receive any story from Scripture, it's the same sacred story infused with the divine, but it's a whole new story based on new scenes and settings.

5. *Every story contains the whole story:* In every story of the Bible, no matter how small, there is a crystal of the whole story. Every story finds its place in another story. You can't tell one story without in some way telling the whole story. Every time we read the Bible with all our hearts and souls and minds, we kneel at the manger and welcome the Incarnation, and we also discover new meanings and insights from the same mysterious and overflowing manger.

6. *Live the story.* You can't escape living in and through a story. All of us are living a story. The only question is, What story and whose story are you living? Madison Avenue's? Wall Street's? Hollywood's? Bethlehem's?

What makes your story compelling is not the theology behind it but the witness in front of it. I am often in profound disagreement with the ideas of philosopher Ivan Illich (1926–2002), but on this point I am in profound agreement:

Neither revolution nor reformation can ultimately change a society, rather you must tell a new powerful tale, one so persuasive that it sweeps away the old myths and becomes the preferred story, one so inclusive that it gathers all the bits of our past and our present into a coherent whole, one that even shines some light into the future so that we can take the next step. . . . If you want to change a society, then you have to tell an alternative story.[5]

> WALKING IN FAITH

1. Paradoxically, a world ruled by algorithms and numbers makes numbers less important, not more. Not surprisingly, change and the future still come from the margins, where two or three are gathered together. How does this idea speak to the future of a church increasingly marginalized in Western culture?

2. Science and philosophy cannot guide one's life in Christ. Our generating story—the story of our origin—does that. How have you lived by trusting the story? How has not trusting the story produced ambiguity in your life?

3. In what specific ways can Curtis Chang's summation of the apologetic strategies of Augustine and Aquinas (enter the challenger's story; retell the challenger's story; capture the story in the wider story of Christianity, exposing the flaw or inadequacy in the challenger's story) open new approaches to today's epochal threats?

Conclusion

Wild Cards, Black Swans, and Game-Changing Super Volcanoes

*A major eruption would be a low-probability, high-consequence event,
a proverbial Black Swan, something that could have
societal and planetary effects.*

JOEL ACHENBACH,
"THE YELLOWSTONE SUPERVOLCANO IS A DISASTER
WAITING TO HAPPEN"

THE FUTURE IS NO PLACE for dilettante discipleship.

Ridges under the oceans are seldom seen or noticed, but we experience their effects long-term. Tectonic plates develop along these oceanic ridges, and in the places where plates collide, called *subduction zones*, there can be both sudden and spectacular volcanic eruptions, creating *super volcanoes*. It is a fatal mistake to see a super volcano as a pendulum swing and not a paradigm shift.

Sometimes what you don't know can be more important than what you do know. Sometimes these sudden-surprise super volcanoes can create whole islands overnight where none existed before. Such is the case with Surtsey, an island in Iceland that didn't exist before 1963, when it was formed by a super volcano that erupted for three years.[1]

Super volcanoes are fire fountains streaming into the sky, "all terror, horror and sublimity, blackness, suffocating gases, scorching heat, crashings, surgings, detonations," as the Victorian travel writer Isabella Bird described the boiling crater of Kilauea, Hawaii, in 1875.[2] As every volcanic eruption has made clear, another world is possible. This wild card, black swan future is enough to give even the most famously stoic immediate spine chills and biohorror thrills.

But just as often, erupting volcanoes can be visual letdowns. What you see for the most part is little more than a dense, choking cloud of ash and smoke, with the occasional stripe of orange lava to relieve the gloom. As the British travel writer Norman Lewis noted in his now-classic account of Vesuvius's eruption in 1944, "I had been prepared for rivers of fire, but there was no fire and no burning anywhere—only the slow, deliberate suffocation of the town under millions of tons of clinkers. . . . The whole process was strangely quiet."[3]

In this book, we have highlighted where the volcanoes are and how they will blow if they do erupt. We can expect future technology to take us places so far outside the range of imagination that they are inconceivable. But "inconceivable" is the natural habitat for the disciple of Jesus. We serve Jesus, the All-Things-Are-Possible Christ.

Impossibility is the only door that opens.

AUSTRALIAN POET LES MURRAY,
"ONE KNEELING, ONE LOOKING DOWN"

Any one of the wild card super volcanoes enumerated in this book could stand alone as a two-hundred-page anxiety attack. They are living examples of what the politician was talking about when he stood to address his fellow parliamentarians: "Friends, yesterday we stood on the edge of the abyss, but today we have taken a great step forward!"

Some things are both inevitable and unforeseen, as Alexis de Tocqueville said of the French Revolution. These "unseens" create unintended consequences for which no one is prepared. That is why we conclude *Rings of Fire* with extended discussions of two of the most fearsome threats to the future that are swept along with the flow of fire.

Paranoia is when you figured out what's going on.

ONE OF STANLEY KUBRICK'S FAVORITE SAYINGS

We will always have problems. Beware what comes bearing the name *progress*. Progress is always ambiguous, often dangerous, at times deadly. The best definition of *progress* may be "when we upgrade our problems." The problem is that the very "solutions" that enable us to tackle the problems of living together in harmony can bring even more dangerous problems in their wake.

Jesus doesn't so much solve our problems as open up new doors to fresh possibilities and better problems. Life is by definition problematic. The best you can hope for in life is to trade up your problems.

Here are some of the wild cards and black swans that loom on the horizon:

1. Global warming could result in sea levels rising and flooding major coastal cities.

2. The Gulf Stream could flip, turning Europe into Siberia.

3. A rise in methane emissions could signify a doomsday feedback loop where the more global warming, the more methane is released.

4. We could lose the evolutionary arms race with antibiotics.

5. Besides influenza,[4] new plagues could spread to slay whole populations, from new zoonotic viruses like SARS and AIDS to viral infections that come from animals, like avian flu. Epidemics and pandemics are endemic wild cards.

6. The race is already on to get ahead of an extremely drug resistant strain of typhoid, an early version of which is already found in much of Southeast Asia, Sub-Saharan Africa, and Oceania, where a lineage known as H58 is resistant to as many as five classes of antibiotics.[5]

7. China's debt binge could come back to bite us all.[6]

8. A few individuals or small groups could carry out biotechnological violence on a scale that was inconceivable in the past.

9. Nuclear meltdown from terrorism or "dirty bombs."[7]

10. New Crusades (against Islam or against Christianity).

What is the difference between throwing innocent people into blazing ovens and throwing blazing ovens at innocent people?

DOROTHY DAY

---

11. Cyberattacks through cyberterrorism and cybercrime: One person has as much power as a nation-state to shut down a city or country.

12. A botox bomb could go off, with a single gram of botulinum in

crystallized form, weaponized to be inhaled, capable of killing one million people.[8]

13. New ways to cheat evolution, like engineered gene drives, are perilous undertakings that open up a Matryoshka nesting doll of Pandora's boxes.

14. Precipitous plunge of trust in establishment institutions, whether politics or religion or business (Big Business, Big Labor, Big Government, Big Church), engendering global anarchy.

15. Collapsing infrastructure: 14,000 of the country's dams are rated "high hazard" by the American Society of Civil Engineers, and 151,238 of its bridges are rated as "deficient"—not to mention the problem with decrepit plumbing and decaying pipes.[9]

16. Surprise release of new infective particles, like the one called a *prion*. You never survive a prion, which is nothing but a protein that destroys the central nervous system. Recent revelations that deadly and highly communicable flu viruses have been engineered in the name of science are not comforting.

17. Pure evil: Some people like to watch the world burn and people die. The sheer enormity of evil that lies at the heart of the human species is always a game changer. Holocaust survivor Primo Levi (1919–87), an Italian Jewish chemist and writer, had slaked his thirst with an icicle hanging off a building upon his arrival at Auschwitz. Immediately a guard chopped the icicle away and out of his hand. Levi asked, "Why?" The guard answered, "Here there is no why!"[10]

18. Popping volcanoes: Unanticipated eruptions could haze the skies in ash, causing a global cooling that would generate a food crisis unlike anything the world has imagined.

What, if anything, is the meaning and purpose of life? This is the question humans used to look to religion to answer. Now everything is in free fall and in a free-for-all. All is up for grabs. When you lose all notion of good and evil, or can no longer tell the difference between the beautiful and the ugly, the costly and the cheap, the sublime and the ridiculous, the real and the fake, you have fallen under the spell of the death spiral.

In a world that bears false witness as easily as it wears a false face or puts on a false front, the future needs those who will bear true witness, whatever the cost.

Thus bad begins and worse remains behind.

WILLIAM SHAKESPEARE,
HAMLET

The satirical phrase "Love your bureaucracy" we steal from Donald R. Keough, former CEO of Coca-Cola. In *The Ten Commandments for Business Failure*, his 8th Commandment of business failure is "love your bureaucracy."[11] Max Weber's forgotten warning of a coming iron cage of a rationalized, bureaucratized world and the mechanization of life seems now almost prophetic.[12]

In the interest of efficiency, bureaucracies build silos ruled by "experts," which inevitably produce turf wars, which hinder the communication and collaboration[13] that keep fertile the mental furrows in which new ideas may take root and not be poisoned by inertia, routine, and kludge. Even webs isolate as much as they connect. We may never be more isolated than when we are networked, as the "weaving" of networks and the "curating" of members has a menacing, mind-manacling quality to it.[14]

Words like *process* and *procedure* are but bureaucratic euphemisms deployed to entrench the powerful. It is not easy to wrest support for new ideas and experimentation from the sepulchre of bureaucratic statism. Just ask the Wright brothers how hard it was to convince their government, even before the days of bloated bureaucracies, that airplanes might be of interest. The Wrights' first government contract was with France, not the US. Or just before you swallow something the government promises is safe, see if it doesn't have a Flinty taste or a 9/11 smell.

A bureaucratic spirit is the opposite of a democratic spirit and will kill true democracy if not checked constantly. The vote for Brexit was not a vote against the European Union so much as it was a voter's rebellion against the bureaucratic, nonmeritocratic elites in Brussels.

The essence of populism, whether right-wing or left-wing, is the people against the powerful. Most "experts" see populism as a boil that will burst. But populism could just as easily be a cauldron that keeps boiling for a long, long time. Populism's revival around the world is an expression of people's anger at being slapped in the face for so long by those for whom the public trust seems more a public trough.

Bureaucratic structures are as lawless in their own way as they are awe-less (indifferent?) of human decency, as resistant to respectfulness as they are "immune to grace."[15] And graceless, disrespectful systems produce graceless reactions and graceless elections.

Democracy means "the power of the people," not majority rules. If democracy does nothing else, it allows people to lead the lives they choose. But democracy depends on the willingness of people to practice deferred gratification, and democracy is becoming dysfunctional partly because people increasingly are unwilling to defer their gratification into the future.

Democracy also mandates a public-spiritedness that can temper rank partisanship and fanaticism. When the only means for settling differences is the annihilation of the other side, how can any democratic society survive, let alone claim to "celebrate difference"? The social fabric that ties "democracy" and "community" together is frayed and ripped. God's mission is now to a world that is coming apart at the seams.

Democracy is first of all a metaphysics and only afterwards a politics.

JEAN-LUC NANCY,
THE TRUTH OF DEMOCRACY

Israeli philosopher and historian Yuval Harari suspects that "as data-processing conditions change again in the twenty-first century, democracy might decline and even disappear."[16] But Plato's greatest worry about democracy was that its citizens would not defer gratification, only live "from day to day, indulging the pleasure of the moment."[17] Everyone now stalks the earth like a god, looking for immediate pleasure and satisfaction, willing to game the system to benefit the few at the expense of the many.

Worldwide democracy has been losing ground at least since the financial crisis of 2007–8.[18] For the twelfth consecutive year, countries that suffered democratic setbacks outnumbered those that registered gains.[19] Eighty-nine countries regressed in 2017; only twenty-seven improved in the quality of democracy.[20]

True democracy yokes two oxymoronic features: the protection of the rights of the individual and the platforming of the voice of the people. When those constituent features of the democratic spirit become separated into individualism and majoritarianism, *democracy* becomes another word for demagoguery.[21]

The Cross tells the story. The high priest Caiaphas, who organized the plot to kill Jesus, had noble motives. He esteemed it worthy to let "one man . . . die for the people."[22] It's the ultimate story of how nothing is so evil that God cannot bring good out of it. But it is *not* okay to commit evil even if good may come out of it. Jesus was crucified by majority vote of the people and by the bureaucratic ideology that says you sacrifice the one to save the many. Establishment hierarchy and bureaucracy, principalities and powers, crucified Jesus.

When the church no longer exists for mission but for the perpetuation of the church, the church has become a bureaucracy. In other words, an ecclesia of missional disciples turns into an ecclesiocracy of arrogant, corrupt, self-serving ecclesiocrats. One litmus test of a church-become-bureaucracy is this: How many times does Jesus count or have any place in our church discussions? The church must move from a regulatory, bureaucratic mind-set to a recivilizing, blessing mind-set. How do you make your church stop some of the things it is doing so it can start doing some new things it is not doing? Lovett Weems, in his book on challenges facing the church, features the way denominations "have often been fundamentalists of structure rather than doctrine."[23]

Nothing, nothing, nothing, no error, no crime is so absolutely repugnant to God as everything which is official; and why? Because the official is impersonal and therefore the deepest insult which can be offered to a personality.

SØREN KIERKEGAARD

Pope Francis was asked about the Irish Catholic Marie Collins, who served on the Pontifical Commission for the Protection of Minors until April 2017, when she resigned because of its slowness and shortcomings in dealing with the victims of abuse. Asked about her decision to resign, the pope applauded her actions, admitted that she "was right about some things," and confessed that the Vatican bureaucracy was woefully and worriedly slow.[24]

Every spirituality in history has become institutionalized. And institutions are ugly. But like low blows and cheap shots and cursing, bureaucracy is inescapable. A good civilization needs a good government, and the power of government to do good or evil is not to be gainsaid. Any government, whether of church or state, brings bureaucracy. Even when decentralization is the goal, and decentralism's wide-as-possible, human-scale distribution of power is put in place, and governing functions are as close to the people as possible, and the individual is not swallowed up by the shark-infested waters of an impersonal Leviathan, and the core beliefs of democracy, liberty, community, and morality are vigilantly protected,[25] there will still be bureaucracy, even if in decentralized form. The best you can hope for is an inefficient, inept, clumsy bureaucracy, for anything else is a danger to the human race. So the next time you spend a frustrating afternoon in a local DMV for something that should have only taken ten minutes, breathe a sigh of relief. You're safe, and the human race is safe.

The bureaucratic impulse must be continually restrained, tamed, challenged, and rebuked if it is not to become a satanic force in the future. We must constantly throw into the bureaucratic anthill some bohemian grasshoppers and push some foxes down the hedgehog holes, outfitting them in protective gear for the period they are there. We must challenge the pieties of bureaucracy (for example, Robert's Rules of Order) with the impieties of Spirit-regulating, Spirit-organizing, Spirit-driven ad-hocracy. The Order of St. Roberts must bow to the spontaneity and serendipity of the Order of the Holy Spirit.

Does anyone really comprehend, or appreciate, how hard, how heroic it is to be a human being in a bureaucratic, technocratic system? There is fast violence that destroys life in the here and now. Then there is slow violence that degrades and defaces life over the long haul. The closing lines of the dramatic monologue in Alfred, Lord Tennyson's "Ulysses" have had many lives. The words have been inscribed on the walls in many Olympic villages as well as tattooed on the bodies of many athletes. In the James Bond film *Skyfall* (2012), Judi Dench, as M, speaks them in defiance to all cyberterrorists and bureaucrats everywhere:

> *That which we are, we are;*
> *One equal temper of heroic hearts,*
> *Made weak by time and fate, but strong in will*
> *To strive, to seek, to find, and not to yield.*[26]

The gospel of Jesus Christ is a healing and cleansing tonic that has the ability to mend the tatters of any bureaucratic tapestry and breathe new life into the bureaucratic kiss of death. But we must do the weaving and the kissing.

Those who cannot see Christ in the poor are atheists indeed.
DOROTHY DAY

Lalta is a scavenger in India. Her job is to clean human excrement out of latrines by hand and carry it in a basket on her head to a dumping ground.[27]

Visitors to New York City line up outside Serendipity 3 to order exquisite desserts, most notably the Golden Opulence Sundae. For $1,000 you get three scoops of Tahitian vanilla ice cream covered in 23-karat gold leaf, layered with caviar from Chicago, chocolate from Tuscany, vanilla beans from Madagascar, and a sugar-forged orchid made from candied fruit from Paris that takes eight hours to build. The dish is served in a $350 Baccarat crystal goblet (lined with more 23-karat gold leaf), with an 18-karat gold spoon on the side.

The fault lines and fissures of the future are volcanic, many, and multiplying, but one of the most dangerous divides is not based on race or gender or nationality but class. In one of the biggest surprises of the "information revolution," digital technologies are widening, not narrowing, the wealth gap,[28] and will continue to do so until corporate accountability and social responsibility become economic and political watchwords. Globalization and the shrinking of the middle class have worsened inequality and widened income disparity to apocalyptic proportions.

We are not the first to be living in a culture of huge inequality. In the history of humanity, there have been times of colossal gulfs between the rich and the poor. There was sizeable inequality in Jesus' day. When Dorothy Wordsworth observed, in her famous *Grasmere Journal*, that in the future "there would be only two ranks of people, the very rich and the very poor,"[29] she was expressing a sentiment that you could find voiced eighteen hundred years earlier.

But there are differences of degree that become differences of kind. The year 2012 stands as a watershed: For the first time in US history, more than half of all income in the US went to the richest 10 percent of the population.[30] Six years later, we reached another watershed: Asia became home to the highest number of billionaires for the first time in history. China leads the field, far outnumbering the US, with two billionaires born every week. What is more unique about the Asian wealth is that virtually all new entrants are self-made instead of originating from multigenerational inheritance, which is common in North America and Europe.[31]

The American dream isn't fading . . . it's being hoarded.

MALCOLM HARRIS,
KIDS THESE DAYS: HUMAN CAPITAL AND THE MAKING OF MILLENNIALS

There is always going to be inequality. A world where everyone is equal, everything is shared, all is fair, is called "utopia" for a reason: It fails to take into account human nature and human difference.[32]

The good news is there is less extreme poverty today than at any other time in the history of the world, and for the first time, poverty is not growing just because the population is.[33] Yet in the context of the West, a small percentage of the population—the corporatocracy, or oligarchy—are creating categories of superwealth never before seen in world history.

Out of this belching economic and social chasm burst forth a host of other burning-hot issues, like how the rich raise their kids versus the poor and the varying resources available to each.[34] Or the scandal of the medication of poverty. Poor children (those on Medicaid) are prescribed antipsychotic and behavior-controlling psychotropic drugs at a rate four times higher than children privately insured.[35] The number one thing that goes with less education, less money, less healthy foods, and less-safe neighborhoods is . . . more pills, especially Schedule II controlled drugs.[36] The consequences of inequality are as much social as economic, with all sorts of mental and physical side effects being incubated by this degree of disparity.[37]

The richest one percent of the world's population own more than the rest of the people on the planet combined. Twenty-six people now own as much wealth as the poorest half of the world's population.[38] The business of producing enhanced humans only raises the stakes of inequalities—the rich can afford "betterment," not the poor. Global warming will drive populations away from the equator, and the one percent will try to wall themselves off from the rest of the world.[39] They will fail.

As much as the poor, the rich will always be with us. The fact that someone else has a better car or a bigger house is of no consequence, or shouldn't be. If Jesus wants to pay some people more who do less, as long as everyone is given a generous wage, why should we be envious that life is more generous to some than to others? Wealth is not the problem. Poverty is. The more we move in directions that favor the powerful, the young, the educated, and the rich to an even greater extent, the poor will lose even more value than they already have. What happens when masses sense that the game is rigged is the gurgling volcano of the future.

What the future holds for wealth inequality will in part depend on the dance between market and state: Markets are necessary to create wealth, but the state is needed to control markets.[40] But it will also depend on the ability of people of faith to get on the dance floor and do their parts. Even small parts. For example, no one should be more known for being "good tippers" than Christians.[41] Where others tip a couple of dollars, we tip $10 or $20, and 40 percent for breakfast, always with a smile and blessing like this one: "This is for you. We've got to stick together."

If we don't stick together, we'll blow up together. Feeding the soul and feeding the body are not the same, but they can never be separate either. The widening chasm between rich and poor[42] and the social polarization that attends the disparity is a more immediate threat to the future than any other wild card, black swan, or game changer.[43] Will the heart of our thinking and dreaming be every person's dignity as a human being, or will it be the economy, wealth, privilege, and protection of vested interests?

The Mount Vesuvius of inequality is a seething anger that can flare up and explode at any moment, just as it has in the past, triggering many forms of civil unrest and pandemonium.

The hand, the head, and the heart of man go together.
ART CRITIC AND PHILOSOPHER JOHN RUSKIN

Can the church battle the narratives of "indulge yourself" with competing biblical narratives that call on us to invest in the future and share the wealth? Bob Dylan's song "Gotta Serve Somebody" (1979) so upset John Lennon that he promptly wrote "Gotta Serve Yourself" (1980). These are the two competing worldviews of our day.[44] The future depends on which soundtrack wins: the one based on the narcissistic cult of self-worship or the one based on the Jewish idea of *tikkun olam*—collective action to repair the world. The self is not the most important aspect of life or the highest ideal. Service is.

Ill fares the land, to hastening ills a prey,
Where wealth accumulates, and men decay.

OLIVER GOLDSMITH,
"THE DESERTED VILLAGE"

There is an extravagance to God's imagination that is breathtaking. Artist and theologian Makoto Fujimura calls it the "creative wastefulness" of God.[45]

By the midpoint of the twenty-first century, we will move into a postscarcity economy in which things such as goods, services, and information are free, or practically free, or want to be free. Such a future will emerge from an abundance of fundamental resources (think nano, AI, alternative energy, etc.) in conjunction with sophisticated automated systems capable of converting raw materials into finished goods (namely by molecular assemblers). In such a world, manufacturing would be as easy as using duplication software or 3-D printers, with every material imaginable the new "paper."

In a postscarcity economy, the primary currency will be experiences and relationships, and the highest levels of both will not come cheap. To move into this world, religious leaders will first have to move their thinking from "great thought" or "nice effort" to "amazing experience." Sometimes God is more active in the world than in the church because God's anointed and appointed instruments are busy conducting their own missions rather than God's mission. But God will not be without a witness, and God will be in this future, whether our tribes are there or not. Jesus went from calling the Temple "my Father's House" to "my House" to—in his next-to-last sentence spoken in the Temple—"your house": "Your house is left to you desolate."[46] Can a church go from "Christ's body" to "your body," which Jesus "leaves desolate" for us to handle? If it happened to Israel, it can happen to a church.

Though he was rich, yet for your sake he became poor,
so that you through his poverty might become rich.

THE APOSTLE PAUL,
2 CORINTHIANS 8:9

Why is wealth such a threat, then and now? First, wealth allows the rich to separate themselves from others—to become independent of others and isolated from the needs of others. The shameless denial of the haves is only matched by the shameful debasement of the have-nots, most of whom tragically go to work and labor the hardest while they live in grinding poverty.[47]

Second, in an outcomes society, there is little time for outcasts, outliers, outsiders, and those on the outskirts of power. No time for outlooks on the future either, only outcomes in the present. Riches aren't bad unless they keep you from becoming rich in faith and things of the Spirit.[48] Hedonism is good unless it leads to henotheism, where you come to worship the "lower gods" rather than the high and holy, the one and only God. What if we revised our economic thinking to reward companies and countries that create the best lives for people, not just the most wealth? The future of capitalism rests on whether it can move the moral needle toward the public good; whether it can become an *ethical* capitalism. The problem is, an ethical capitalism requires ethics—including ethical families, ethical communities, ethical individuals, and so on.

Nature is never spent;
There lives the dearest freshness deep down things.
GERARD MANLEY HOPKINS,
"GOD'S GRANDEUR"

Every time Jesus hosted a table or performed a food miracle, there were leftovers. The church needs a theology of leftovers. We don't know why he sent his disciples ahead while he remained to dismiss the crowd after miraculously feeding thousands of people,[49] but we suspect it had something to do with teaching them what to do with the leftovers. After God has filled us, what do we do with all the leftovers? Do we take them home and hoard them for ourselves? Or do we share them with those in need?

The Jewish tradition of leaving corners of fields unharvested for the poor is a good place to start. The Scriptures call us to be gleaners of the fields, to gather the leftovers and distribute them among leftover people, or to let others glean the fields. Our concern is not to pray for the harvest. That is the business of the Lord of the Harvest. Our concern is to pray for the laborers of the harvest, for them to bring in the sheaves and to gather up the leftovers for those left over. There is plenty for everyone if we learn how to share.

*I believe that in the end it is kindness and generous accommodation
that are the catalysts for real change.*

NELSON MANDELA,
LAUNCHING "THE ELDERS," JULY 18, 2007

So, what do we do when the wild cards are dealt, the black swans show up, and the game changers go into motion?

When Jesus heard of the beheading of John the Baptist, he did a couple of things.[50] First, he withdrew. He regrouped. He needed solitude. Some grieving needs to be private. Second, Jesus moved out of his grief and into compassion for the crowd. With a stronger resolve for God than ever before, he returned to his mission and began healing the sick.

One of Martin Luther's favorite sayings was *Omnis homo mendax*, or "All men are liars." By this phrase Luther meant that sin will corrupt everything we touch, everywhere and always. Philosopher John Gray has shown how the worst atrocities in history, especially in modernity, have come from crusades stemming from utopian visions of eradicating evil from the world, which is most often translated as eradicating people defined as evil from the world.[51] And evil looks different to a Nazi than a Nazarene.

When Sir Kenneth Clark was making episode six ("Protest and Communication") of his groundbreaking 1969 television series, *Civilisation*, the shoot took place at the Castle Church door in Wittenberg, where Clark was to speak Martin Luther's three words that launched the Reformation in particular and the modern era in general: "Here I stand!" This one shoot took six takes, because Clark kept breaking down in tears. Clark understood the power of those three words to bring in the future.[52]

Each one of those words is wrong for the twenty-first century. It is no longer "Here" but "There." It is no longer "I" but "we." It is no longer "stand" but "go." It is time to less "take a stand" than to "take a hike" and walk together into the future.

Martin Luther King Jr. based his civil rights movement on freedom marches. Whether it be Walk Selma to Montgomery, or Walk Chicago, or Walk in Washington, King insisted, "if you can't fly, run; if you can't run, walk; if you can't walk, crawl; but by all means keep moving."[53]

Nelson Mandela (1918–2013) picked this up in his Walk On movement. In 2007, Mandela founded The Elders, an international group of fourteen governmental leaders, business leaders, and peace activists who would carry forward Mandela's mission of human rights, peace, and justice.[54] To honor the hundredth anniversary of Mandela's birth, The Elders sponsored a "Walk Together" competition to collect the one hundred best ideas for world betterment in the arenas of health, education, peace, and justice.

This metaphor of Walk On, rather than Stand Against, is also a favorite of Pope Francis. A church that "walks together" is one of Pope Francis's favorite phrases.

Moses was walking in the desert when he saw something strange and out of place—a burning bush. Instead of running away, he walked close and encountered the divine. Mary was walking through the garden when she saw something strange and out of place at the tomb of her Lord—the stone covering rolled away. Instead of running away, she walked in and got close and encountered the divine.

When you see something strange and out of place, which is inevitably what the future holds, don't run. Walk forward and get close. Don't back up. Step in to the strange and step up to the divine. We must lock arms and walk together in humble confidence, always in pursuit of solutions, always cognizant that any solution in an imperfect, fragile, fearful world is itself imperfect and fragile. And yet we walk with the mantra of the most repeated biblical phrases always in our mouths and on our lips: "Fear not."

———————

His resurrection is like the first erupting of a volcano, which shows that the fire of God is already burning inside the world and its light will eventually bring everything else to a blessed glow. He is risen to show that it has already started.

KARL RAHNER,
THE MYSTICAL WAY IN EVERYDAY LIFE

———————

> WALKING IN FAITH

1. Progress is when we upgrade our problems. Life is problematic by definition. The best you can hope for is to "trade up" your problems. How are we to respond to this predicament, and how does our response affect the intractability of the "problem"?

2. How can the "blink" of the human conscience be represented (to those whom have written off God, religion, the church, and even the trustworthiness of truth) as an invitation to new realms of possibility rather than a sign of rejection?

Afterword

Mark Chironna

IN 1992, PETER DRUCKER SAID, "Every few hundred years throughout Western history, a sharp transformation has occurred."[1] He added, with seeming prophetic insight, that within fifty years of such shifts, a new world would exist. Drucker applied the principle to the late-twentieth-century "shift to a knowledge society." Yet what he expected to take fifty years happened even more quickly.

Such is the 2020 landscape.

As the cycles of human history attest, the fundamental shifts Drucker describes cannot happen without convulsions. Empires come and empires go. Companies come and companies go. Conquests begin and end. Some surrender to current reality. Others see the shifts coming. The exiled prophet Daniel saw life beyond his lions' den experience and beyond the fiery furnace his friends faced. He anticipated the promise of a new future emerging for his people and for the nations. He followed instructions to "seal the book until the time of the end," and he noted the warning that "many will dash about, and knowledge will increase."[2]

There seems to be no avoiding the dashing about, the running to and fro, the roaming here and there, when knowledge increases. Disruptions occur and accelerate. Eruptions are triggered when unseen tectonic plates shift beneath the seen global culture. Cracks and fault lines widen and deepen with the shaking, quaking, and fiery upheavals described in this book. The powerful pull of the future releases a level of chaos in a present reality that wants to be stable but can't.

The world *is* on fire. We would prefer calm, sunny days and are willing to tolerate a little rain. But fiery days? Those are not in our preferred forecasts of the now-present future. Amid the chaos and fear, however, we can choose to expand the breadth of our expectations to embrace a new reformation, a renaissance that reflects Augustine's *semper reformanda*—the "always reforming" heart of a people whose horizon is Christ. They are the "hopers" who countenance wild cards with the same self-possession that embraces former and latter rains, because they see past the eruptions and infernos to a future that is as bright as God's promises.

These promises are not only found in the future but also in the voices from our collective past—people who described their own times and fiery conditions and saw past them to our day.

Amazingly, with every fiery cultural eruption, we get to know more than we knew before. Yet even as knowledge increases, there is still more to know. St. Paul corrected the Corinthians, who in their hubris saw themselves as a people "in the know," by saying that even at their prophetic best they (and we) "know in part and . . . prophesy in part."[3]

We can indeed know something of the future, but our knowing is not prediction. The future cannot be predicted. For the faithful followers of Jesus, the future is a promise from the One who keeps every promise he gives. In him "are hidden all the treasures of wisdom and knowledge,"[4] and only he knows it all. Yet we can act on what we know and are indeed *called* to do so—to act in faith on the knowledge we have been given, taking the next necessary steps into a future that wants to unfold with our cooperation.

Keeping up with what we must come to know and have yet to learn involves what sociologist Roberto Poli calls the "discipline of anticipation" and "anticipatory thinking."[5] Even in the world of positive psychology, Martin Seligman and others remind us that we are "prospective" beings,[6] meaning we anticipate the future before it arrives. Seligman's book is described as follows: "It is anticipating and evaluating future possibilities for the guidance of thought and action that is the cornerstone of human success."[7]

By divine design, our minds and hearts are teleological. We are inherently goal- and outcome-oriented. Therefore the pull of the future continually grips our human psyche in order to move us toward that which wants to unfold. This very human trait has divine origins; it is encoded in us as image bearers of the Most High God.

The idea that Len Sweet has perhaps most successfully embedded in my psyche is this one: "Jesus is calling us from the future to the future." While many great minds have used the term *futurology*, the quintessential

futurologist is none other than Jesus, the incarnate Logos, the Word made
flesh, "the Alpha and the Omega" who declares "the end from the beginning."[8]

All creation is moving toward the glorious future goal that St. Paul calls
"the summing up of all things in Christ."[9] He is creation's *telos*.[10] Whatever
fundamental shifts and cycles of history occur, all things are shaken by the
Voice that declares all things future.[11] Christ the Ultimate Judge has been
appointed and ordained by the Father. He is *the* Horizon: our way and our
destination.[12]

Our capacity to anticipate, expect, and intentionally move toward the
future is woven into the fabric of our humanness by the Creator, "who gives
life to the dead and calls into being that which does not exist."[13]

Creation's groans and convulsions are its travailing,[14] a sort of birthing
prayer that causes tectonic-plate shifts and volcanic eruptions. We groan
deeply within our own hearts and minds,[15] precisely because we don't know
all there is to know but are groping to see beyond the fires raging around
us to the bright future God has promised.

We aren't deserted in this groaning; nor are our frustrations and travails
random. The Creator has subjected the planet to them, not in desertion
but in hope.[16] The Spirit, who is from the Father, helps our weaknesses as
he wordlessly groans within us and pushes our prayers into the very throne
room of grace.[17] Through that Spirit, the Father searches the depths of the
tectonic plates, cracks, and fault lines within our humanity, and the Son
intercedes through us for what he wants to happen in us, through us, and
for us.

By the Spirit in us, the Son is praying for that which is possible in
heaven and seemingly impossible on earth. More is possible than is probable. Yet within the scope of true prayer, there is the preferable—what really
wants to happen. We can try to control every outcome and engineer a sense
of certainty, but we can only "succeed" by reducing God and ourselves to
the mundane and predictable, so that the mystery of faith is no longer
relevant, being replaced by techniques and how-to's.

The prospect is both dehumanizing and demonic.

Rings of Fire has presented us with metaphors to enter. These metaphors
can shift the deeply held but inaccurate mental models that dictate to us
how the world works and restrict us to the recurring patterns that further
alienate us. The metaphors of possible and preferable futures—and even
wild card futures—overcome that which is predictable by invoking the
mystery of faith. Such metaphors have the power to shift our false and

jaded conspiracy theories and uproot the systems and schemas that tell us we have it all figured out.

Instead, we will be gripped by compelling questions on a glorious quest for God's dream, which seems as impossible to us as Don Quixote's dream of Dulcinea's transformation from prostitute to queen. We have not all sold ourselves short and prostituted his glorious image in us for what is convenient. We have not all forgotten that we are destined for the regal beauty of the *totus Christus*, the bride of Christ adorned to meet the Bridegroom at an hour we cannot predict. We seek to emulate not the foolish virgins who missed the future when it arrived but the wise virgins who waited expectantly with oil in their lamps because they were rooted in a promise and the full assurance of faith, ready for any eventuality.[18]

Though our faith is tried by fire, it is refining us as pure gold and preparing us for a great feast with our Bridegroom, in whom "we live and move and have our being."[19] He is continually bringing the future into the present for those who cry out, "Even so, come, Lord Jesus!"[20]

Let every question raised in this tome lead you on a glorious quest. Live with the questions long enough, and you just might bump—accidentally on purpose—into some answers!

Acknowledgments

The changes that have occurred in my lifetime have been hard to keep track of, much less keep up with or stay ahead of. Unless you live happily in the retirement subdivision of *Animal Farm* or have found refuge in a nostalgic bubble of retromania or retrotopia, you are transitioning less into an era of change than into a change of era, whether you're talking about laws or lawns.

One of the hardest parts of this book to write was the requiem on the American Dream. The degradation of that dream is apparent not just in our public schools, physical environment, and social inequality but is also inescapably present in the homeless who stake their claims to the sidewalks of our greatest cities. A special thanks to a unique manna-mañana prophet in our midst, colleague and friend Dr. Daniel Daves. From his prototype farm in Panama, he both confirms my fears about the prospect of erupting volcanoes (not just the metaphorical kind) and my hopes about lava-rich soil being the best soil on which to build a hazy, ashen future. I wish I had already read his upcoming book on the *Global Food Revolution* (2019) for the writing of *Rings of Fire*.

It is indisputable that the faith of our fathers and mothers, the church I write about in *Mother Tongue* (2017), is close to extinction. A whole new way of following Jesus is being born, some of it better and quite exciting, some of it worrisome. If Paul were to show up in one of our churches today, I think we would get more than a letter. Like every other arena of life, religion now is a cavalcade of matchless hope with unimagined possibilities, alongside follies, falsehoods, false claims, and fake everything. Simply

259

turning the pages of a daily newspaper or opening the weekly *Economist* is like tripping a bomb.

My family has borne the brunt of living in that blast radius. Elizabeth Rennie has hazarded the front lines for thirty years and has always been there to shame me out of my foxholes and critique my advance from atom-scapes (*Quantum Spirituality*) to landscapes (*FaithQuakes*) to waterscapes (*AquaChurch, SoulTsunami*, and *The Church of the Perfect Storm*) to moun-tainscapes (*Rings of Fire*).

My greatest joys in life have come from being a father to our three kids—Thane, Soren, and Egil—and now their spouses: Margaret ("Maggie") Mauer Sweet, Daniel Briggs, and Hollie Johnson Sweet, who know all my waysides, waywardness, holloways, and hiding places. I trust the six of them to keep my secrets and to keep advancing. I thank them for never indulging my "Cassandra pity parties," named after a mythological Greek princess Apollo punished by making no one believe her prophetic forecasts would come true.

You don't need set routines and fixed schedules for writing. You don't need seclusion and the absented life to be a writer. What you do need is people who love you and defend you and support your ravenous appetite for research and reading, whether books, goods, or looks. Irish historian Hugh Jackson Lawlor (1860–1938), who taught at Trinity College Dublin, instructed his divinity students to read at least six hours a day. A century earlier, John Wesley insisted on no less than five hours a day of "reading" for his lieutenants. My library is lugubrious with all media forms of audio, video, print, and internet—books, magazines, movies, YouTube, radio, TV, web, and so on, many of which were recommended by my friends Landrum Leavell, Jesse Caldwell, David Wahlstedt, and colleagues in the eighteen (so far) cohorts in the semiotics, church, and culture (SCC) doctoral program at Portland Seminary of George Fox University. My literary agent, Mark Sweeney, believed in this book even when I lost the nerve. My editor, David Zimmerman, has shown heroic restraint on an author who believes, along with one of the greatest living stylists of our era, screenwriter Frederic Raphael, that "grammatical niceties are a form of nostalgia."[1]

The 1991 eruption of Mount Pinatubo spewed so much ash and sul-fur dioxide that it blocked enough sunlight to briefly lower world tem-peratures. This future prospect became a personal present during the final twelve months of writing and editing *Rings of Fire*. The fallout of dust has been blinding—tears from the deaths of three canine family members (Yuki, Haiku, and Saami) and a life-threatening family illness, as well as the pixie dust from the weddings of all three of our children, two of whom wed their literal "one and onlys," their one-and-done dream mates.

I could not have walked these mountains and valleys without the prayerful abidance of friends James Davis, Ken Ulmer, Jules and Peg Glanzer, Melinda Smith, Eric Peterson (who himself lost both his father and mother during this time), Ken and Arlene Dove, Joanna Reynolds, Karen Louise Palmbaum Claassen, and my Drew University colleague Gary Simpson, himself a pastor to preachers (who too often are pastorless).

My Salvation Army family, in which I include Klon Kitchen, were stalwarts of support and bulwarks of blessing. Debra and William Mockabee of the USA Southern Territory took me under their pastoral wings, sent me periodic prayer lifts to keep me going, and enlisted members of the corps to remember me during this time. I consider all The Salvation Army as my extended family. My preacher-mom, Mabel Boggs Sweet, always said that the true Wesleyans today were found serving in The Salvation Army, and she often took my brothers, John and Phil, and I to Salvationist meetings. I'm proud to be a self-avowed if silent member of the tribe.

A grant from the Windgate Foundation enabled me to teach doctoral students interested in New Reformation semiotics and post-critical studies at five universities while continuing to speak and write. Only the trust and confidence of Dede Hutcheson of Fort Smith, Arkansas, put this on the horizon, and the tireless efforts of Anne Mathews-Younce (to whom I dedicated *The Bad Habits of Jesus*) and Jennifer Tyler of the E. Stanley Jones Foundation made this a reality. My dedicated travel agent Ginny O'Neal deserves a yearly bonus and daily blessing just by having me as a client.

This book would not have been possible without the prodding, protection, and patronage of my colleague, contributor, and friend Dr. Mark Chironna. When I worried that the book was turning into a five-hundred-page anxiety attack, he reminded me that the twentieth anniversary of *SoulTsunami* was a "seminal moment" for a new semiotic slant on the *Zeitgeist* ("spirit of the times") and the *Heilige Geist* ("Holy Spirit"). After all, Emily Dickinson's "certain Slant of light" inflicts a "Heavenly Hurt" as it works its revelatory internal changes on the mind and soul of the one who encounters it at the seminal moment.[2] Mark's fearless spearheading of the Issachar Initiative and Institute and his creation of the new Issachar Publishing House kept my own feet to the lava-and-magma fire. I owe him great debt for his multiple contributions to this book, to my ministry, and, most importantly, to my life during the writing of this book.

No one has reached out to me with more consistency and compassion than Mark. I dedicate this book to him with deep affection and gratitude.

It's said that the Beatles' first visit to the United States was met with panic at Tin Pan Alley: "These boys are geniuses," one songwriter supposedly lamented. "They're going to ruin everything." This is what the Pharisees said when Jesus arrived on the scene. They were right. In Mark Chironna, I have found a friend who sticks closer than a brother on The Jesus Way, the way that "ruins" the world as we know it by giving us a better way—the way of simple gifts and narrow paths, higher ground and lowered knees, upper rooms and downward heavens.

Leonard Sweet
Father's Day 2019
Dolphin Cay, Orcas Island

Notes

PREFACE

1. This is especially true of the San Andreas Fault zone.
2. Alexis de Tocqueville, quoted in David Ohana, *The Intellectual Origins of Modernity* (New York: Routledge, 2019), 80–82.
3. See 1 Chronicles 12:32.
4. See Roger Scruton, *On Hunting* (South Bend, IN: St. Augustine's Press, 2001), 155. Scruton is right on about the past while missing the mark about the future, at least in the church: "Nostalgia is an unhealthy state of mind. But the study, love and emulation of the past are necessary to our self-understanding. All that has gone most wrong in our century has proceeded from a morbid obsession with the future—a belief in 'new dawns', 'revolutionary transformations', and resurrected nations on the march. The past, unlike the future, can be known, understood and adapted to our current uses. When we cast ourselves free from it, we are swept away by outside forces, adrift on the oceanic tide of happening. The future, which we cannot describe, begins to seem inevitable. This surrender to the unknown persists, despite all the crime and destruction that have been wrought in its name."
5. Gregory Boyle, *Barking to the Choir: The Power of Radical Kinship* (New York: Simon & Schuster, 2017), 117–18.
6. Borrowed from Roger Stronstad and J. Deotis Roberts, *The Prophethood of All Believers: A Study in Luke's Charismatic Theology* (Cleveland, TN: CPT Press, 2010).
7. William Blake, *Letters from William Blake to Thomas Butts, 1800–1803* (Oxford: Clarendon, 1926).
8. Bill Emmott, *The Fate of the West: The Battle to Save the World's Most Successful Political Idea* (London: Profile Books, 2017), 207.
9. See Hosea 1.
10. Some scholars believe a volcanic eruption led to Icelandic Vikings leaving paganism and becoming Christian. For the metaphor "walking on lava," see The Dark Mountain Project, *Walking on Lava: Selected Works for Uncivilised Times*, eds. Charlotte Du Cann, Dougald Hine, Nick Hunt, and Paul Kingsnorth (White River Junction, VT: Chelsea Green, 2017).
11. Toni Morrison, *Beloved* (New York: Knopf, 1987), 255.
12. Revelation 22:20, NKJV.
13. Ephesians 5:14.

INTRODUCTION

1. Culture is a constricting complex of values, concepts, and ideas imposed on the individual in the interests of uniformity. But culture can also be a creative framework for unlimited human potential if it is constantly filtered through a biblical mesh of thought and expression.
2. For this countercultural view, see Terence McKenna's lecture "Culture Is Not Your Friend," video, 6:05, posted by AMP3083, July 24, 2015, https://www.youtube.com/watch?v=OdUCa5TrC9Q: "Culture is for other people's convenience and the convenience of various institutions, churches, companies, tax collection schemes, and what have you. It is not your friend. It insults you, it disempowers you, it uses and abuses you."
3. See Acts 17:26.
4. Esther 4:14.
5. Cambridge University historian Eamon Duffy is (we think) the source of the "angle" metaphor, but we don't know where he said it.
6. See Matthew 4:19.

7. Rebecca Leung, "'Star Wars' Goes to Hell: George Lucas Talks about 'Dark, Emotional' Finale," interview by Lesley Stahl, *60 Minutes*, March 10, 2005, https://www.cbsnews.com/news/star-wars-goes-to-hell/. Read this transcript and pretend it's about church leadership.

8. Stephen Witt, *How Music Got Free: The End of an Industry, the Turn of the Century, and the Patient Zero of Piracy* (New York: Viking, 2015), 130.

9. Ian Mortimer, *Centuries of Change: Which Century Saw the Most Change and Why It Matters to Us* (London: Bodley Head, 2014).

10. Tim Urban, "The AI Revolution: The Road to Superintelligence," Wait But Why, January 22, 2015, https://waitbutwhy.com/2015/01/artificial-intelligence-revolution-1.html.

11. Mortimer, *Centuries of Change*.

12. Steven Pinker, *Enlightenment Now: The Case for Reason, Science, Humanism and Progress* (New York: Viking, 2018), 323.

13. Steven Pinker, *The Better Angels of Our Nature: Why Violence Has Declined* (New York: Viking, 2011).

14. Justin Welby, *Dethroning Mammon: Making Money Serve Grace* (London: Bloomsbury Continuum, 2016), chap. 6, e-book. Even though some degrees of inequality are built into free enterprise, the argument goes, it is better than state intervention in economic affairs leaving the masses breadless.

15. Goldman Sachs estimate. See Matt Jancer, "The Transformer of Autonomous Farmbots Can Do 100 Jobs on Its Own," *Wired*, March 2018, 20.

16. Most have argued that this global lift out of poverty is because of global trade, technological innovation, and capitalism, although not everyone agrees.

17. For example, in England you can't buy a banana at the supermarket chain Sainsbury's without a fair trade designation.

18. "The Death Penalty in 2016: Facts and Figures," Amnesty International, April 11, 2017, https://www.amnesty.org/en/latest/news/2017/04/death-penalty-2016-facts-and-figures/.

19. The best critique of Pinker is John Gray's "Unenlightened Thinking: Steven Pinker's Embarrassing New Book Is a Feeble Sermon for Rattled Liberals," *New Statesman*, February 22, 2018.

20. For the nightmares of atheism, see Aurel Kolnai's classic *The War against the West* (London: Victor Gollancz, 1938)—sheer genius, each page written in a Vienna café, and Nazism is presented as a neopagan movement that aimed to destroy the Christian West. The best book from a Christian perspective on atheism today is David Bentley Hart, *Atheist Delusions: The Christian Revolution and Its Fashionable Enemies* (New Haven: Yale University Press, 2009).

21. Amos Tversky and Daniel Kahneman, "Availability: A Heuristic for Judging Frequency and Probability," *Cognitive Psychology* 5, no. 2 (September 1973): 207–32.

22. See Tim Dee, ed., *Ground Work: Writings on People and Places* (London: Jonathan Cape, 2018), for an example of pessimism among distinguished writers and academics.

23. Mark 8:36.

24. Luke 12:15.

25. This is the secret behind the success of David Borgenicht et al., The Worst-Case Scenario Survival Handbook series (San Francisco: Chronicle, 1999–2019).

26. René Girard, *When These Things Begin: Conversations with Michel Treguer*, trans. Trevor Cribben Merrill (East Lansing: Michigan State University Press, 2014).

27. Girard, *When These Things Begin*, 88.

28. As Gustave Flaubert said at the time of the Franco-Prussian war, "When this is over we shall still be stupid."

29. Umberto Eco, *Inventing the Enemy and Other Occasional Writings*, trans. Richard Dixon (Boston: Houghton Mifflin Harcourt, 2012).

30. See Albert Hirschman's classic *The Rhetoric of Reaction: Perversity, Futility, Jeopardy* (Cambridge, MA: Belknap, 1991).

31. Tony Wright, "Reform! The Fight for the 1832 Reform Act by Edward Pearce," *Independent*, January 26, 2004, https://www.independent.co.uk/arts-entertainment/books/reviews/reform-the-fight-for-the-1832-reform-act-by-edward-pearce-75392.html.

1—HOSTILE CULTURE

1. "21 Books You Don't Have to Read," *GQ*, April 19, 2018, https://www.gq.com/story/21-books-you-dont-have-to-read. Jesse Ball wrote the entry about the Bible.

2. Acts 3:13, DRA.

3. One of the few charities to support persecuted Christians is the Catholic charity Aid to the Church in Need.

4. See Hebrews 12:1.

5. See "The Second Moment of Creation," *Civilisations*, directed by Tim Niel, written and presented by Simon Schama, aired March 1, 2018, on PBS. This story is told in this first episode of the update of Kenneth Clark's 1969 television series, *Civilisation*.

6. Francis Robinson, "Present Shadows, Past Glory: Islamic Responses to Centuries of Western Power," *Times Literary Supplement*, September 6, 2002, 14.

7. Nassim Nicholas Taleb, *Antifragile: Things That Gain from Disorder* (New York: Random House, 2012).

8. Luke 6:22-23.

9. See Isaiah 5:26; Zechariah 10:8.

10. David Bentley Hart, *The New Testament: A Translation* (New Haven: Yale University Press, 2017).

11. Matthew 3:2, NKJV.

12. Pope John Paul II made repeated apologies on behalf of the church as an institution, and Benedict XVI apologized to Irish victims of clerical abuse. In April 2018, Francis apologized to Chilean sexual abuse survivors, not on behalf of the church, but personally, because of his failure to take their claims seriously enough. The point is, everyone now needs to learn to apologize, even the pope.

13. For the losses in the Church of England and the Church of Scotland, see Ian Bradley, "The Strange Death of Protestant Britain: The Near-Loss of Religious Sensibilities," *Tablet*, December 13, 2017.

14. "Reformation: A Time of Renewal and Division," Anglican Community News Service, January 19, 2017, https://www.anglicannews.org/blogs/2017/01/reformation-a-time-of-renewal-and-division.aspx. The archbishops suggested that Luther's 95 Theses were "both renewal and division." They praised it for its "clear proclamation of the gospel of grace" but regretted "the lasting damage done five centuries ago to the unity of the Church."

15. Mark 1:15, NKJV.

16. Acts 2:38.

17. Acts 17:30.

18. See Leonard Sweet, *I Am a Follower: The Way, Truth, and Life of Following Jesus* (Nashville: Thomas Nelson, 2012).

19. Augustine of Hippo, "Sermon 32 on the New Testament," *Nicene and Post-Nicene Fathers*, First Series, vol. 6, ed. Philip Schaff, trans. R. G. MacMullen. Revised and edited by Kevin Knight, New Advent, accessed June 21, 2019, http://www.newadvent.org/fathers/160332.htm.

20. Romans 2:4, NKJV.

21. William Temple, quoted in L. William Countryman, *Forgiven and Forgiving* (Harrisburg, PA: Morehouse, 1998), 2.

22. C. S. Lewis, *Mere Christianity*, rev. ed. (New York: HarperCollins, 2001), 56–57.

23. Jeremiah 31:17, NKJV.

24. See Susan Owens, *The Ghost: A Cultural History* (London: Tate, 2017).

25. See Tim Shah and Tom Farr, "Defending Religion in the Public Square," *New York Times*, December 27, 2011, https://www.nytimes.com/roomfordebate/2011/12/22 /is-americans-religious-freedom-under-threat/defending-religion-in-the-public-square.

26. I know this firsthand, since I am married to a person who was brought up in just such a pagan household.

27. The interview took place in 1776 and is recounted in Peter Gay, "A Passion for Liberty," review of *Enlightenment: Britain and the Creation of the Modern World*, by Roy Porter, *Times Literary Supplement*, October 6, 2000, https://www.the-tls.co.uk/articles/private/a-passion-for-liberty/.

28. See Bernadette Kehoe, "Cardinal Rejects Accusation that Faith Schools Are Socially Divisive," *Tablet*, April 7, 2018, 29.

29. *Pakistan* literally means the "land of the pure [Muslim]."

30. Tom Heneghan, "French Parliament Bans 'Conspicuous Religious Signs," *Tablet*, January 30, 2018, https://www.thetablet.co.uk/news/8477/french-parliament-bans-conspicuous-religious-signs-.

31. John Molyneux, "More Than Opium: Marxism and Religion," *International Socialism* 2, no. 119 (Summer 2008), https://www.marxists.org/history/etol/writers/molyneux/2008/xx/religion.html.

32. For illiberal liberalism and a new Puritanism, see John Gray, "The Problem of Hyper-Liberalism," *Times Literary Supplement*, March 27, 2018, https://www.the-tls.co.uk/articles/public/john-gray-hyper-liberalism -liberty/.

33. Elizabeth Pisani, *Indonesia, Etc.: Exploring the Improbable Nation* (New York: Norton, 2014).

34. Matthew 10:8.

35. 1 Chronicles 29:14, NKJV.

36. Rowan Williams, quoted by Telegraph View, "Wise Words from Rowan Williams on Christianity in

Britain," *Telegraph*, April 27, 2014, https://www.telegraph.co.uk/news/religion/10789477/Wise-words -from-Rowan-Williamson-on-Christianity-in-Britain.html.

37. Matthew Parris, "Millions of Us Honestly Don't Know What Our Duty Is to Migrants—and Christianity Doesn't Help," *Spectator*, September 5, 2015, https://www.spectator.co.uk/2015/09/millions-of-us-honestly -dont-know-what-our-duty-is-to-migrants-and-christianity-doesnt-help/. Alister McGrath has also made the case that Western culture is living off the borrowed moral capital of a religion it rejected, in his *Why God Won't Go Away: Engaging with the New Atheism* (Nashville: Nelson, 2011), and *The Big Question: Why We Can't Stop Talking about Science, Faith, and God* (New York: St. Martin's Press, 2015). See also Larry Siedentop, *Inventing the Individual: The Origins of Western Liberalism* (Cambridge, MA: Belknap, 2017).

38. This sentence serves as the title of a chapter in Dominic Erdozain, *The Soul of Doubt: The Religious Roots of Unbelief from Luther to Marx* (Oxford: Oxford University Press, 2016).

39. Sebastian Castellio, quoted in Stanford Rives, *Did Calvin Murder Servetus?* (North Charleston, SC: Booksurge, 2008), 344.

40. Mark 16:15.

41. See Matthew 13:1-23; Mark 4:1-20; Luke 8:4-15.

42. In April 2018, Facebook banned a Franciscan ad showing Jesus on the cross because it was "shocking and excessively violent."

43. Edwin Hanton Robertson, *Bishop of the Resistance: A Life of Eivind Berggrav, Bishop of Oslo, Norway* (St. Louis: Concordia, 2000).

44. Lisa Cron, *Wired for Story: The Writer's Guide to Using Brain Science to Hook Readers from the Very First Sentence* (New York: Ten Speed, 2012), 6.

HOT TAKE—PEDAGOGICAL AND ANDROPOLOGICAL REVOLUTIONS

1. Chloe Pfeiffer, "Vietnam's Students Perform Mysteriously Well on Tests, and Researchers Have Figured Out Why," Business Insider, July 14, 2016.

2. You shalt have no other subject higher than the student. You shalt treat students as subjects, not objects— more as apples than oranges: wholes to respect, not assemblages to be taken apart—as whole-brained humans, not left-brained lobes with right-brained lobotomies. When you are educated in parts, is it any wonder that the different parts of our lives do not fit together? Corollary to Commandment 1: Thou shalt kill the industrial "classroom," where big-jug, little-mug/lecture-drill-test methods of instruction have reigned for far too long. The separation of the learning environment from the living and working environment must be ended. The classroom metaphor carries too much baggage: test anxiety and so on. Delivery mechanisms have become destinations. Thou shalt only conduct "courses," a journey metaphor: Like a river takes its "course" by meandering and changing direction depending on what it encounters on the journey, so is learning a pilgrimage. The ultimate classroom is the world, the universe, so education in the future will take place not in centralized houses of learning and other formal educational settings, but in decentralized sites and natural environments where peer-to-peer learning is a primary driver. The student-student relationship is now as important as the teacher-student relationship. Teach the student, not the book. If you end a "course" where the syllabus says you should end, it will have been a "class," not a "course." Each student should shape the direction of the "course." Likewise, the concept of a "major" is outdated for a liberal arts education. The question is not "What's your major?" but "What's your mission?" The industrial model of gardening of hearts has more often led to the hardening of hearts. Nothing in life comes straight or cut-and-dried—not even cut-and-dried flowers. *(There is spaghetti, but it's not ready until you cook it and add sauce!)*

3. Thou shalt not make for yourself graven images of any technology, nor bow down to any tablet, whether print or digital, nor worship any culture, whether Gutenberg or Google. Thou shalt learn to speak and communicate in the language of the culture in which you serve. There are worlds of knowledge that transcend cultures (such as various languages or basic math). But like the gospel, these mean nothing to real people without incarnation within their own distinct cultures. New technologies don't replace old technologies; they just reinvent them. Soon all our bills will be delivered electronically, which means that we will shortly talk nostalgically about the mail carrier the way we talked nostalgically about the milkman who came by every morning to drop some bottles in the milk box. One media form does not give way right away to another media form. Latin did not give way to the vernacular languages without a fight. Even the first sermons delivered to the laity in English were recorded in Latin, and some sermons were delivered with Latin and English alternating with great rapidity, even in single sentences.

4. Thou shalt not take the name of your profession in vain. Thou shalt not teach. Thou shalt organize learning instead. This means that just as the book was the primary delivery system for learning and human development in the Gutenberg era, the web is the primary delivery system for learning and human

development in the TGIF (Twitter-Google-Instagram-Facebook) era. Stop the fetishizing of books or writing. Writing is just a technology. Why do we require "papers"? Reading is not conversation. The web, not the book, is the delivery system for education now: low-residency but high-relationship, heavily immersive, and intensive face-to-face studies. The notion that you learn by sitting in a chair for a couple of hours a week for thirteen weeks while someone encases themselves in chalk will go down in history as one of the worst pedagogical methods ever invented. A two-day intensive "advance" (Christians don't "retreat") has more face-to-face time than a semester course. "Classroom" learning gives way to 3-D online learning (preferably in cohorts) and almost monastic learning advances where the students do everything together (eat, play, worship, study, learn) for short periods of time. Students don't need authority figures for access to information in a TGIF world. But they need authority figures more than ever to process and assess the information they're accessing. Faculty are less "instructors" or "lecturers" than enchanters, mentors, and coaches. In a coaching approach to learning, who you study with will be more important than where you studied. There will be a decoupling of credentialing and learning: The mentor relationship will surpass the diploma as the ultimate and preferred credential among employers and everyone else. Nevertheless, *blended* is a metaphor we don't like or use. Here is the most-used definition of *blended learning*: "A blended learning approach combines face to face classroom methods with computer-mediated activities to form an integrated instructional approach. For example, a blended approach to a traditional, face to face course might mean that the class meets once per week instead of the usual three-session format. Learning activities that otherwise would have taken place during classroom time can be moved online" ("Blended Learning," ICT Tutor Support, accessed July 17, 2019, https://www.educatorstechnology.com/2016/10/here-is-good -visual-on-blended-learning.html). But if you're doing the same thing face-to-face as you've already done, and only doing online what you've done in the classroom, then it's a double disaster waiting to happen. The University of Phoenix is the dinosaur empire as well as the evil empire.

5. Remember the sandbox, where learning is fun. Keep the playground holy. We don't know which is more important or harder: to learn to play or to play to learn. If it's too much work, it's not learning. Turn classrooms into playgrounds or "play stations." The gamification of education will be one of the cottage industries of the future. As I wrote in *The Well-Played Life: Why Pleasing God Doesn't Have to Be Such Hard Work*, "Play is oxygen for the imagination, which sparks creativity, which ignites innovation, which combusts in paradigm shifts" (Carol Stream, IL: Tyndale Momentum, 2014), 6. Anthony de Mello's *Awakening: Conversations with the Masters* puts it a little differently: "The aim of spirituality . . . is to make all life play. . . . Work becomes spiritual only when it is transformed into play" (New York: Doubleday, 2003), 110.

6. There are two corollaries to Commandment 6: First, change has changed; change is no longer incremental but exponential. Second, learn a living over a lifetime: Lifelong learning is not optional. For AI processors, see "Hyenas and Cheetahs: Artificial Intelligence Is Awakening the Chip Industry's Animal Spirits," *Economist*, June 9, 2018, 54–56.

7. There are many out there who say that the Massive Open Online Course is the right paradigm for the future. This free, high-quality online education appears to democratize knowledge and was pioneered by MIT, Stanford, Harvard, and TED. More than fifty highly rated US colleges are piloting free online non-course-credit educational learning. MOOCs are different from blended programs like The University of Phoenix, DeVry, and others. But both are straitjacketing education. There are two corollaries to this commandment: First, thou shalt not commit to a general (universal) before committing to a local (artisanal, provincial, parochial, particular). Second, the Well Curve replaces the Bell Curve as the "normal distribution system." For an elaboration of the difference between a Bell Curve World and a Well Curve World, see Leonard Sweet, *Carpe Mañana: Is Your Church Ready to Seize Tomorrow?* (Grand Rapids, MI: Zondervan, 2001). Also see see my predictions about today's world in *SoulTsunami: Sink or Swim in New Millennium Culture* (Grand Rapids, MI: Zondervan, 1999).

8. Matthew 10:14.

2—DEVOLUTION REVOLUTIONS AND THE COLLAPSE OF NATION-STATES

1. Denis O'Donoghue, *Brendaniana: St. Brendan the Voyager in Story and Legend* (Dublin: Browne & Nolan, 1895), 162. Whether this was on Iceland or the Azores remains a matter of debate.

2. One of the earliest recorded usages of the word *state* was from the late 1530s, coming from the English political theorist Thomas Starkey (ca. 1495–1538).

3. Winthrop S. Hudson, "Denominationalism as a Basis for Ecumenicity: A Seventeenth Century Conception," *Church History* 24, no. 1 (March 1955): 32–50.

4. Thomas L. Friedman, *The World Is Flat: A Brief History of the Twenty-First Century* (New York: Farrar, Straus and Giroux, 2005).

5. Graeme Wearden, "My Goodness: Nigeria Overtakes Ireland in Guinness Sales," *Guardian*, August 30, 2007, https://www.theguardian.com/business/2007/aug/30/9.

6. John Maynard Keynes, *A Tract on Monetary Reform* (London: Macmillan, 1923), 80.

7. See also Albert Einstein, "What Life Means to Einstein: An Interview by George Sylvester Viereck," *Saturday Evening Post* (October 1929). The German poet Viereck later became a pro-Nazi propagandist. Viereck: "Do you look upon yourself as a German or as a Jew?" Einstein: "It is quite possible to be both. I look upon myself as a man. Nationalism is an infantile disease. It is the measles of mankind." The exact quotation in the original language has not been preserved. Einstein echoes his words in "My Credo," adding, "I am against any nationalism, even in the guise of mere patriotism. Privileges based on position and property have always seemed to me unjust and pernicious, as did any exaggerated personality cult." Albert Einstein, "My Credo" (speech to the German League of Human Rights in Berlin, Autumn 1932).

8. See paper by economists Gharad T. Bryan, James J. Choi, and Dean Karlan, "Randomizing Religion: The Impact of Protestant Evangelism on Economic Outcomes," National Bureau of Economic Research, February 2018, https://www.nber.org/papers/w24278.

9. Jean Tirole, *Economics for the Common Good*, trans. Steven Rendall (Princeton, NJ: Princeton University Press, 2017).

10. The collapse of the nation-state forces us to look afresh at neglected connections between continents and hidden continuities between periods.

11. M. Cherif Bassiouni, "Searching for Peace and Achieving Justice: The Need for Accountability," *Law and Contemporary Problems* 59, no. 4 (Fall 1996): 10.

12. The Syrian Civil War alone has resulted in more than 5 million refugees.

13. Alan Boyle, "#CalExit Gets Some Northwesterners Dreaming about Cascadia Region," GeekWire, November 15, 2016, https://www.geekwire.com/2016/northwest-cascadia-calexit/.

14. For more on this, see Göran Therborn, *Cities of Power: The Urban, the National, the Popular, and the Global* (New York: Verso, 2017). Also see Richard Schragger, *City Power: Urban Governance in a Global Age* (New York: Oxford University Press, 2016).

15. Whether water will put a brake on this city-state expansion is a question to keep in mind.

16. Philip R. Berke, "Catastrophe," in *The Encyclopedia of Urban Studies*, vol. 1, ed. Ray Hutchison (Thousand Oaks, CA: SAGE, 2010), 120.

17. Four major civilizational streams are found in Singapore: Chinese, Indian, Islamic, and Western.

18. Brookings Institution Metropolitan Policy Program, as referenced in William A. Galston, "Why Cities Boom While Towns Struggle," *Wall Street Journal*, March 14, 2018, A15.

19. See Don Peck, *Pinched: How the Great Recession Has Narrowed Our Futures & What We Can Do about It* (New York: Crown, 2011).

20. Few quotes have been as misinterpreted as this one. See Matt Werner, "Gertrude Stein's Oakland," HuffPost, updated December 6, 2017, https://www.huffpost.com/entry/oakland-in-popular -memory_b_1560227. Or for the original nostalgic context, see page 298 of Stein's *Everybody's Autobiography* (New York: Random House, 1937).

21. Jonathan Taplin, *Move Fast and Break Things: How Facebook, Google, and Amazon Cornered Culture and Undermined Democracy* (New York: Little, Brown, 2017). See also Samuel Earle, "Vatican 2.0," *Times Literary Supplement*, November 14, 2017, https://www.the-tls.co.uk/articles/public/technology-companies -facebook-god-earle/.

22. Sergey Brin, quoted at James B. Rule, "The Search Engine, for Better or for Worse," *New York Times*, March 18, 2013, https://www.nytimes.com/2013/03/19/opinion/global/the-search-engine-for-better-or-for-worse.html.

23. Thomas Frey, "Owning Your Own Country," Futurist Speaker, November 26, 2008, https://futuristspeaker.com/business-trends/owning-your-own-country/.

24. Ulrich Beck's most famous book is *Ecological Politics in an Age of Risk*, trans. Amos Weisz (Malden, MA: Polity, 1995).

25. See Pierre Manent, "Repurposing Europe," *First Things*, April 2016, https://www.firstthings.com/article/2016/04/repurposing-europe.

HOT TAKE—GLOBAL REFUGEES AND MIGRANTS

1. Raul Hilberg, *Perpetrators, Victims, Bystanders: The Jewish Catastrophe, 1933–1945* (New York: Aaron Asher, 1992). Note that online searches usually reveal one. Numbers vary because recorded lists vary per jewishgen.org.

2. See Dave Smith, *Refugee Stories: Seven Personal Journeys behind the Headlines* (Herts, UK: Instant Apostle, 2016) for the voices of the refugees themselves.

3. Phillip Connor, "International Migration: Key Findings from the U.S., Europe and the World," Pew Research Center Fact Tank, December 15, 2016, http://www.pewresearch.org/fact-tank/2016/12/15 /international-migration-key-findings-from-the-u-s-europe-and-the-world/.

4. Tom Heneghan, "Christians in Western Europe 'More Likely to Be Anti-Immigrant,'" *Tablet*, June 7, 2018, https://www.thetablet.co.uk/news/9208/christians-in-western-europe-more-likely-to-be-anti-immigrant-.

5. Slavoj Žižek, *Against the Double Blackmail: Refugees, Terror and Other Troubles with the Neighbours* (London: Allen Lane, 2016).

6. Ambrose, "Letter 18," *Nicene and Post-Nicene Fathers*, Second Series, vol. 10, ed. Philip Schaff and Henry Wace, trans. H. de Romestin, E. de Romestin, and H. T. F. Duckworth. Revised and edited by Kevin Knight, New Advent, accessed June 22, 2019, http://www.newadvent.org/fathers/340918.htm.

7. Caitríona O'Reilly, *Geis* (Hexham, UK: Bloodaxe, 2015), 46.

8. This is the phrase of Peter J. Hoffman and Thomas G. Weiss, *Humanitarianism, War, and Politics: Solferino to Syria and Beyond* (Lanham, MD: Rowman & Littlefield, 2017), 271–72.

9. See Galatians 2:11-13.

3—CHINAFICATION

1. "Christianity in China," Council on Foreign Relations, last updated October 11, 2018, https://www.cfr.org /backgrounder/christianity-china.

2. "Christianity in China," Council on Foreign Relations. Christians will still only form under 5 percent of the Chinese population.

3. See Ian Johnson, *The Souls of China: The Return of Religion after Mao* (London: Allen Lane, 2017), 30-31.

4. For older figures, see Lian Xi, *Redeemed by Fire: The Rise of Popular Christianity in Modern China* (New Haven: Yale University Press, 2010) and Vincent Goossaert and David A. Palmer, *The Religious Question in Modern China* (Chicago: University of Chicago Press, 2012). In Bryan T. Froehle and Mary L. Gautier, *Global Catholicism: Portrait of a World Church* (Maryknoll, NY: Orbis, 2003), the number of Catholics in mainland China is put at 7.5 million.

5. He was also chairman of the Central Military Commission from 1989 to 2004 and president of the People's Republic of China from 1993 to 2003. The quote is found in Lamin Sanneh, "Religion's Return," *Times Literary Supplement*, October 13, 2006, https://www.the-tls.co.uk/articles/private/religions-return/.

6. "The Pope and China May Be Close to a Deal on Appointing Bishops," *Economist*, April 28, 2018, 42.

7. Simon Scott Plummer, "St. Peter and the Dragon: What's in a China-Vatican Deal for Beijing?" *Tablet*, March 10, 2018, 12.

8. Imagine the surprise of the medieval papacy when it realized that the Chinese-invented paper used in its transactions all came from the Muslim world and was stamped "Allah is great."

9. The Starbucks is in the wall at Badaling, forty-seven miles north of Beijing.

10. Eliot Weinberger, "Diary," *London Review of Books* 27, no. 18, September 22, 2005, 34.

11. According to the latest research statistics published by the US National Science Foundation, as reported in Jeff Tollefson, "China Declared World's Largest Producer of Scientific Articles," *Nature*, January 18, 2018, https://www.nature.com/articles/d41586-018-00927-4. China produced 18.6 percent of the world's published papers in science and engineering in 2016, up from 11 percent in 1988. The US share of papers slipped from 38 percent to 18 percent during that same time.

12. Michael Schuman, "What If China Really Is Exempt from the Laws of Economics?" *Bloomberg Businessweek*, January 29, 2018, 64–65.

4—WORLD RELIGIONS, ESPECIALLY ISLAM

1. Malcolm Guite, *What Do Christians Believe? Belonging and Belief in Modern Christianity* (New York: Walker, 2008), 96.

2. Acts 17:23-24, NKJV.

3. Pope John Paul II, *Fides et Ratio*, September 14, 1998. "In India particularly, it is the duty of Christians now to draw from this rich heritage the elements compatible with their faith, in order to enrich Christian thought."

4. Mohandas Gandhi, quoted in Ramin Jahanbegloo, *The Global Gandhi: Essays in Comparative Political Philosophy* (New York: Routledge, 2018), 3.

5. See Matthew 8:10-13; Luke 17:18-19.

6. See John 4:22.

7. "Pray continually" (1 Thessalonians 5:17); "anxious for nothing" (Philippians 4:6, NKJV); "consider the lilies" (Matthew 6:28, NKJV).

8. For more on this, see historian Cemil Aydin's *The Idea of the Muslim World: A Global Intellectual History* (Boston: Harvard University Press, 2018).

9. The Shia minority of Islam amounts to between 10 and 15 percent of the world's Muslim population of 1.8 billion, making for an overall population of 200 million. The majority reside in Iran, Iraq, Pakistan, and India, along with a sizable minority in Saudi Arabia. See Pew Research Center, "Mapping the Global Muslim Population," October 7, 2009, https://www.pewforum.org/2009/10/07/mapping-the-global-muslim-population/.

10. See Leonard Sweet, *Me and We: God's New Social Gospel* (Nashville: Abingdon, 2014), for a Christian response to world domination by consumerism.

11. Mark Steyn, *America Alone: The End of the World as We Know It* (Washington, DC: Regnery, 2008), 79. "Islamism is now the ideology of choice for the world's grievance-mongers."

12. Michael Binyon, "Softly, Softly Is the Way to Reconciliation between the Catholic and Orthodox Churches," *Tablet*, July 7, 2018, 9. This eye-popping revival of the Orthodox Church in Russia since 1991 is by and large coming from cultural Christians and a new Russian civil religion, or from self-styled "Orthodox atheists."

13. Quoted in Steyn, *America Alone*, 35–36.

14. Some of the most rabid demonizations of Muslims can be found in the writings of the new atheists: See Christopher Hitchens, "Putting It Mildly," *God Is Not Great: How Religion Poisons Everything* (New York: Twelve, 2007), chap. 1. "I leave it to the faithful to burn each other's churches and mosques and synagogues, which they can always be relied upon to do."

15. Islam means "submission." Israel means "struggle." In Islam the "greater jihad" is the internal struggle for spiritual betterment; war against unbelievers is the "lesser jihad." There is an old Ottoman joke that the greater jihad is to make love to your wife. Only one (extremist) Muslim sect, the Kharijites, puts jihad among the pillars (*arkan*), or pivotal precepts, of Islam.

16. Lamin Sanneh, *Beyond Jihad: The Pacifist Tradition in West African Islam* (New York: Oxford University Press, 2016).

17. Islam isn't monolithic in its expression, and there have always been civil-religion equivalents. For example, even though alcohol was forbidden in Islamic culture, there were still Muslims who drank, especially the aristocracy. Robert Irwin, "Wines in the Koran," *Times Literary Supplement*, January 26, 2007, 3. Kaikakavus is a Persian prince from Gorgan in Muslim Iran, who wrote a guide on how aristocrats should act: "'Wine drinking is a transgression; if you wish to commit a transgression it should at least not be a flavorless one. If you drink wine, let it be the finest—so that even though you may be convicted of sin in the next world, you will at any rate not be branded a fool in this.' There is a rich body of wine poetry in Persian, as well as in Turkish and Arabic literature."

18. Surah 19.

19. George Sale (1697–1736), best known for his translation of the Koran into English, believed that the tenet of Mary being born free of original sin was borrowed from the Koran.

20. Bruce B. Lawrence, *The Koran in English: A Biography* (Princeton: Princeton University Press, 2017), 158.

21. Bernard Lewis, *Faith and Power: Religion and Politics in the Middle East* (Oxford: Oxford University Press, 2010).

22. Lewis, *Faith and Power*, 200.

23. Lewis, *Faith and Power*. "From the very beginning of Islam, from the lifetime of its founder, religion and the state are one and the same." Also see Mohsen Kadivar, "Freedom of Religion and Belief in Islam," in *The New Voices of Islam: Rethinking Politics and Modernity*, ed. Mehran Kamrava (Berkeley: University of California Press, 2006), 126. The reformist Iranian scholar Kadivar asserts that "most available interpretations of Islam do not welcome the freedom of religion and belief." A more correct interpretation of Scripture, he argues, accepts the principle of "no compulsion in religion" (see 2:256 in the Koran). Kadivar has been punished with eighteen months in an Iranian prison for his exegesis of Scripture, and many other reformists in Iran and elsewhere have suffered worse. But in Islam, that word—*reformist*—covers a wide swath.

24. Nigeria is twice the size of California, about 25 percent larger than the state of Texas. It is comprised of thirty-six states, twelve of which have now instituted Sharia law.

25. Hilaire Belloc, *The Great Heresies* (New York: Start Publishing, 2017), 42: "Islam was the one heresy that nearly destroyed Christendom through its early material and intellectual superiority."

26. Ziauddin Sardar, *Islam beyond the Violent Jihadis: An Optimistic Muslim Speaks* (London: Biteback, 2016), "What I Know," e-book.

27. Christie Watson, *The Language of Kindness: A Nurse's Story* (New York: Tim Duggan, 2018), chap. 1, Kindle.

28. As quoted in Zachary Lockman, *Contending Visions of the Middle East: The History and Politics of Orientalism* (Cambridge, UK: Cambridge University Press, 2010), 26.

29. William Johnston, *"Arise, My Love . . .": Mysticism for a New Era* (Maryknoll, NY: Orbis, 2000), 201.

30. See Bob Roberts Jr., *Lessons from the East: Finding the Future of Western Christianity in the Global Church* (Colorado Springs: David C Cook, 2016); Carl Medearis, *Muslims, Christians, and Jesus: Gaining Understandings and Building Relationships* (Minneapolis: Bethany House, 2008); and Carl Medearis, *Speaking of Jesus: The Art of Not-Evangelism* (Colorado Springs: David C Cook, 2011).

31. Thanks to Jonathan Wright, "Respectful Adversaries," *Tablet*, August 11, 2007, 20.

32. The prophet Muhammad mounted about seventy military expeditions against unbelievers during his rule in Medina, many of which he commanded himself. Jihad ideology focuses on the martial side of the prophet's life, and warfare against unbelievers, or "jihad in the name of God," is a theme prominent in the Koran and Sunna. There was no martial side to Jesus' life and mission. You can't be a follower of Jesus and be a terrorist. Can you be a follower of Muhammad and be a terrorist? That is a question Muslims must answer to other Muslims.

33. See John 1:38; 18:7.

5—THE PUBLIC SQUARE

1. Numbers 11:29, NKJV.

2. Islamism is the ideology that politics is an extension of faith.

3. Nick Spencer, *The Evolution of the West: How Christianity Has Shaped Our Values* (Louisville, KY: John Knox, 2018).

4. If truth is culturally constructed, then how does one oppose *suttee*, the convention of Indian wives throwing themselves on their husbands' funeral pyres? Or dowry murder, where wives are burned alive because their dowries weren't as large as expected? Or honor killings? The list is endless.

5. Thanks to Teri Hyrkas for this death-row insight.

6. Oliver Letwin, *The Purpose of Politics* (London: Social Market Foundation, 1999). See also Ruth Kelly, "Is Civilization the Only Value?" *Times Literary Supplement*, December 10, 1999, 27.

7. See Exodus 7:1; Deuteronomy 18:18; Jeremiah 1:5; Malachi 4:5.

8. 1 Thessalonians 5:19-20, KJV.

9. Hebrews 1:1.

10. 1 Chronicles 25:1, AMP.

11. See 2 Samuel 23:2.

12. See Ecclesiastes 3:7.

13. Charles T. Mathewes, *A Theology of Public Life* (Cambridge, UK: Cambridge University Press, 2007), 165. "The various political theologies of the last century, from the Social Gospel to Christian realism, liberation theology and radical orthodoxy, while rightly proclaiming the public or worldly character of Christianity, nevertheless have proven unable to elicit a sustained response for the churches."

14. The fourth law of politics is this: If you have found something that everyone agrees on, you're wrong.

HOT TAKE—ACID BATHS OF IRONY

1. See Mary Ellen O'Connell, "On Drone Killings, Brennan Doesn't Uphold Our Values," CNN, January 14, 2013, https://www.cnn.com/2013/01/14/opinion/oconnell-brennan/index.html.

2. Keith Houston, "The Five-Hundred-Year-Long Battle to Make Written Irony Easier to Understand," New Statesman America, October 24, 2013, https://www.newstatesman.com/2013/10/rain-your-wedding-day.

3. Lauren Dassow Walls, quoted in Jay Parini, "Huckleberries on Hot Summer Days," *Times Literary Supplement*, July 4, 2017.

4. Luke 10:21, NKJV.

5. Mark Brazaitis's *The Incurables* (Notre Dame, IN: Notre Dame University Press, 2012) includes a short story called "Afterwards" in which he defends incongruous laughter—laughing when the situation doesn't seem to call for it.

6. See 2 Corinthians 11 for an example.

7. Reinhold Niebuhr, "Humour and Faith," in *Discerning the Signs of the Times* (New York: Charles Scribner's Sons, 1946), 111–12.

6—THE DISUNITING STATES OF AMERICA

1. Joseph Nye's book *Is the American Century Over?* (Malden, MA: Polity, 2015) contends that it is distinctly American to worry about decline and collapse. He does admit that the greatest threat to the US is from within, specifically people disillusioned with government.

2. See "The 'Change the World' Schtick Is a Front" in *Trends Journal* (Winter 2016): 40–44.
3. Daniel O'Leary, "Pursuing Purest Gold," *Tablet*, August 16, 2017, 10.
4. See David Bond, "How Nelson Mandela Used Sport to Transform South Africa's Image," BBC Sport, December 6, 2013, https://www.bbc.com/sport/25262862.
5. Jesse Owens, quoted in Derwombat, "Jesse Owens and Luz Long, a Friendship That Defied the 1936 Nazi Olympics," *Old Guv Legends* (blog), October 7, 2017, https://derwombat.net/2017/07/10/1936-jesse-owens-and-luz-long-olympic-heroes/.
6. O'Leary, "Pursuing Purest Gold," 10.
7. Enzo Traverso, *The End of Jewish Modernity*, trans. David Fernbach (London: Pluto, 2016). See also his *Left-Wing Melancholia: Marxism, History, and Memory* (New York: Columbia University Press, 2016).

7—TOLERANCE OF DIVERSITY, TOUTING OF UNITY

1. Psalm 46:4.
2. Ephesians 4:6, NKJV.
3. For more on the church's obedience to the Spirit, see my *Soul Salsa* (Grand Rapids, MI: Zondervan, 2000) and *I Am a Follower* (Nashville: Thomas Nelson, 2012).
4. W. B. Yeats, "The Second Coming," Poetry Foundation, https://www.poetryfoundation.org/poems/43290/the-second-coming.
5. For more on this, see Flemming Rose, "I'm Not Willing to Sacrifice Freedom of Expression on the Altar of Cultural Diversity," interview by Nick Gillespie, *Reason*, May 2017, https://reason.com/2017/04/11/im-not-willing-to-sacrifice-fr/.
6. Romans 12:5, NKJV.
7. Stephen L. Carter, "Kavanaugh Protesters Come Dangerously Close to Self-Indulgence," Bloomberg Opinion, September 6, 2018, https://www.bloomberg.com/opinion/articles/2018-09-06/kavanaugh-protesters-need-to-rethink-their-strategy.
8. See Bernard Cooke, *Power and the Spirit of God: Toward an Experience-Based Pneumatology* (New York: Oxford University Press, 2004), 7. "The paradigm shift in the theological view of 'power,' in the context of the twentieth-century reappraisal of soteriology, represents what may be the most radical shift in mentality to touch Christianity in eighteen hundred years."
9. Kurt Vonnegut, *Kurt Vonnegut: Letters*, ed. Dan Wakefield (New York: Delacorte, 2012), "The Sixties," e-book.
10. Patricia Nelson Limerick, "Insiders and Outsiders: The Borders of the USA and the Limits of the ASA: Presidential Address to the American Studies Association," 31 October 1996, *American Quarterly* 49, no. 3 (September 1997) 449–69, American Studies at the University of Virginia, http://xroads.virginia.edu/~DRBR2/limerick.html.
11. Limerick, "Insiders and Outsiders."
12. Limerick, "Insiders and Outsiders."
13. Limerick, "Insiders and Outsiders."
14. Limerick, "Insiders and Outsiders."
15. Limerick, "Insiders and Outsiders."

HOT TAKE—IDENTITY CRISES GALORE AND GALLOPING

1. In Haitian folklore, there was a figure called the *zombi*, which was unknown in Western culture until 1929. See John Cussans, *Undead Uprising: Haiti, Horror and the Zombie Complex* (London: Strange Attractor, 2017) and Greg Garrett, *Living with the Living Dead: The Wisdom of the Zombie Apocalypse* (New York: Oxford University Press, 2017).
2. Aaron Antonovsky, *Unraveling the Mystery of Health: How People Manage Stress and Stay Well* (San Francisco: Jossey-Bass, 1987).
3. Robert Irwin, *Ibn Khaldun: An Intellectual Biography* (Princeton, NJ: Princeton University Press, 2018), chap. 3.
4. Matthew 19:14.
5. For more on the importance of table, see Leonard Sweet, *From Tablet to Table: Where Community Is Found and Identity Is Formed* (Colorado Springs: NavPress, 2015).

8—SEXULARISM

1. See Joan Wallach Scott, *Sex and Secularism* (Princeton: Princeton University Press, 2017). The word *sexularism* was coined by Scott. I am using it very differently than she does, and I apologize to her for doing so.
2. Although not as negative as in certain times past. Some fifth-century bishops had to restrain their clerics

from castrating themselves. One eleventh-century ascetic was so anti-body that he was renowned for his terrible personal hygiene, ankle-length hair, and two pet snakes. For more such stories, see William North and Laura L. Gathagan, eds., *The Haskins Society Journal 24: 2012*, Studies in Medieval History (Suffolk, UK: Boydell, 2013).

3. Maureen Dowd, "Erotic Vagrancy, Anyone?" editorial, *New York Times*, July 9, 2011, https://www.nytimes.com/2011/07/10/opinion/sunday/10dowd.html.

4. Perhaps the best thing ever written about sex from a Christian perspective is Philip Yancey's "Designer Sex," in *Rumors of Another World: What on Earth Are We Missing?* (Grand Rapids, MI: Zondervan, 2003), 73–95.

5. Sarah Coakley, *God, Sexuality, and the Self: An Essay 'on the Trinity'* (Cambridge, UK: Cambridge University Press, 2013).

6. Ann Pellegrini, as quoted in J. C., "From the Top," *Times Literary Supplement*, December 28, 2012, 21. The question came from the professor of performance studies and director of the Center for the Study of Gender and Sexuality at New York University (Ann Pellegrini).

7. James Brabazon, *Albert Schweitzer: A Biography*, 2nd ed. (Syracuse, NY: Syracuse University Press, 2000), 58.

8. Orson Welles, quoted in Grace Jones, *I'll Never Write My Memoirs: Graces Jones as Told to Paul Morley* (New York: Gallery, 2015), 263.

9. See Sara Moslener, *Virgin Nation: Sexual Purity and American Adolescence* (New York: Oxford University Press, 2015), 1. This historian argues that sexual abstinence teachings to teens are really political projects "to maintain . . . ties to Republican supporters by asserting ostensibly biblical ideals of marriage, family, and sexuality as integral to national well-being."

10. Donald M. Joy's *Parents, Kids & Sexual Integrity* (Waco, TX: Word, 1988) has not received the attention it deserves. It should have been required reading in every parenting class or seminar the day it was published.

11. Children raised in homosexual families fare as well as those residing with different-sex parents in terms of academic performance, cognitive development, social development, and psychological health. They are no more likely to engage in early sexual activity or substance abuse than children of heterosexual couples. Most become heterosexuals, although they are more likely than children raised by different-sex parents to be open to the possibility of same-sex attraction. Thus far, children and teenagers conceived through various forms of ART (assisted reproductive technology) exhibit few differences in adjustment and achievement from those naturally conceived.

12. Russell L. Dicks, *Pastoral Work and Personal Counseling* (New York: Macmillan, 1944).

13. Hans Urs von Balthasar, *Truth Is Symphonic: Aspects of Christian Pluralism*, trans. Graham Harrison (San Francisco: Ignatius Press, 1987).

14. See David M. Halperin and Trevor Hoppe, eds., *The War on Sex* (Durham, NC: Duke University Press, 2017). This collection of essays by lawyers, scholars, journalists, and activists presents the argument that through the latter half of the twentieth century the US has spearheaded a global "war on sex."

15. Wendell Berry, *Sex, Economy, Freedom & Community* (New York: Pantheon, 1993), 142.

16. Alison Wolf, *The XX Factor: How Working Women Are Creating a New Society* (London: Profile, 2013), 182. Wolf contends that more academically successful girls begin sexual activity at a later age, on average. She writes, "[Of] American women aged twenty-five to forty-four surveyed . . . who went on to gain a higher degree, more than half reported that they were over nineteen when they first had intercourse. Among high-school dropouts, by contrast, half reported having had intercourse before their sixteenth birthday."

17. Gil Bailie, in Brian Volck, "A Conversation with Gil Bailie," *Image* 41 (Winter 2003): 70.

9—GENDERS AND GENDERING

1. Queer theory is less about sex and gender than it is about disruption of the dominant paradigms, departure from the "normal." Replace the word *transgressive* for *queer*, or even the word *disorienting* or *subversive*, and you'll gain in clarity but lose in chill and frisson what is really going on in this "new discipline."

2. This is the coinage of Mari Ruti in her *Penis Envy and Other Bad Feelings: The Emotional Costs of Everyday Life* (New York: Columbia University Press, 2018).

3. Vicky Beeching, *Undivided: Coming Out, Becoming Whole, and Living Free from Shame* (New York: HarperOne, 2018); Jayne Ozanne, *Just Love: A Journey of Self-Acceptance* (London: Darton, Longman & Todd, 2018). Check out the stories of these two prominent evangelical singers for the abysmal failure of the church in this regard.

4. Jude 1:3, NKJV.

5. 1 Corinthians 6:19-20; see also Romans 8:9.

6. David Firestone, "While Barbie Talks Tough, GI Joe Goes Shopping," *New York Times*, December 31, 1993, https://www.nytimes.com/1993/12/31/us/while-barbie-talks-tough-g-i-joe-goes-shopping.html.

7. Chris Green, "'Cisgender' Has Been Added to the Oxford English Dictionary," *Independent*, June 25, 2015, https://www.independent.co.uk/incoming/cisgender-has-been-added-to-the-oxford-english-dictionary-10343354.html.

8. Jenny Audring, "Gender," Oxford Research Encyclopedias: Linguistics, July 2016, https://oxfordre.com/linguistics/view/10.1093/acrefore/9780199384655.001.0001/acrefore-9780199384655-e-43.

9. Australian Government Attorney-General's Department, *Australian Government Guidelines on the Recognition of Sex and Gender*, updated November 2015, https://www.ag.gov.au/Publications/Documents/AustralianGovernmentGuidelinesontheRecognitionofSexandGender/AustralianGovernmentGuidelinesontheRecognitionofSexandGender.pdf.

10. Peter Hasson, "New York City Lets You Choose from 31 Different Gender Identities," May 24, 2016, https://dailycaller.com/2016/05/24/new-york-city-lets-you-choose-from-31-different-gender-identities/.

11. See Matthew 19:12.

12. See Council on Biblical Manhood and Womanhood, Nashville Statement (article 6), 2017, https://cbmw.org/nashville-statement.

13. Leonard Sax, "How Common Is Intersex?" *Journal of Sex Research*, August 1, 2002, https://www.leonardsax.com/how-common-is-intersex-a-response-to-anne-fausto-sterling/.

14. Anthropologists call these *berdache*, from a French word for catamite.

15. Congregation for Catholic Education, *"Male and Female He Created Them": Towards a Path of Dialogue on the Question of Gender Theory in Education* (Vatican City, 2019).

16. See Deuteronomy 23:1.

17. Isaiah 56:3-5, NKJV.

18. See Galatians 3:28.

10—SUICIDE CULTURE

1. *First Reformed* begins with a suicide. It is written and directed by Paul Schrader, who was himself rescued from Russian roulette in a hot tub by his roommates and a psychiatrist. For suicidology, see Andrew Bennett, *Suicide Century: Literature and Suicide from James Joyce to David Foster Wallace* (Cambridge, UK: Cambridge University Press, 2017). Bennett approaches suicide paradoxically and sensitively as a survival mechanism but stresses the toll on those it leaves behind.

2. The suicide rate has increased 60 percent in the last forty-five years, according to Jennifer Michael Hecht in *Stay: A History of Suicide and the Philosophies against It* (New Haven: Yale University Press, 2013), 4.

3. See Mission 22, accessed June 26, 2019, https://www.Mission22.com.

4. See "11 Facts about Suicide," DoSomething.org, accessed June 25, 2019, https://www.dosomething.org/us/facts/11-facts-about-suicide. As of this writing, one person in the US commits suicide every 16.2 minutes (per DoSomething.org: https://www.dosomething.org/us/facts/11-facts-about-suicide). But there are twenty-five attempts for every one death. Also see "Facts & Stats," Jason Foundation, accessed June 25, 2019. "More teenagers and young adults die from suicide than from cancer, heart disease, AIDS, birth defects, stroke, pneumonia, influenza, and chronic lung disease, combined."

5. Dr. John D. Sweet gave us this idea of using the number 22 to talk about suicide.

6. Judges 16:23-31; 1 Samuel 31:3-5; 2 Samuel 17:23; 1 Kings 16:18-19; Matthew 27:5. Was Samson a suicide? In a warrior culture, like samurai, 22 can be the last resort for restoring one's honor after being disgraced.

7. 1 Kings 19:4.

8. Some say women are twice as prone to depression as men, although Tim Grayburn's *Boys Don't Cry: A Story of Love, Depression, and Men* (London: Hodder & Stoughton, 2017) challenges that as a cliché. On the other hand, one Scottish study found that "the more housework you do, the more depression you report." See Frank Furedi, *Therapy Culture: Cultivating Vulnerability in an Uncertain Age* (London: Routledge, 2003), 109.

9. Terrence Real, *I Don't Want to Talk about It: Overcoming the Secret Legacy of Male Depression* (New York: Fireside, 1998), 34.

10. "Critical Mental Health Resources for College Students," Center for Online Education, accessed June 26, 2019, https://www.onlinecolleges.net/for-students/mental-health-resources/.

11. Furedi, *Therapy Culture*, 110.

12. The way Rick and Kay Warren handled the suicide of their son Matthew in 2013 is exemplary.

13. Cited in Furedi, *Therapy Culture*, 116. It is estimated that one-third of all staff and clergy of the sixty-two thousand Baptist churches "suffer from depression because their jobs are so demanding."

14. The 1983 Code of Canon Law in the Roman Catholic Church retains a permanent exclusion from ordained ministry for anyone who has "attempted suicide" or "mutilated" themselves, even, it appears, after recovery.

15. Corey Adwar, "The Role of Impulsiveness Is One of the Saddest Things about Suicide," Business Insider, August 13, 2014, https://www.businessinsider.com/many-suicides-are-based-on-an-impulsive-decision-2014-8.

16. "The Sorrows of Werther," *Economist*, June 16, 2018, 24. In 1998, Britain switched to blister packs that require users to punch pills out one by one, and deaths from overdoses of paracetamol (Tylenol) dropped by 44 percent in eleven years.

17. Stefan Timmermans, *Postmortem: How Medical Examiners Explain Suspicious Deaths* (Chicago: University of Chicago Press, 2007), 8.

18. Kay, in Patricia Cornwell, *Black Notice* (New York: Penguin, 2001), chap. 21, e-book.

19. See Anthony Bourdain, "Anthony Bourdain on *Appetites, Washing Dishes and the Food He Still Won't Eat*," interview by with Dave Davies, *Fresh Air*, NPR, October 20, 2017, https://www.npr.org/2017/10/20 /558792269/anthony-bourdain-on-appetites-washing-dishes-and-the-food-he-still-wont-eat.

20. See "Wheatfield with Crows, 1890 by Vincent Van Gogh," VincentVanGogh.org, https://www.vincent vangogh.org/wheat-field-with-crows.jsp. Methodist Vincent Van Gogh's last painting, done when he was physically and mentally broke, was a garden ["countryside"? "farm"?] in spring, showing nature caught up in the very act of creation. When *Wheatfield with Crows* was finished, Van Gogh took his own life. The crucible of despair and pain can be a conduit of great beauty.

21. William Cowper, "Walking with God," *Olney Hymns*, 1779.

22. Sheldon Metcalfe, *Building a Speech*, 8th ed. (Boston: Wadsworth, 2012), 98.

23. In his *Reflections on the Psalms* (London: Harcourt, Brace, 1958), C. S. Lewis waxed nostalgic about the days when communities still banished undesirables from their midst—one of his less charitable moments.

24. See John 10:10.

25. See Kay Redfield Jamison, *Night Falls Fast: Understanding Suicide* (New York: Knopf, 1999). These are the four biggest reasons for committing suicide, as found by a scholarly study of suicide notes.

26. Exodus 20:13, KJV.

27. Roland H. Bainton, *Church of Our Fathers* (Philadelphia: Westminster, 1950). Bainton mentions the practices of the Cathari. Thanks to John Sweet for reminding us of the Cathars.

28. Jeremiah 31:17, NKJV.

29. See Megan Brenan, "Americans' Strong Support for Euthanasia Persists," Gallup, May 31, 2018, https:// news.gallup.com/poll/235145/americans-strong-support-euthanasia-persists.aspx. According to Gallup in May 2018, 65 percent of USAmericans are in favor of legalizing doctor-assisted suicide for the terminally ill—72 percent if the question does not include the word *suicide*.

30. Only in Pennsylvania was voluntary death not criminalized.

31. John Donne's *Biathanatos*, written in 1608 but published posthumously in 1644, vindicates (mutely) self-homicide. David Hume's frigid essay "Of Suicide" (1783) justifies self-destruction on the horrid basis that the loss of an individual life "is of no greater importance to the universe than an oyster."

32. David Foster Wallace, "This Is Water by David Foster Wallace (Full Transcript and Audio)," Farnam Street, accessed July 30, 2019, https://fs.blog/2012/04/david-foster-wallace-this-is-water/.

33. Robinson Jeffers, quoted in Michael Broomfield, *His Place for Story: Robinson Jeffers: A Descriptive Bibliography* (New Castle, DE: Oak Knoll, 2015).

34. Fred Craddock, "Mark 4:35-41—Lord, I'm Tired," May 6, 2018, in Sermons from Evergreen Community Church, read by Josh Friend, podcast, 23:18, https://podpoint.com/Sermons-from-Pastor-Josh-Friend /mark-435-41-lord-im-tired-rev-dr-fred-craddock.

HOT TAKE—PRENATAL SCREENING AND "WRONGFUL LIFE"

1. Wm. Robert Johnston, comp., "Historical Abortion Statistics, United States," Johnston's Archive, last updated December 2, 2018, http://www.johnstonsarchive.net/policy/abortion/ab-unitedstates.html.

2. See Jerry Toner, *Popular Culture in Ancient Rome* (Malden, MA: Polity, 2010).

3. Ezekiel 16:4-5, NLT.

4. Stephen M. Miller, *Understanding Jesus: A Guide to His Life and Times*, j repr. (Uhrichsville, OH: Barbour, 2013). See the end of the chapter titled "Escape to Egypt."

5. Quickening was when Aristotle said the fetus became a fully animated human. Of course, "quickening" is a subjective moment for the woman, not the child. A fetus "quickens" and kicks long before the mother feels it.

6. See the hour-long documentary *A World without Down's Syndrome?* directed and presented by Sally Phillips, October 5, 2016, on BBC Two. Phillips, whose son, Olly, has Down syndrome, was criticized in the media and especially social media for questioning the unqualified goodness of noninvasive prenatal testing, since she said that whether her child had Down syndrome or not, no child of hers would go unlived or unloved

in the world. Our growing callousness toward people of disabilities can easily creep toward people of weakness and woundedness, even to children.

7. See McKay v. Essex Area Health Authority, 2 All ER 771 (1982). An English court rejected a wrongful life case on the grounds that recognizing the claim would "mean regarding the life of a handicapped child as not only less valuable than the life of a normal child, but so much less valuable that it was not worth preserving."

8. "Parents Sue Doctors for 'Wrongful Birth' of Disabled Child," Fox News, last updated January 13, 2005, https://www.foxnews.com/story/parents-sue-doctors-for-wrongful-birth-of-disabled-child.

9. Heidi Ledford, "CRISPR Fixes Disease Gene in Viable Human Embryos," *Nature*, October 3, 2017, https://www.nature.com/news/crispr-fixes-disease-gene-in-viable-human-embryos-1.22382.

HOT TAKE—HOT SPRINGS INCAPACITATIONS

1. Jean Vanier, "Jean Vanier: 'The Strong Need the Weak as Much as the Weak Need the Strong,'" interview by Maggie Fergusson, *Economist: 1843*, July/August 2014, https://www.1843magazine.com/content/features/maggie-fergusson/jean-ark. There are now, in thirty-seven countries, 154 L'Arche (The Ark) communities of, for, and by the disabled around the world—thanks to the vision in 1964 of this one Canadian Catholic theologian and philosopher, "Jean of Ark."

2. See Ezekiel 3:26; Acts 9:79; 2 Corinthians 12:6-7.

3. Vladimir Nabokov suffered from epilepsy, as did other Nabokov family members. Dostoyevsky also had epilepsy. Other writers and artists include Vachel Lindsay, Karen Armstrong, and George Inness.

4. See 2 Kings 7.

5. Alyson C. Huntly, *Open Hearts: Resources for Affirming Ministries in the United Church of Canada* (Ottawa: Affirm United, revised 2017), accessed June 20, 2019, http://ause.ca/wp-content/pdf/OpenHearts.pdf, 12. With thanks to Jason Sedore for pointing me to this resource.

11—RACE RELATIONS

1. Ed Yong, "The New Story of Humanity's Origins in Africa," *Atlantic*, July 11, 2018, https://www.theatlantic.com/science/archive/2018/07/the-new-story-of-humanitys-origins/564779/; James Owen, "Modern Humans Came Out of Africa, 'Definitive' Study Says," *National Geographic*, July 18, 2007, https://news.nationalgeographic.com/news/2007/07/modern-humans-came-out-of-africa-definitive-study-says/.

2. Marjorie Perloff, "Hey, There Goes O. J.," *Times Literary Supplement*, September 7, 2016, https://www.the-tls.co.uk/articles/public/hey-there-goes-o-j/.

3. In his classic history of slavery, *Roll, Jordan, Roll: The World the Slaves Made* (New York: Vintage, 1976), Eugene Genovese reminds us that to reobjectify slaves in our historical memory and not appreciate slaves' own agency and actions, initiative and industry, is to focus on mere "lives" and not whole beings. For an alternative view of slavery as a business, see Sven Beckert and Seth Rockman, eds., *Slavery's Capitalism: A New History of American Economic Development* (Philadelphia: University of Pennsylvania Press, 2016).

4. The word *duologue* was invented by Abraham Kaplan. He added that if you multiply a duologue by a roomful of people, you have a conference.

5. Leonard Sweet, *From Tablet to Table: Where Community Is Found and Identity Is Formed* (Colorado Springs: NavPress, 2015).

6. Leonard Sweet, *Me and We: God's New Social Gospel* (Nashville: Abingdon, 2014). See for an extended discussion of this and a complexification of black as good and white as evil.

7. Celsus, *On the True Doctrine: A Discourse against the Christians*, trans. R. Joseph Hoffmann (New York: Oxford University Press, 1987), 79.

8. See Frank Tallis, *The Incurable Romantic and Other Unsettling Revelations* (London: Little, Brown, 2018), preface. Psychotherapist Tallis contends that there is power in narrative healing: "Psychotherapy is as much about narrative as it is about science or compassion."

9. See Cathleen Kaveny, *A Culture of Engagement: Law, Religion, and Morality* (Washington, DC: Georgetown, 2016), 128.

10. We might want to consider this as a principle of how to handle bad reviews or critical comments by those who don't want discussion, only execration. Whatever you do or think, you are going to get criticized.

11. See 2 Corinthians 1:20.

12. The Rule "Life is not fair" can be called "Rule 174.465" after Patent 174,465, issued on March 7, 1876, to Alexander Graham Bell. It was maybe the most profitable patent in history. Yet there is strong evidence that a rival inventor, Elisha Gray of Western Electric, got his patent registered before Bell, or at least was the true inventor of the telephone.

13. 2 Chronicles 20:15.

14. Luke 11:4, NLT.
15. E. P. Thompson, *The Making of the English Working Class* (New York: Vintage, 1966), 12.

12—STEAMY INCARCERATIONS

1. Alan Elsner, *Gates of Injustice: The Crisis in America's Prisons*, 2nd edition (Upper Saddle River, NJ: Prentice Hall, 2006). This is up from 2006, when the US had 5 percent of the world's population but 20 percent of the world's prisoners.
2. NAACP, "Criminal Justice Fact Sheet," accessed June 28, 2019, https://www.naacp.org/criminal-justice-fact-sheet/.
3. See Naomi Murakawa, *The First Civil Right: How Liberals Built Prison America* (New York: Oxford University Press, 2014) for more of how liberals put blacks behind bars through the bureaucratic engineering of society. The Boggs Act of 1952 imposed mandatory sentences for drug-related offenses, which led to a massive escalation of incarcerations. Lyndon Johnson's Omnibus Crime Control and Safe Streets Act of 1968 spelled huge increases to police departments and the beginning of the militarization of the police, eventually paying for helicopters, gas masks, riot gear, smoke and gas grenades, flares, and infrared cameras. But the greatest push to criminalize and incarcerate came from Bill Clinton, who pushed more mandatory minimum sentences than any other president, funded state prison construction (both public and private), and applied the death penalty to sixty crimes. During the Clinton years, the black-to-white ratio for incarceration went from 3–1 to 6–1.
4. James Forman Jr., *Locking Up Our Own: Crime and Punishment in Black America* (New York: Farrar, Straus and Giroux, 2017).
5. Michelle Alexander, *The New Jim Crow: Mass Incarceration in the Age of Colorblindness*, rev. ed. (New York: New Press, 2012).
6. Michael Tonry, *Thinking about Crime: Sense and Sensibility in American Penal Culture* (New York: Oxford University Press, 2004), 10–11.
7. "Addiction as a Disease," Center on Addiction, last updated April 14, 2017, https://www.centeronaddiction.org/what-addiction/addiction-disease.
8. Bruce Anderson, "Mr. Blair Could Have His Own Problems with the Liberal Elite," *Spectator*, December 30, 2000, 8.
9. See Matthew 25:36. Or in positive form, "I needed clothes and you clothed me, I was sick and you looked after me, I was in prison and you came to visit me."
10. See Matthew 25:40-45.
11. Hebrews 13:3.
12. Acts 1:8.
13. Scott Larson, "Does Your Church Have Enough Samaritans?" *The Exchange with Ed Stetzer* (blog), *Christianity Today*, June 22, 2018, https://www.christianitytoday.com/edstetzer/2018/june/does-your-church-have-enough-samaritans.html.
14. Edward Gibbon, quoted in W. B. Carnochan, *Gibbon's Solitude: The Inward World of the Historian* (Stanford, CA: Stanford University Press, 1987), 150.
15. Harold B. Segel, *The Walls behind the Curtain: East European Prison Literature, 1945–1990* (Pittsburgh: University of Pittsburgh Press, 2012), ix, 37–49.

13—ECOLOGICAL EXTINCTIONS AND HOTHOUSE HOME

1. See Genesis 9:9-10.
2. David George Haskell, *The Songs of Trees: Stories from Nature's Great Connectors* (New York: Penguin, 2018), 40.
3. Jared Diamond, *Collapse: How Societies Choose to Fail or Succeed*, rev. ed. (New York: Penguin, 2011), 23.
4. See the hate sites generated by my book *Quantum Spirituality: A Postmodern Apologetic* (Dayton, OH: Whaleprints, 1991).
5. See Matthew Griffiths, *The New Poetics of Climate Change: Modernist Aesthetics for a Warming World* (London: Bloomsbury, 2017).
6. Bernie Krause, "The Voice of the Natural World," filmed June 2013 at a TED Global conference, video, 14:45, https://www.ted.com/talks/bernie_krause_the_voice_of_the_natural_world#t-940323.
7. See John Bellamy Foster, Brett Clark, and Richard York, *Ecological Rift: Capitalism's War on the Earth* (New York: Monthly Review, 2010), 14. The study's authors said they didn't yet know enough to measure the planetary boundaries for chemical pollution and aerosol levels.
8. Frances Moore Lappé and Jeffrey Perkins, "The Two Sides of Fear: A Dreaded Emotion Can Save Lives, but First We Have to Turn and Face It," *Utne Reader*, May/June 2004, 68. "What used to mean life now means death—for our spirits, and ultimately for our planet."

9. Mark 4:35-36.

10. See William Ryan and Walter Pitman, *Noah's Flood: The New Scientific Discoveries about the Event That Changed History* (New York: Touchstone, 2000). In 1993, marine geologists William Ryan and Walter Pitman proposed that around 5600 BC, the melting of the glaciers caused a sudden crisis that changed the face of the planet in under two years, not more than five. The Black Sea flood could have been recalled millennia later as the Flood of Noah (or of Utnapishtim, in Mesopotamian sources). Alternatively, the biblical story could be about the flood that is known to have created the Persian Gulf in much the same way, at a similar date.

11. For hymns repenting of our misuse of creation, see Shirley Erena Murray of New Zealand, "Sing Green" (1992), where she mentions acid rain and the "plastic plague"; "Where Are the Voices for the Earth?" (1999); "Touch the Earth Lightly" (1992); "God of the Galaxies" (1992), with the refrain "Let us care for your garden and honor the earth"; and two of our favorites—Ruth Duck's "Creative God, You Spread the Earth" (1991) and Brian Wren's "Thank You, God, for Water, Soil, and Air" (1975).

12. "99 Percent of the Earth's Species Are Extinct—but That's Not the Worst of It," Curiosity, January 11, 2017, https://curiosity.com/topics/99-percent-of-the-earths-species-are-extinctbut-thats-not-the-worst-of-it-curiosity/.

13. Scott Atran and Douglas Medin, *The Native Mind and the Cultural Construction of Nature* (Cambridge, MA: MIT Press, 2008).

14. Referenced in Stanley L. Jaki, *Universe and Creed* (Milwaukee, WI: Marquette University Press, 1992), 17.

15. See Numbers 3:7-8; 8:26; 18:5-6.

16. Isaiah 51:1, NKJV.

17. Genesis 1:3; John 8:12; 9:5; 12:46.

18. One of the best resources on the web for ecologizing your church is Web of Creation, https://www.webofcreation.org. See also "A Litany of Sorrow," Let All Creation Praise, http://www.letallcreationpraise.org/liturgy/litanies. This litany, written for Earth Day 2000 and provided by the North American Conference on Religion and Ecology, ends with the penitent response "We have forgotten who we are."

19. For one hundred such ideas, see Paul Hawken, ed., *Drawdown: The Most Comprehensive Plan Ever Proposed to Reverse Global Warming* (New York: Penguin, 2017).

20. George M. Ella, *William Cowper: The Man of God's Stamp* (Dundas, Ontario: Joshua Press, 2000).

21. Jeremy Bentham, quoted at "Jeremy Bentham on the Suffering of Non-Human Animals," Utilitarianism, accessed June 28, 2019, https://www.utilitarianism.com/jeremybentham.html.

22. See Alan E. Lewis, *Between Cross and Resurrection: A Theology of Holy Saturday* (Grand Rapids, MI: Eerdmans, 2001) and Shelly Rambo, *Spirit and Trauma: A Theology of Remaining* (Louisville, KY: Westminster John Knox, 2010).

23. "VIPs (Very Important Pets)," *American Demographics* 23 (March 2001): 16.

24. Wojtek Rozdzenski, "Picasso, Monet and Pigeons—An Unlikely Trio," DailyArt, February 2, 2018, http://www.dailyartmagazine.com/monet-and-pigeons/.

25. P. Dadvand et al., "The Association between Lifelong Greenspace Exposure and 3-Dimensional Brain Magnetic Resonance Imaging in Barcelona Schoolchildren," *Environmental Health Perspectives* 126, no. 2 (February 2018).

14—SOLUTIONISM, DATAISM, SCIENTISM (SDS)

1. Thanks to Will Clegg for finding this gem from William Hone, *The Every-Day Book* (1868), quoted at "Dueling Servilities," *Futility Closet* (blog), July 7, 2018, https://www.futilitycloset.com/2018/07/07/dueling-servilities/.

2. For a similar perspective, see Susan Haack, *Defending Science—within Reason: Between Scientism and Cynicism* (Amherst, NY: Prometheus, 2003), chap. 10. Her chapter called "Point of Honor: On Science and Religion" is devoted to the incompatibility of religion and science. According to Haack, the "fundamental appeal" of religion is "to the side of the human creature that craves certainty, likes to be elevated by mysteries, dislikes disagreeable truths, and clings to the flattering idea that we are not just remarkable animals, but the chosen creatures." In defense of religion, what about the idea of faith (which eschews certainty), the conviction of human imperfection (which can be highly "disagreeable"), and the virtue of humility—all of which are key components of many religions?

3. Stephen Hawking and Leonard Mlodinow, *The Grand Design* (New York: Bantam, 2010), 5.

4. Neil deGrasse Tyson, *Astrophysics for People in a Hurry* (New York: W. W. Norton, 2017), 12.

5. Some artists, musicians, and novelists are already doing this. John Updike's *Roger's Version* (New York: Knopf, 1986) attempts to show the religious significance of modern physics. A computer science student

tells his theology professor, "God is *breaking through*. They've been scraping away at physical reality all these centuries, and now the layer of the little left we don't understand is so fine God's face is staring right out at us" (chap. 1).

6. W. V. Quine, quoted in Mark Booth, ed., *What I Believe: 13 Eminent People of Our Time Argue for Their Philosophy of Life* (London: Firethorn, 1984), 74.
7. Oliver Sacks, *The River of Consciousness* (New York: Vintage, 2018), 24.
8. Thomas Burnett, "What Is Scientism?" BioLogos, June 11, 2012, https://biologos.org/blogs/guest/what-is-scientism. For C. S. Lewis's warnings about the alliance of government and scientism, which he called "scientocracy," see John G. West, ed., *The Magician's Twin: C. S. Lewis on Science, Scientism, and Society* (Seattle, WA: Discovery Institute Press, 2012). Thanks to Terry Rankin for this last Lewis reference.
9. Yuval Noah Harari, *Homo Deus: A Brief History of Tomorrow* (New York: Harper, 2017), 399.
10. Wikisource, s. v. "Darwin Journal of Researches," chap. 13, 280, last edited April 11, 2018, https://en.wikisource.org/wiki/Page:Darwin_Journal_of_Researches.djvu/302.
11. For the difference between the bird in the bush versus the bird in the pan, see Leonard Sweet's foreword ("Battle of the Birds") to Eric E. Peterson's *Wade in the Water: Following the Sacred Stream of Baptism* (Eugene, OR: Cascade, 2018). R. D. Laing, in his classic work *The Divided Self: An Existential Study in Sanity and Madness* (New York: Penguin, 1965), chap. 1, pointed out that in English the word *merely* never precedes the word *objective*, only *subjective*.
12. See Michael Polanyi, *Personal Knowledge: Towards a Post-Critical Philosophy* (Chicago: University of Chicago Press, 1958).
13. So argues David Wootton, in "Facts," chap. 7, *The Invention of Science: A New History of the Scientific Revolution* (New York: Harper, 2015).
14. Randy Alfred, "Dec. 30, 1924: Hubble Reveals We Are Not Alone," *Wired*, December 30, 2009, https://www.wired.com/2009/12/1230hubble-first-galaxy-outside-milky-way/. The founder of semiotics, Charles Sanders Peirce, once remarked that universes are not as plentiful as blackberries. It appears now they are. See Martin Gardner's *Are Universes Thicker than Blackberries? Discourses on Gödel, Magic Hexagrams, Little Red Riding Hood, and Other Mathematical and Pseudoscientific Topics* (New York: Norton, 2004).
15. The phrase *the heretical question of our time* comes from Welsh scholar David Hawkes, "Backwards into the Future," *Times Literary Supplement*, August 30, 2013, 7.

15—GENETIC ENGINEERING, ROBOTICS, ARTIFICIAL INTELLIGENCE, INFORMATION TECHNOLOGY, NANOTECHNOLOGY (GRAIN)

1. In Chaldean numerology, *Io* represents the number nine and is considered sacred.
2. Quoted in Michael Mayne, *Learning to Dance* (London: Darton, Longman & Todd, 2001), 5.
3. Jim Boulton, "Everything That Can Be Digital, Will Be," Digital Archaeology, November 26, 2012, https://digital-archaeology.org/anything-that-can-be-digital-will-be/.
4. Leonard Nimoy's Mr. Spock can be seen consulting Spinoza's *Ethics* in an early episode of *Star Trek*.
5. Peter J. Bowler, *A History of the Future: Prophets of Progress from H. G. Wells to Isaac Asimov* (Cambridge, UK: Cambridge University Press, 2017).
6. Ellen Ullman, *Life in Code: A Personal History of Technology* (New York: MCD, 2017), 16.
7. Molly Crabapple, *Drawing Blood* (New York: Harper, 2018), 312.
8. In response to Bill Joy's "Why the Future Doesn't Need Us" (April 1, 2000), Kevin Kelly makes a good suggestion: "We should devise an Intended Effects Impact Report to be issued with each new technology. What do we expect from X in 5 years, in 10 years, or one generation? Then measure it in five years, or one generation, and evaluate the results of X" ("Rants & Raves," *Wired*, July 2, 2000, https://www.wired.com/2000/07/rants-raves-134/).
9. See Enrico Moretti, *The New Geography of Jobs* (Boston: Houghton Mifflin Harcourt, 2012).
10. Virginia Woolf, *A Room of One's Own* (New York: Harcourt, Brace, 1929), chap. 6.
11. See Mark Harris, "Inside the First Church of Artificial Intelligence," *Wired*, November 15, 2017, https://www.wired.com/story/anthony-levandowski-artificial-intelligence-religion/. Anthony Levandowski's nonprofit religious organization, The Way of the Future, seeks to develop and promote "the realization, acceptance, and worship of a Godhead based on Artificial Intelligence" that will contribute to the "betterment of society."
12. Most of these "I've been chipped" humans live in Sweden. See "Why Swedes Are Inserting Microchips into Their Bodies," *Economist*, August 2, 2018, 45.
13. Anyone else remember the spiritual rush you got the first time you played Myst?
14. John Brandon, "An AI God Will Emerge by 2042 and Write Its Own Bible. Will You Worship It?"

VentureBeat, October 2, 2017, https://venturebeat.com/2017/10/02/an-ai-god-will-emerge-by-2042-and -write-its-own-bible-will-you-worship-it/. "In the next 25 years, AI will evolve to the point where it will know more on an intellectual level than any human. In the next 50 or 100 years, an AI might know more than the entire population of the planet put together. At that point, there are serious questions to ask about whether this AI—which could design and program additional AI programs all on its own, read data from an almost infinite number of sources, and control almost every connected device on the planet—will somehow rise in status to become more like a god, something that can write its own bible and draw humans to worship it."

15. Brandon, "An AI God Will Emerge by 2042." Yuval Harari, in *Homo Deus*, argues for the emergence of two new religions: technohumanism and dataism, a new ethical system that says there is now a higher level of ethical system in the universe than humans.

16. The etymology of the word *Vatican* comes from *vatis*, meaning "prophecy" or "divination." Who will prophesy and divine the future more: the old or the new Vatican?

17. Nick Bostrom, "Predictions from Philosophy? How Philosophers Could Make Themselves Useful," Nick Bostrom's website, April 9, 1997, https://nickbostrom.com/old/predict.html. The term *autopotent* was coined by Oxford philosopher Nick Bostrom to indicate an ability for superintelligence to be self-aware and to self-modify.

18. The ethical dilemma of double effect is this: While it is wrong to give a lethal dose of a drug in order to terminate life, is it acceptable to give, in order to relieve suffering, a dose of a painkiller that will, in fact, shorten the patient's life?

19. Charles Darwin, the greatest scientist of the nineteenth century, was an amateur. He did his science for love and not for money. He also grieved a "curious and lamentable loss of the higher aesthetic tastes" and confessed that he felt "nauseated" by reading Shakespeare. See "Darwin's Reading and the Loss of Delight in Poetry and Painting," Victorian Web, last modified July 28, 2012, http://www.victorianweb.org/science /darwin/reading.html.

20. J. B. S. Haldane, *Daedalus; or, Science and the Future* (London: K. Paul, Trench, Trubner, 1924).

21. Bruce Sterling, *Tomorrow Now: Envisioning the Next Fifty Years* (New York: Random House, 2002), 26.

22. Yuval Noah Harari, *Homo Deus: A Brief History of Tomorrow* (New York: Harper, 2017), 14.

23. Michael Specter, "Rewriting the Code of Life," *New Yorker*, December 25, 2016, http://www.newyorker.com /magazine/2017/01/02/rewriting-the-code-of-life.

24. Jennifer A. Doudna and Samuel H. Sternberg, *A Crack in Creation: Gene Editing and the Unthinkable Power to Control Evolution* (Boston: Houghton Mifflin Harcourt, 2017).

25. Joanna Moorhead, "Monk at the Cutting Edge," *Tablet*, March 25, 2017, 17.

26. Gregory Votolato, *Car* (London: Reaktion, 2015).

27. World Health Organization, *Global Status Report on Road Safety 2015*, https://www.who.int/violence_injury _prevention/road_safety_status/2015/en/.

28. *Autopia* is a term invented by Reyner Banham to describe the car culture of California in particular and suburbia in general. See Reyner Banham, *Los Angeles: The Architecture of Four Ecologies* (London: Allen Lane, 1971).

29. "A Handy Collaborator," *Economist*, June 6, 2015, 73.

30. Jennifer Smith, "Self-Driving Technology Threatens Nearly 300,000 Trucking Jobs, Report Says," *Wall Street Journal*, September 4, 2018, https://www.wsj.com/articles/self-driving-technology-threatens-nearly -300-000-trucking-jobs-report-says-1536053401.

31. US employers report 6 million unfilled job openings at mid-2017, the most in sixteen years of record keeping. See Patrick Gillespie, "U.S. Has Record 6 Million Job Openings, Even as 6.8 Million Americans Are Looking for Jobs," CNN Business, June 6, 2017, https://money.cnn.com/2017/06/06/news/economy /us-job-openings-6-million/index.html.

32. Economist James Bessen, *Learning by Doing: The Real Connection between Innovation, Wages, and Wealth* (New Haven, CT: Yale University Press, 2015), 107. Tellers will continue to decrease once a saturation point of branches is reached, but the numbers are not apocalyptic.

33. See James Surowiecki, "The Great Tech Panic: Robots Won't Take All Our Jobs," *Wired*, September 2017, https://www.wired.com/2017/08/robots-will-not-take-your-job/.

34. Tim Harford, *Messy: The Power of Disorder to Transform Our Lives* (New York: Riverhead, 2017).

35. Akiko Fujita, "GPS Tracking Disaster: Japanese Tourists Drive Straight into the Pacific," ABC News, March 17, 2012, https://abcnews.go.com/blogs/headlines/2012/03/gps-tracking-disaster-japanese-tourists-drive -straight-into-the-pacific/.

36. Rob Thubron, "Musk, Hawking and Wozniak Urge AI Weapons Ban," Techspot, July 28, 2015, https:// www.techspot.com/news/61539-musk-hawking-wozniak-urge-ai-weapons-ban.html.

37. See "Facial Recognition Software by Churchix for Biometric Attendance," Churchix, accessed June 30, 2019, http://churchix.com/.

38. Kevin Kelly, *Inevitable: Understanding the 12 Technological Forces That Will Shape Our Future* (New York: Viking, 2016), chap. 2.

39. For the dangers of AI, see Jerry Kaplan, *Humans Need Not Apply: A Guide to Wealth and Work in the Age of Artificial Intelligence* (New Haven: Yale University Press, 2015).

40. See Max Tegmark, *Life 3.0: Being Human in the Age of Artificial Intelligence* (New York: Vintage, 2018), 32. MIT professor Max Tegmark relates the chat between Google cofounder Larry Page and Tesla CEO Elon Musk.

41. Christopher Frayling, *Frankenstein: The First 200 Years* (London: Reel Art, 2017).

42. Sam Barsanti, "MIT Scientists Create a 'Psychopath' AI by Feeding It Violent Content from Reddit," Newswire, AV Club, June 6, 2018, https://news.avclub.com/mit-scientists-created-a-psychopath-ai-by-feeding-it-1826623094.

43. The iPhone's depth-sensing camera to facilitate AR (augmented reality) apps ensures its doom. We're probably at least a decade away from the move from smartphones, but groundwork for the eventual demise is being laid by Elon Musk, Microsoft, Facebook, Amazon, and a countless number of startups.

44. These forms of AR include Galaxy S8 Bixby (voice) and Gear VR (headset); Facebook Oculus; iPhone Siri; Amazon Echo and Alexa; Microsoft Cortana; Sony PlayStation VR; and Apple Watch.

45. The degree to which companies are controlling what you see around you will be a major ethical issue of the future.

46. Marcello Ienca, "The Right to Cognitive Liberty," *Scientific American*, July 2017, 10.

47. For more along these lines, see Martin Heidegger, *The Question concerning Technology, and Other Essays* (Munich: 1954; repr., New York: Harper Perennial, 2013), in which the author discusses the essence of technology.

48. "From A&E to AI," *Economist*, June 7, 2018, 68–69.

49. See Jeremy Bailenson, *Experience on Demand: What Virtual Reality Is, How It Works, and What It Can Do* (New York: Norton, 2018).

50. Jaron Lanier, *Dawn of the New Everything: Encounters with Reality and Virtual Reality* (New York: Holt, 2017), 1.

51. Tom Rachman, "What Is It to Be a Cow?" *Times Literary Supplement*, March 13, 2018, https://www.the-tls.co.uk/articles/public/what-is-it-to-be-a-cow-vr/.

52. See Leonard Sweet, *The Well-Played Life: Why Pleasing God Doesn't Have to Be Such Hard Work* (Carol Stream, IL: Tyndale, 2014).

53. Check out Zooniverse at https://Zooniverse.org/, which celebrated its tenth anniversary in 2017.

54. Alfie Bown, *The PlayStation Dreamworld* (Malden: MA: Polity, 2017).

55. Clive Thompson, "Face It, Meatsack: Pro Gamer Will Be the Only Job Left," *Wired*, February 22, 2017, https://www.wired.com/2017/02/clive-thompson-future-of-work-is-gaming/.

56. Plato, *Phaedrus*, trans. Benjamin Jowett (CreateSpace, 2018), 94. Socrates never wrote anything. Everything he said we get from Plato.

57. See Scott Galloway, *The Four: The Hidden DNA of Amazon, Apple, Facebook, and Google* (New York: Penguin, 2017), 268.

58. Ukrainian reporter Mustafa Nayyem called for a nonvirtual demonstration at Maidan, Kyiv's main square. "Likes don't count." See Marci Shore, *The Ukrainian Night: An Intimate History of Revolution* (New Haven: Yale University Press, 2018), 32.

59. Andrew McAfee and Erik Brynjolfsson, *Machine, Platform, Crowd: Harnessing Our Digital Future* (New York: W. W. Norton, 2017).

60. Jonathan Haskel and Stian Westlake, *Capitalism without Capital: The Rise of the Intangible Economy* (Princeton: Princeton University Press, 2018).

61. Stuart Hameroff, "Is Your Brain Really a Computer, or Is It a Quantum Orchestra?" HuffPost, updated July 8, 2016, https://www.huffpost.com/entry/is-your-brain-really-a-co_b_7756700.

62. David Deutsch, "Quantum Theory, the Church-Turing Principle and the Universal Quantum Computer," *Proceedings of the Royal Society of London A: Mathematical, Physical and Engineering Sciences* 400, no. 1818 (July 1985): 97–117.

63. If 77,000 people in three states had voted differently in 2016, or stayed at home, Hillary Clinton would have been elected president. The margin of victory in the 2000 presidential election (.045 percent) was smaller than the margin of error.

64. "St. David of Wales," Catholic News Agency, accessed July 1, 2019, https://www.catholicnewsagency.com/saint/st-david-of-wales-163.

65. See 1 John 4:19.

66. This is the argument of T. S. Eliot, "Tradition and the Individual Talent," in *Selected Essays, 1917–1932* (New York: Harcourt, Brace, 1932), 13–22 (chap. 1).

67. Michael Saler, "The Central Story of Our Lives," *Times Literary Supplement*, October 19, 2017, https://www.the-tls.co.uk/articles/public/philip-pullman-book-of-dust-review/. "His Dark Materials [series] was an inversion of John Milton's account of Adam and Eve in *Paradise Lost*."

68. See David E. Cole, *What the Church Can Learn from Harley-Davidson: Connecting with Today's Culture* (Duvall, WA: Outward-Focused Network, 2017). Some of this appears in the foreword.

69. See Isaiah 51:1.

70. Genesis 16:8.

71. David Tracy calls this "mutually-critical correlation between a still authoritative religious tradition and the particular cultural context we inhabit." See Mary Doak, "The American Spiritual Culture: And the Invention of Jazz, Football, and the Movies," review of *The American Spiritual Culture: And the Invention of Jazz, Football, and the Movies*, by William Dean (New York: Continuum, 2002), and *Spiritus: A Journal of Christian Spirituality* 5, no. 1 (Spring 2005): 118.

16—GENERATIONS AND THE SILVER RUSH

1. Alvin Silverstein, *Conquest of Death* (New York: Macmillan, 1979), 3.

2. This is not factoring in digital resurrection technology, which creates chatbots of the deceased who can interact with you every day. Then there will be robotic avatars of a beloved one, created out of texts, photos, sound messages, and emails, which can then interact with the living on a daily basis in every form imaginable, including, in the distant future, a response to touch.

3. *National Life Tables, UK: 2013 to 2015*, prepared by the Office for National Statistics for the UK Statistics Authority, September 29, 2016, https://www.ons.gov.uk/peoplepopulationandcommunity/birthsdeathsandmarriages/lifeexpectancies/bulletins/nationallifetablesunitedkingdom/20132015.

4. Leonard Sweet, *Quantum Spirituality: A Postmodern Apologetics* (Dayton, OH: Whaleprints, 1991) is dedicated to her.

5. E. Mazareanu, "Cremation Rate in the United States from 1960 to 2035," last edited July 18, 2018, https://www.statista.com/statistics/251702/cremation-rate-in-the-united-states/. In 1960 less than 4 percent of USAmericans were cremated. That figure is now well over 50 percent.

6. Lori Cuthbert and Douglas Main, "Orca Mother Drops Calf, after Unprecedented 17 Days of Mourning," *National Geographic*, August 13, 2018, https://www.nationalgeographic.com/animals/2018/08/orca-mourning-calf-killer-whale-northwest-news/.

7. For more, see Frank Furedi, *Therapy Culture: Cultivating Vulnerability in an Uncertain Age* (London: Routledge, 2003), 14–15.

8. See Barbara Ehrenreich, *Natural Causes: An Epidemic of Wellness, the Certainty of Dying, and Killing Ourselves to Live Longer* (New York: Twelve, 2018).

9. "The Kin and I," *Economist*, August 29, 2015, 36.

10. This is the argument of former French president Valéry Giscard d'Estaing in his memoirs, *Le Pouvoir et La Vie, vol. 2* (Paris: Compagnie 12, 1991), 110, as quoted in Manfred F. R. Kets de Vries, *Leaders, Fools and Impostors: Essays on the Psychology of Leadership*, rev. ed. (Lincoln, NE: iUniverse, 2003), 30–31.

11. This is the thesis of my book *The Well-Played Life: Why Pleasing God Doesn't Have to Be Such Hard Work* (Carol Stream, IL: Tyndale, 2014).

12. See Fyodor Dostoyevsky, *Crime and Punishment*, trans. Oliver Ready (New York: Penguin, 2014).

13. W. B. Yeats, "When You Are Old," first published in his *The Rose* (1893), in *The Collected Poems of W. B. Yeats*, rev. ed., ed. Richard J. Finneran (New York: Scribner, 1996), 41.

14. Alban, "Wanted: Young Ministers," January 24, 2007, https://alban.org/archive/wanted-young-ministers/. Previously published in James P. Wind, *Congregations*, March/April 2001, 5. For more on the various missions of life's three ages, see Leonard Sweet, *The Well-Played Life*.

15. Bono, "Notes from the Chairman," *New York Times*, editorial, January 9, 2009, https://www.nytimes.com/2009/01/11/opinion/11bono.html?mtrref=www.google.com&gwh=8D96D6D5BD93D395971911D184B6A489&gwt=pay.

16. Tara Bahrampour, "Creativity Can Last Well into Old Age, as Long as Creators Stay Open to New Ideas," *Washington Post*, November 21, 2013, https://www.washingtonpost.com/local/creativity-can-last-well-into-old-age-as-long-as-creators-stay-open-to-new-ideas/2013/11/21/31487172-52ca-11e3-a7f0-b790929232e1_story.html?utm_term=.f50a6c081d2d.

17—RAPIDIFICATION

1. Frederick A. Norwood, "When They All Sat Together in Dayton," *Methodist History* 25, no. 1 (October 1986): 34–40.
2. See "Free Hand," Andrea del Sarto at the Frick, *Economist*, October 17, 2015, 90.
3. Tyler Cowen, *The Complacent Class: The Self-Defeating Quest for the American Dream* (New York: St. Martin's, 2017). Cowen sees the US losing its vim and vitality, sinking into stagnation and status quoism, partly for this reason. Entrepreneurialism is floundering in the vacuum of messiness and vaulting of efficiency.
4. Pope Francis, *Laudato Sí*, May 24, 2015. The term *rapidification*, invented by Pope Francis, first appears in this encyclical.
5. The world's largest library, the Library of Congress in Washington, DC, adds ten thousand items to its collection every day. Also see Jeff Davidson, *Breathing Space: Living and Working at a Comfortable Pace in a Sped-Up Society* (New York: MasterMedia, 1991), 24–26.
6. Much of the same argument can be found in Thomas L. Friedman, *Thank You for Being Late: An Optimist's Guide to Thriving in the Age of Accelerations* (New York: Farrar, Straus and Giroux, 2016).
7. See Shelly Banjo, "Over 30? You're Too Old for Tech Jobs in China," *Bloomberg Businessweek*, May 1, 2018, https://www.bloomberg.com/news/features/2018-05-02/china-s-tech-industry-wants-youth-not-experience. Ironically, those very cultures that have most revered and honored age in the past have been some of the quickest to run on youth, not experience, in the transition to a digital age. According to China's largest jobs website, Zhaopin.com, three-quarters of tech workers are younger than thirty. The arena of technology is one where the church should be drawing on the ministry of its own kids.
8. Even though he doesn't use the word *motern*, James W. Geiger, in *The Gospel according to Relativity: Constant Value in a Changing World* (Xulon Press, 2005), separates pluralism from relativity and wants us to think in terms of motion (*moto*) rather than time (*modo*).
9. Leonard Sweet, *Carpe Mañana: Is Your Church Ready to Seize Tomorrow?* (Grand Rapids, MI: Zondervan, 2001).
10. Abraham Joshua Heschel, *God in Search of Man: A Philosophy of Judaism* (New York: Farrar, Straus and Giroux, 1955), 3.
11. Pope Francis, *Gaudete et Exsultate*, March 19, 2018.
12. Thomas Aquinas, *De Potentia*, 7.5, quoted in Paul Hedges and Alan Race, eds., Christian Approaches to Other Faiths, (London: SCM Press, 2008), 94.
13. Thomas Aquinas, *Summa Theologica*, 1.12.13.
14. George Bernard Shaw, *Major Barbara, act 3* (New York: Penguin, 1957), 128.
15. See Acts 2:42.
16. Compare Matthew 16:22-25 and 1 Peter 2:19-24.
17. See Kathryn Schulz, *Being Wrong: Adventures in the Margin of Error* (New York: Ecco, 2011). Schulz introduces a new discipline of "wrongology."
18. "Victorian" or "Philistine" are more historically precise characterizations of this phenomenon than "Puritan." Puritans (in their strictest forms) sought to purify the church of any residues of Roman Catholicism. They would relentlessly punish offenses against Calvinist dogma and bring the full weight of church and state down on every stain of impurity or impiety, banishing violators from all contact with the community—even family members. The contemporary resurgence of Puritanism is not limited to the Taliban (the Puritans of Islam) but shows up in secular popularist religion that seeks to purify culture of transgressions of its "isms" and enforces dogma to the fullest extent of law and social media, with no regard to the personal, social, or economic consequences.
19. The best theologies of failure are found in J. R. Briggs, *Fail: Finding Hope and Grace in the Midst of Ministry Failure* (Downers Grove, IL: InterVarsity Press, 2014); Alan Jamieson, *Journeying in Faith* (London: SPCK, 2004), 87–95; and Leonard Sweet, "The Nerve of Failure," *Theology Today* 34, no. 2 (July 1977).
20. See Matthew 10:14.

18—REPRODUCTION CRISIS

1. Hal Whitehead and Luke Rendell, *The Cultural Lives of Whales and Dolphins* (Chicago: University of Chicago Press, 2015), 12.
2. Genesis 1:28, NKJV.
3. Matthew 7:16, NKJV.
4. See the Paris-based Ipsos poll on whether people see religion as good or bad in the world. "Ipsos Global @dvisory: Is Religion a Force for Good in the World? Combined Population of 23 Major Nations Evenly

Divided in Advance of Blair, Hitchens Debate," Ipsos, November 25, 2010, https://www.ipsos.com/en-us/ipsos-global-advisory-religion-force-good-world-combined-population-23-major-nations-evenly-divided.

5. So argues Rupert Shortt, *God Is No Thing: Coherent Christianity* (London: Hurst, 2016), 93.

6. Grace Davie, *Religion in Britain: A Persistent Paradox*, 2nd ed. (Chichester, West Sussex, UK: Wiley Blackwell, 2015), 5, 162, largely rewritten from her *Religion in Britain Since 1945: Believing without Belonging* (Oxford: Blackwell, 1994).

7. Alister McGrath, *The Twilight of Atheism: The Rise and Fall of Disbelief in the Modern World* (New York: Doubleday, 2004), 173.

8. Ian Bradley, "The Strange Death of Protestant Britain: The Near-Loss of Religious Sensibilities," *Tablet*, December 16, 2017, 4.

9. See Allison de Jong, "Protestants Decline, More Have No Religion in a Sharply Shifting Religious Landscape (Poll)," ABC News, May 10, 2018, https://abcnews.go.com/Politics/protestants-decline-religion-sharply-shifting-religious-landscape-poll/story?id=54995663.

10. The first person to warn of the menace of this phrase was the historian Robert Orsi: "The phrase 'I am spiritual but not religious' unwittingly encodes this memory: it means 'my religion is interior, self-determined and determining, free of authority,' the opposite that other thing, which in the history of the modern West means first 'I am not like Catholics,' later 'I do not belong to any church.'" Robert A. Orsi, "2 + 2 = Five, or the Quest for an Abundant Empiricism," *Spiritus: A Journal of Christian Spirituality* 6, no. 1 (Spring 2006): 113–121.

11. Laurie Hays Coffman, Facebook response to my post on December 26, 2018.

12. Gina A. Bellofatto, "Religious Belief in 2100," *Futurist*, September/October 2012, 45. "In 1900, 99.8% of the world's population belonged to a religious tradition and 0.2% were unaffiliated (agnostic or atheist). The year 2012 marked a drop in the world's religious population to 88.2% and a rise of unaffiliated populations to 11.8%."

13. See Tim Crane, *The Meaning of Belief: Religion from an Atheist's Point of View* (Cambridge: Harvard University Press, 2017). Crane argues that religion is about relationships more than beliefs, and about trying to find meaning—both meaning in life and the meaning of life—through relationships to "something transcendent" (p. 6).

14. For more on this, see Leonard Sweet, *Nudge: Awakening Each Other to the God Who's Already There* (Colorado Springs: David C Cook, 2010).

15. John 13:35, NLT.

16. We use the language of transfiguration over transformation because transformation suggests change from the outside in, whereas transfiguration suggests change from the inside out. There is also an element of colonialism still inherent in that word *transform*, since the "transformation" in mind usually ends up looking like the one doing the talking about the "transformation."

HOT TAKE—THE DECLINE AND FALL OF SEMINARIES

1. See 2 Corinthians 11:19, KJV.

2. See Leonard Sweet, *Viral: How Social Networking Is Poised to Ignite Revival* (Colorado Springs: WaterBrook, 2012).

3. William Muehl, *Why Preach? Why Listen?* (Philadelphia: Fortress, 1986).

4. See Matthew 10:39.

5. Karl Rahner, "I Believe in Jesus Christ," in Theological Investigations, Vol. 9: *Writings of 1965–67*, trans. Graham Harrison (London: Darton, Longman & Todd, 1972), 167.

19—SACRALIZATION AND IDOLS

1. Peter L. Berger, "Secularism in Retreat," *National Interest*, December 1, 1996, https://nationalinterest.org/article/secularism-in-retreat-336.

2. See Bryan Appleyard, "He Is Risen," *Sunday Times*, November 2, 2014, https://www.thetimes.co.uk/article/he-is-risen-2t9hsgl7gv9. British journalist Bryan Appleyard recommended Marilynne Robinson's three novels *Gilead, Home*, and *Lila* to his British readers but warned that the works will seem odd to them "because what is going on here is religion" and "many, probably most, British people—artists, writers, audiences—will find this exotic because to them, religion has been embarrassed out of existence."

3. There are shower gels like Tom Daxon's Resin Sacra and Commes des Garçons 2-Him. Some of the best cathedral fragrances are the Unum LAVS candle, Roja Dove's Essence of Christmas candle, Heeley's Benediction candle, Cire Trudon Spiritus Sancti and Carmelite candles, and Frédéric Malle's unsurpassable Notre Dame candle. In terms of cologne and perfume, Etro's Messe de Minuit and Les Liquides Imaginaires'

Sancti bring to mind Midnight Mass. Comme des Garçons's "Incense" series of colognes, the last one featuring Avignon (also celebrated in Phaedon's Rouge Avignon cologne), are as divine of smells as one can inhale. Odin's 10 Roam is a cologne that brings coffee into the cathedral. Jovoy's La Liturgie des Heures is a sacred combination of musk and myrrh that you will never want to leave your body. It is now a pilgrimage ritual to go to Paris and visit L'Officine Universelle Buly's store to purchase the mystical Mount Athos incense.

4. Not to mention the more nettlesome and narcotic "all the smelly little orthodoxies which are now contending for our souls," as George Orwell liked to call them ("Charles Dickens," George Orwell website, last modified September 24, 2015, http://orwell.ru/library/reviews/dickens/english/e_chd). See science journalist Chet Raymo, *When God Is Gone, Everything Is Holy: The Making of a Religious Naturalist* (Notre Dame, IN: Sorin Books, 2008).

5. For more on GOOD Christianity, see Leonard Sweet, *11 Genetic Gateways to Spiritual Awakening* (Nashville: Abingdon, 1998); *The Jesus Prescription for a Healthy Life* (Nashville: Abingdon, 1996); and *The Bad Habits of Jesus: Showing Us the Way to Live Right in a World Gone Wrong* (Carol Stream, IL: Tyndale, 2016).

6. You get a small sense of this in Walter Isaacson's masterful *Steve Jobs* (New York: Simon & Schuster, 2011).

7. JAMA Network Journals, "High Prevalence of Diabetes, Prediabetes in China," Medical Xpress, June 27, 2017, https://medicalxpress.com/news/2017-06-high-prevalence-diabetes-prediabetes-china.html.

20—HELL, HEAVEN, AFTERLIFE

1. Psalm 139:7-8, NKJV.

2. For a rather grim picture of Sheol, a place where death's shadow covers all, see Ecclesiastes 9:10: "Whatever your hand finds to do, do it with all your might, for in the realm of the dead, where you are going, there is neither working nor planning nor knowledge nor wisdom."

3. "Unequal Zeal," *Economist*, July 7, 2011, https://www.economist.com/international/2011/07/07 /unequal-zeal. The same survey revealed that "the vast (94%) majority of respondents in the three mainly Muslim countries studied (Saudi Arabia, Turkey and Indonesia) said religion was important in their lives, whereas, among self-described Christians in 19 countries, only 66% said likewise. But among the 65% of Americans who called themselves Christian, some 86% deemed faith important, whereas among Christians in France and Sweden, the figures were 36% and 42%."

4. Rupert Shortt, "At the Prow of History," *Times Literary Supplement*, December 16, 2016, 3–5.

5. Questions about eternal damnation and eternal life are not as pressing in other religious traditions like Islam or Hinduism or Buddhism, where there are as many as thirty-three different hells, with each one notching up the torment a bit. A Swedish DJ and musician, born Tim Bergling, took the stage name Avicii, which is the Buddhist term for lowest hell. The Buddhist concept of Nirvana is not beatific but nihilistic. The Sanskrit word originally meant "extinction," with the metaphor for Nirvana being the snuffing out of a candle.

6. Matthew 16:18, ESV. The phrase *pulai hadou* ("gates of hell") is a Greek translation of a Jewish expression meaning "realm of the dead," but there was a physical structure behind the saying, a real cave with a gate known as the Gates of Hell found at Caesarea Philippi, the very place Jesus took his disciples to have this encounter with Peter and found his church.

7. See Albert B. Hakim, "Hell, Population Zero," *Commonweal*, December 2, 2015, https://www.commonweal magazine.org/hell-population-zero. Hakim provides a survey of theological reflections on universalism from Origen to Karl Barth.

8. Saul Bellow, *Ravelstein* (New York: Viking, 2000), 223.

9. 2 Corinthians 3:17.

10. John Milton, "Paradise Lost" (1667), bk. 1, line 263.

11. James M. McLachlan, "Hell Is Others and Paradise Is Others," in Benjamin W. McCraw and Robert Arp, eds., *The Concept of Hell* (New York: Palgrave Macmillan, 2015), 42.

12. Dallas Willard, *The Divine Conspiracy* (San Francisco: HarperOne, 2018), 302.

13. Emanuel Swedenborg, *Heaven and Hell*, trans. George F. Dole (West Chester, PA: Swedenborg Foundation, 2010).

14. Robert Capon, quoted in Bert Gary, *Jesus Unplugged: Provocative, Raw, and Fully Exposed* (Grand Haven, MI: FaithWalk, 2005), 162.

15. For self-love as self-enclosure, see Anthony Kelly, *Eschatology and Hope* (Maryknoll, NY: Orbis, 2006).

21—#CHURCHTOO

1. John Robinson, "On Prophesying or Preaching," *The Works of John Robinson*, vol. 2, chap. 3, Online Library of Liberty, accessed July 7, 2019, https://oll.libertyfund.org/titles/robinson-the-works-of-john -robinson-vol-2.

2. Joanna Williams, *Women vs. Feminism: Why We All Need Liberating from the Gender Wars* (Bingley, UK: Emerald, 2017). For the Asian exposure of everyday subtle sexism, see this bestselling book of 2017 in Korea: Cho Nam-Joo, *Kim Jiyoung, Born 1982* (English ed. New York: Scribner, 2020).

3. See Roseann Lake, *Leftover in China: The Women Shaping the World's Next Superpower* (New York: Norton, 2018) for more on this continuing Chinese notion of unmarried women as living failures, no matter how successful in any or all other arenas of life.

4. It is an open question whether the pay gap has less to do with gender than social stratification of an elite corps of men (and a few women) in professional positions as opposed to low-paying and temporary jobs.

5. See OECD, *The ABC of Gender Equality in Education: Aptitude, Behaviour, Confidence*, March 5, 2015, OECD Publishing, OECD iLibrary, https://www.oecd-ilibrary.org/education/the-abc-of-gender-equality -in-education_9789264229945-en. Up until the 1960s, boys spent longer and went further in school than girls and were more likely to graduate from a university. Now the stats have tilted in the other direction. There is a new gender gap in the sixty-four countries and economies assessed in the triennial international survey PISA, used to develop the report compiled by the Paris-based think tank Organisation for Economic Cooperation and Development (OECD). The report found that girls outperform boys in reading by on average a year of study. Some nations, like Sweden, openly talk about its "boy crisis," and Austria has a crash reading program called "Boys, Blokes, Books, and Bytes."

6. Shubhomita Bose, "Only 20% of Tech Jobs Are Held by Women," Small Business Trends, December 26, 2018, https://smallbiztrends.com/2018/03/women-in-technology-statistics.html.

7. Rebecca Solnit, *Men Explain Things to Me* (Chicago: Haymarket, 2014), 23.

8. The ordination of women in Roman Catholicism will come sooner than most people imagine, especially with the cardinals Pope Francis is appointing (which is a pope's way of choosing his successor). A nun has already presided at a Catholic wedding in Canada with the permission of the local hierarchy and of Rome (July 22, 2017). Pierrette Thiffault of the Sisters of Providence stood behind the altar but did not exercise any priestly functions. The top futurist in the Roman Catholic church would most likely disagree with me: See John L. Allen Jr.'s fantastic survey, *The Future Church: How Ten Trends Are Revolutionizing the Catholic Church* (New York: Doubleday, 2009), especially 178–216.

9. Joan Taylor, inaugural lecture, King's College London, May 1, 2014.

10. Olivia Rudgard and Victoria Ward, "Early Church Found Place for Female Bishops, Experts Claim," *Telegraph*, March 31, 2018, https://www.telegraph.co.uk/news/2018/03/31/early-church-found-place -female-bishops-experts-claim/.

11. Fran Bigman, "Girl-Prevention," *Times Literary Supplement*, February 3, 2012, 24.

12. So named by British psychologists Michelle K. Ryan and S. Alexander Haslam, "The Glass Cliff: Exploring the Dynamics Surrounding the Appointment of Women to Precarious Leadership Positions," *Academy of Management Review* 32, no. 2 (April 2007): 549–72.

13. David McDonald, *Then. Now. Next. A Biblical Vision of the Church, the Kingdom, and the Future* (published in association with Westwinds Community Church, Jackson, MI, 2017), 170.

22—POLITICAL RELIGION

1. See Matthew 4:8-10.

2. So argues John Gray in *Black Mass: Apocalyptic Religion and the Death of Utopia* (New York: Farrar, Straus and Giroux, 2007).

3. Robert Nozick, *Philosophical Explanations* (Cambridge: Harvard University Press, 1981), 5.

4. See Christopher Dillon, *Dachau and the SS: A Schooling in Violence* (Oxford: Oxford University Press, 2015).

5. Ansgar Hillach, Jerold Wikoff, and Ulf Zimmerman, "The Aesthetics of Politics: Walter Benjamin's 'Theories of German Fascism,'" in special Walter Benjamin issue, *New German Critique* 17 (Spring 1979): 99–119.

6. Vernard Eller, *Christian Anarchy: Jesus' Primacy over the Powers* (Grand Rapids, MI: Eerdmans), 1987, 186–87.

7. Paul Tillich, *The Protestant Era*, trans. James Luther Adams (Chicago: University of Chicago Press, 1948).

8. "Benjamin Disraeli, the Earl of Beaconsfield," History, Gov.UK, accessed July 7, 2019, https://www.gov.uk /government/history/past-prime-ministers/benjamin-disraeli-the-earl-of-beaconsfield. Two-term British prime minister Benjamin Disraeli (1804–81) talked about politics as the "greasy pole," whose scaling was the only purpose of politics. Many centuries earlier, St. Bonaventure is said to have commented about the climbing of poles: "The higher a monkey climbs, the more you see of its behind."

9. See Acts 25:21. See also Matthew Henry, *Matthew Henry's Commentary on the Whole Bible*, vol. 6-1,

Romans, chap. 13: "Never did a sovereign prince pervert the ends of the government as Nero did, and yet to him Paul appealed."

10. Jedidiah Morse, quoted at "Sermon—Fasting—1798, Massachusetts (Morse)," Wall Builders, accessed July 7, 2019, https://wallbuilders.com/sermon-fasting-1798-massachusetts-morse/.

11. John Betjeman, quoted at Richard John Neuhaus, "While We're at It," *First Things*, January 2009, https://www.firstthings.com/article/2009/01/002-while-were-at-it.

23—PARADOX: PURGATORY OR PARADISE?

1. Ray Oldenburg, *The Great Good Place: Cafés, Coffee Shops, Community Centers, Beauty Parlors, General Stores, Bars, Hangouts, and How They Get You through the Day* (New York: Paragon, 1989), 294.

2. Simon Winchester, *The Perfectionists: How Precision Engineers Created the Modern World* (New York: Harper, 2018), n.p.

3. Raphaël Liogier, *Souci de soi, conscience du monde: Vers une religion globale? ["Self-Care, Conscience of the World: Towards a Global Religion?"]* (Paris: Armand Colin, 2012).

4. Banksy, *Wall and Piece* (London: Century, 2007).

5. Another artist who has made a name and fortune for himself by going against the grain of popularity is Bob Dylan. Dylan went through a phase when he did everything he could to make himself unpopular: He announced his decision to retire from music; he got himself photographed on a pilgrimage to Jerusalem; he released a country-and-western album.

6. See Columbia professor Mark Lilla's *The Once and Future Liberal: After Identity Politics* (New York: Harper, 2017).

7. This is the argument of "post-liberal" David Goodhart, *The Road to Somewhere: The Populist Revolt and the Future of Politics* (London: Hurst, 2017), chap. 2.

8. Matthew 18:3, NKJV.

9. For more on this, see Leonard Sweet, *The Bad Habits of Jesus: Showing Us the Way to Live Right in a World Gone Wrong* (Carol Stream, IL: Tyndale, 2016).

10. Nicholas of Cusa in his essay, *De Docta Ignorantia* (1440).

11. This is similar to the Ignatian practice of *tensionante*, or the synthesis of apparently contradictory ideas, which Pope Francis uses masterfully. See biblical scholar Kathleen M. O'Connor's exploration of a proverb (*mashal*) from this vantage in *The Wisdom Literature* (Collegeville, MN: Liturgical Press, 1993), esp. 131.

12. E. M. Forster, *Howards End*, quoted at Emily Buchanan, "'Only Connect? Forsterian Ideology in an Age of Hyperconnectivity," Humanist Life, April 9, 2014, http://humanistlife.org.uk/2014/04/09/only-connect-forsteran-ideology-in-an-age-of-hyperconnectivity/.

13. See Luke 19:41-44.

14. Of course, the parochial can either be trivial or substantial; the provincial can be manorial or celestial.

15. William Blake, "Auguries of Innocence," Poetry Foundation, accessed July 7, 2019, https://www.poetryfoundation.org/poems/43650/auguries-of-innocence.

HOT TAKE—SALT, LIGHT, AND THE SIMPLEX CHURCH

1. David McDonald, *Then. Now. Next.: A Biblical Vision of the Church, the Kingdom, and the Future* (published in association with Westwinds Community Church, Jackson, MI, 2017), 287.

2. Gerard Manley Hopkins to Robert Bridges, May 30, 1878, in *The Letters of Gerard Manley Hopkins to Robert Bridges*, https://archive.org/stream/in.ernet.dli.2015.182404/2015.182404.The-Letters-Of-Gerard-Manley-Hopkins_djvu.txt.

24—CONSCIENCE

1. If you don't understand what Manichaeanism is, or the essence of Manichaean cosmology, just go to a *Star Wars* movie. Might there even be a connection?

2. Joshua Greene, *Moral Tribes: Emotion, Reason, and the Gap between Us and Them* (New York: Penguin, 2013).

3. Julian Baggini, "Time to Abandon Grand Ethical Theories?" *Times Literary Supplement*, May 22, 2018, https://www.the-tls.co.uk/articles/public/ethical-thinking-baggini/.

4. Paul Bloom, *Against Empathy: The Case for Rational Compassion* (New York: Ecco, 2018).

5. E. M. Forster, quoted in Frank Kermode, *Concerning E. M. Forster* (New York: Farrar, Straus and Giroux, 2009), 54.

6. See 1 Corinthians 13:12.

7. See David Daggett's charming oration; "Sun-beams may be extracted from cucumbers, but the process is

tedious," July 4, 1799, Fourth of July Oration, New Haven, Connecticut, https://quod.lib.umich.edu/cgi/t/text/text-idx?c=evans;cc=evans;rgn=main;view=text;idno=N26595.0001.001.

8. Vladimir Nabokov, *Lectures on Literature* (San Diego: Harvest, 1982), 64.

25—NUMBERS AND NARRATIVES

1. Matthew 18:20.
2. See David Lodge, *Consciousness and the Novel* (Cambridge: Harvard University Press, 2002), 87. "In a world where nothing is certain, in which transcendental belief has been undermined by scientific materialism, and even the objectivity of science is qualified by relativity and uncertainty, the single human voice, telling its own story, can seem the only authentic way of rendering consciousness."
3. Edward Said, "The One-State Solution," *New York Times Magazine*, January 10, 1999, https://www.nytimes.com/1999/01/10/magazine/the-one-state-solution.html.
4. Curtis Chang, *Engaging Unbelief* (Downers Grove, IL: InterVarsity Press, 2000).
5. Ivan Illich, quoted in Patrick Scriven, "Telling an Alternative Story," Lewis Center for Church Leadership, February 25, 2015, https://www.churchleadership.com/leading-ideas/telling-an-alternative-story/.

CONCLUSION

1. Rugile, "There Is an Island That Nobody Can Visit and It Didn't Exist Until 1963," Bored Panda, accessed July 8, 2019, https://www.boredpanda.com/forbidden-places-on-earth-surtsey-island-iceland/.
2. Isabella L. Bird, *The Hawaiian Archipelago: Six Months among the Palm Groves, Coral Reefs, and Volcanoes of the Sandwich Islands* (London, 1875; Project Gutenberg, 2004), Kilaueau, June 5, https://www.gutenberg.org/files/6750/6750-h/6750-h.htm.
3. Norman Lewis, *Naples '44* (New York: Pantheon, 1978), 104.
4. After the First World War, when Europeans were weakened by hunger and exhaustion, people succumbed to influenza in greater numbers than had died on the battlefields from 1914 to 1918.
5. Typhoid spreads through contaminated water or food, which means the greatest preparation for preventing the outbreak is doing what we should already be doing: providing access to clean water and sanitation.
6. Dinny McMahon, *China's Great Wall of Debt: Shadow Banks, Ghost Cities, Massive Loans, and the End of the Chinese Miracle* (Boston: Houghton Mifflin Harcourt, 2018).
7. See John Mueller, "Fire, Fire," *Times Literary Supplement*, March 7, 2014, 26. The very possibility that Saddam Hussein's regime in Iraq might obtain nuclear weapons resulted in a war with far more deaths than were suffered at Hiroshima and Nagasaki combined.
8. Stephen S. Arnon et al., "Botulinum Toxin as a Biological Weapon," *Journal of the American Medical Association* 285, no. 8 (February 2001): 1059–70. See also Cynthia Koons, "The Botox Margin of Error," *Bloomberg Businessweek*, October 30, 2017, 50–53.
9. "Building Works," *Economist*, August 27, 2015, https://www.economist.com/finance-and-economics/2015/08/27/building-works. This is not just a US problem but a global problem. These crumbling infrastructures weren't addressed when interest rates were at rock bottom and construction projects were bottoming out. It will go down as a lost opportunity.
10. Primo Levi, quoted at Benjamin Balint, "Here There Is No Why," *Claremont Review of Books*, May 11, 2016, https://www.claremont.org/crb/article/here-there-is-no-why/.
11. Donald Keough, *The Ten Commandments for Business Failure* (New York: Portfolio, 2008), 115.
12. See Max Weber, *The Protestant Ethic and the Spirit of Capitalism* (New York: Oxford University Press, 2002).
13. See Gillian Tett, *The Silo Effect: The Peril of Expertise and the Promise of Breaking Down Barriers* (New York: Simon & Schuster, 2015).
14. For more on this, see Anne-Marie Slaughter, *The Chessboard and the Web: Strategies of Connection in a Networked World* (New Haven: Yale University Press, 2018).
15. These are the words of Austrian philosopher and priest Ivan Illich (1926–2002), interviewed by David Cayley, ed., *The Rivers North of the Future: The Testament of Ivan Illich* (Toronto: House of Anansi Press, 2005), 225.
16. Yuval Noah Harari, *Homo Deus: A Brief History of Tomorrow* (New York: Harper, 2017), 373.
17. Plato, *Republic* 561c.
18. See "Democracy's Retreat," *Economist*, June 16, 2018, 50–51.
19. See the report from the US think tank Freedom House: Michael J. Abramowitz, *Freedom in the World 2018: Democracy in Crisis*, https://freedomhouse.org/report/freedom-world/freedom-world-2018. See also "BTI 2018 Transformation Index," Bertelsmann Stiftung, https://www.bti-project.org/en/data/. The Bertelsmann Foundation, another think tank, looks at democracy successes and setbacks in emerging economies.

20. According to the Economist Intelligence Unit, a sister company of the *Economist*. See "Democracy Index," Economist Intelligence Unit, accessed July 9, 2019, https://www.eiu.com/topic/democracy-index.

21. Yascha Mounk, *The People vs. Democracy: Why Our Freedom Is in Danger and How to Save It* (Cambridge: Harvard University Press, 2018).

22. John 11:50, NLT.

23. Lovett H. Weems Jr., *Focus: The Real Challenges That Face the United Methodist Church* (Nashville: Abingdon, 2012), 36.

24. Pope Francis, quoted in Joanna Moorhead, "Women like Marie Collins and Sheila Hollins Model a Different Way of Working," *Tablet*, May 18, 2017, 12.

25. See Jeff Taylor, *Politics on a Human Scale: The American Tradition of Decentralism* (Lanham, MD: Lexington Books, 2013).

26. Alfred, Lord Tennyson, "Ulysses," Poetry Foundation, accessed July 9, 2019, https://www.poetryfoundation.org/poems/45392/ulysses.

27. Michael Marmot, in *The Health Gap: The Challenge of an Unequal World* (London: Bloomsbury, 2016), tells her story in chap. 6.

28. Erik Brynjolfsson and Andrew McAfee, *The Second Machine Age: Work, Progress, and Prosperity in a Time of Brilliant Technologies* (New York: Norton 2014), chap. 11.

29. She wrote this in 1800. Dorothy Wordsworth, as quoted in Janet C. Gornick and Markus Jäntti, eds., *Income Inequality: Economic Disparities and the Middle Class in Affluent Countries* (Stanford, CA: Stanford University Press, 2013), xiv.

30. Benjamin Landy, "Income Inequality Reached Record Level in 2012," The Century Foundation, September 18, 2013, https://tcf.org/content/commentary/income-inequality-reached-record-level-in-2012/?session=1.

31. Pamela Ambler, "Asia Is Now Home to the Most Billionaires, with China Leading the Pack, Report Says," *Forbes*, October 30, 2017, https://www.forbes.com/sites/pamelaambler/2017/10/30/where-young-chinese-billionaires-are-making-their-wealth-and-spending-it/#5747afa77fb6.

32. For example, we don't have nor should we have equal linguistic rights. Black authors and rappers have the right to exploit certain words that, if any white author or rapper used them, would be and should be the kiss of death. We also don't have equal pregnancy rights. The list of "unequal rights" is a long one.

33. Johan Norberg, *Progress: Ten Reasons to Look Forward to the Future* (London: Oneworld, 2017), 78.

34. See Robert Putnam, *Our Kids: The American Dream in Crisis* (New York: Simon & Schuster, 2015).

35. "Attention Deficit," *Economist*, May 12, 2018, 28–29.

36. Dinci Pennap et al., "Patterns of Early Mental Health Diagnosis and Medication Treatment in a Medicaid-Insured Birth Cohort," *JAMA Pediatrics* 172, no. 6 (June 2018): 576–84, https://jamanetwork.com/journals/jamapediatrics/fullarticle/2678192.

37. So argue Richard Wilkinson and Kate Pickett, *The Inner Level: How More Equal Societies Reduce Stress, Restore Sanity and Improve Everyone's Well-Being* (New York: Penguin, 2019). This is a follow-up to their bestseller of a decade earlier, *The Spirit Level: Why Greater Equality Makes Societies Stronger* (New York: Bloomsbury, 2009), but it goes further in its indictment of capitalism and support of socialism, coming across at times as a socialist manifesto.

38. Larry Elliott, "World's 26 Richest People Own as Much as Poorest 50%, Says Oxfam," *Guardian*, January 21, 2019, https://www.theguardian.com/business/2019/jan/21/world-26-richest-people-own-as-much-as-poorest-50-per-cent-oxfam-report.

39. The bottom 20 percent of the world's population earn less than $550 a year in US purchasing power. If you make $52,000+ per year in US currency, you're in the top one percent globally.

40. See Eric A. Posner and E. Glen Weyl, *Radical Markets: Uprooting Capitalism and Democracy for a Just Society* (Princeton: Princeton University Press, 2018), one of the most exciting books to explore how markets can elevate the poor. This sizzlingly iconoclastic book explores how only revolutionary thinking will solve the problems of inequality, from the self-assessment of property values, to quadratic voting, to citizen sponsorship of one guest worker, to no minimum wage, to straitjacketing asset managers.

41. Riley Griffin, "When It Comes to Tipping, Millennials Are Cheapest," *Bloomberg*, June 18, 2018, https://www.bloomberg.com/news/articles/2018-06-18/when-it-comes-to-tipping-millennials-are-cheapest.

42. See Robert Arnott et al., "The Myth of Dynastic Wealth: The Rich Get Poorer," *Cato Journal* 35, no. 3 (Fall 2015): 447–85. Inequality is in fact increasing, but not by a simple "the rich are getting richer and the poor are getting poorer" formula. The poor are getting poorer relative to the accelerating richness of the rich. Increasing inequality is coming primarily from new wealth created by technology and by the unprecedented increase in executive compensation lavished on CEOs. Three-fifths of the top 0.1 percent of American earners come from the world of corporate executives.

43. Scholars who have written incisively but variously on increased inequality in our world include Thomas Piketty, Anthony Atkinson, Branko Milanovic, and Walter Scheidel.

44. With thanks to Peter Balaban for this bit of musicology.

45. Makoto Fujimura, "Mako Fujimura: Art, 'Seeing,' and the Creative Wastefulness of God," And Sons Magazine, SoundCloud audio, 01:05:48, June 5, 2018, https://soundcloud.com/andsonsmagazine/mako -fujimura-art-seeing-and-the-creative-wastefulness-of-god.

46. "My Father's house," Luke 2:49; "my house," Matthew 21:13; "your house," Matthew 23:38.

47. James Bloodworth, *Hired: Six Months Undercover in Low-Wage Britain* (London: Atlantic, 2018).

48. See Luke 12:21.

49. See Matthew 14:22.

50. See Matthew 14:6-14.

51. John Gray, *Black Mass: Apocalyptic Religion and the Death of Utopia* (New York: Farrar, Straus and Giroux, 2007).

52. "Protest and Commission," *Civilisation*, written and presented by Kenneth Clark, episode 6, aired 1969 on BBC.

53. Martin Luther King Jr., "Keep Moving from This Mountain," speech at Spelman College, April 10, 1960, Stanford University, Martin Luther King Jr. Research and Education Institute, https://kinginstitute.stanford .edu/king-papers/documents/keep-moving-mountain-address-spelman-college-10-april-1960.

54. The Original Elders, besides honorary member Nelson Mandela, included Kofi Annan, Jimmy Carter, Mary Robinson, and Desmond Tutu. The idea for The Elders came from musician Peter Gabriel.

AFTERWORD

1. Peter F. Drucker, "The New Society of Organizations," *Harvard Business Review*, September/October 1992, https://hbr.org/1992/09/the-new-society-of-organizations.

2. Daniel 12:4, NET.

3. 1 Corinthians 13:9, NASB.

4. Colossians 2:3, NASB.

5. Roberto Poli, *Introduction to Anticipation Studies* (New York: Springer, 2017).

6. Seligman et al., *Homo Prospectus* (New York: Oxford University Press, 2016).

7. Seligman et al., *Homo Prospectus*.

8. See John 1:14; Revelation 1:8, NASB; Isaiah 46:10, NASB.

9. Ephesians 1:10, NASB.

10. See Romans 10:4.

11. See Haggai 2:6; Hebrews 12:27.

12. Acts 17:26. "3724 *horízō* (from *horos*, 'boundary, limit')—properly, to set boundaries (limits)—literally, 'determine *horizons*' (*boundaries*)." James Strong, *Enhanced Strong's Lexicon*, under "ordained" (Elmira, Ontario: Woodside Bible Fellowship, 1995).

13. Romans 4:17, AMP.

14. See Romans 8:19-23.

15. See Romans 8:23.

16. See Romans 8:20.

17. See Romans 8:26.

18. See Matthew 25:1-13.

19. Acts 17:28, NKJV.

20. Revelation 22:20, NKJV.

ACKNOWLEDGMENTS

1. Frederic Raphael, "1981" in *Against the Stream: Personal Terms 7* (Manchester: Carcanet, 2018).

2. Emily Dickinson, "There's a certain Slant of light," lines 1, 5, in Emily Dickinson, *Emily Dickinson's Poems as She Preserved Them*, ed. Christanne Miller (Cambridge, MA: Harvard University Press, 2016), 153.